ROBERT F. KENNEDY

IN THE STREAM OF HISTORY

ROBERT F. KENNEDY

IN THE STREAM OF HISTORY

Terrence Edward Paupp

With a foreword by Richard Falk

LONDON AND NEW YORK

First published 2014 by Transaction Publishers

2 Park Square, Milton Park, Abingdon, Oxfordshire OX14 4RN
711 Third Avenue, New York, NY 10017

Routledge is an imprint of the Taylor & Francis Group, an informa

First issued in paperback 2017

Library of Congress Catalog Number: 2013029678

Library of Congress Cataloging-in-Publication Data

Paupp, Terrence Edward.
Robert F. Kennedy in the stream of history/Terrence Edward Paupp; with a foreword by Richard Falk.
pages cm
1. Kennedy, Robert F., 1925-1968--Influence. 2. United States--Politics and government--1945-1989. 3. Legislators--United States--Biography. 4. United States. Congress. Senate--Biography. I. Title.
E840.8.K4P36 2014
973.92--dc23

2013029678

ISBN 13: 978-1-4128-5362-0 (hbk)
ISBN 13: 978-1-138-51424-9 (pbk)

JOHN FITZGERALD KENNEDY
(1917–1963)

ROBERT FRANCIS KENNEDY
(1925–1968)

MARTIN LUTHER KING, JR.
(1929–1968)

Contents

Foreword

Richard Falk

The killings of John F. Kennedy, Malcolm X, Martin Luther King, Jr., and Robert F. "Bobby" Kennedy were the most devastating attacks on American democratic prospects in the entire history of the country. These assassinations inflicted more enduring damage than either Pearl Harbor or the 9/11 attacks. It is not entirely comprehensible, but the elimination of these four public figures created a moral vacuum at the core of American political life that remains unfilled in any comparable manner. What instead filled this vacuum has been greed, cynicism, anger, demoralization, and, worst of all, a complete collapse of any collective faith in a better future.

It is not that the situation of the country was so positive before these men were violently removed from the scene. During these years, the Vietnam War was proceeding with unabated fury; the Cold War, with its attendant arms race, showed no signs of coming to an end; racism and poverty persisted; women were victimized in countless ways; gays faced homophobic violence and persecution; and the United States was using its muscle overtly and covertly to deny Third World peoples the possibilities of a progressive outcome of their struggles against oppression and colonialism.

And yet there was an atmosphere of hope and struggle, and a widespread endorsement of the phrase "we shall overcome" as expressive of prophetic words. There was a sense that the American narrative was moving, however sluggishly, toward solving its deepest problems. Was not slavery finally repudiated? Was not the struggle for civil rights eventually successful? Was not "a war on poverty" being waged? And was not the antiwar movement, formed in opposition to the Vietnam War, gaining ground? And were not women and gays raising their voices and finally being heard? Goethe's remark seemed to capture the spirit of the times: "Him who strives, he may we save."

It is within this overall setting that the life and death of Robert F. Kennedy assumes such an epic stature. It is this Kennedy's assassination, the last of the four, that marks the boundary between collective moods of hope and despair. After Kennedy's death, and the dying of his message of solidarity with the vulnerable and victimized in America and beyond its shores, came the dirty presidency of Richard Nixon, which, although it ended in disgrace and resignation, unfortunately set the political tone of the future. Jimmy Carter came along next, and did his best at first to revive American self-esteem, championing human rights as the centerpiece of American foreign policy, but quietly and quickly regressing when the Iranian opposition took his words to heart and mounted a successful revolution against the Shah's regime—the most valuable U.S. strategic ally in the region. Later Carter was humiliated by the seizure of the American Embassy and the taking of its entire staff as hostages. Next came the Reagan presidency, with its anti-labor, pro-capitalist, pro-militarist, and anti-welfare ethos. Instead of being lamented, the Reagan legacy is now celebrated across the spectrum of mainstream American politics. In this era of American crony capitalism, the entire country has become captive of the machinations of Enron, J. P. Morgan, and Goldman Sachs.

The 1960s language and policies of hope and compassion have virtually disappeared, and what we have in their place is a furious struggle between the center/right (Democratic Party) and the extreme right (Republican Party/Tea Party). The center/right is moving toward the institutionalization of authoritarian democracy, while the far right is drifting toward a previously unknown plutocratic fascism. Imagine a president, accused of being wimpy and socialist, who seems proud of personally selecting the persons to be killed by drone attacks and never finds a bad word to say about hedge funds, banks, and Wall Street. And then imagine his opposition that wants to lower taxes for the rich while cutting entitlements for the poor, cut to the bone government expenditures while embarking on yet another disastrous war (Iran), and acts as if deference to Israeli militarism has become a patriotic duty. All in all, it is a dreary spectacle!

Coming to the rescue is this magnificent book that both chronicles and celebrates the life of Bobby Kennedy, giving us unforgettably iconic glimpses of his personal life and political style, as well as probing assessments of his approach to the public concerns of his time that linger on in our time. Author Terrence Paupp has produced a noble and notable effort to revive the Kennedy legacy when it is urgently needed. More than anyone in recent American history, Bobby Kennedy epitomized our better angels by his own journey from hardcore Cold War Warrior to passionate advocate of peace, justice, and liberation. It reminds us about the political vistas that once were present, and ignites our imagination with hopes for a better future.

Paupp's admirable text reminds us that toward the end of his life, Kennedy cast aside the pragmatic playbook that seems to be guiding the presidency of a closet liberal like Obama. For instance, Kennedy spurned his savvy political advisors by dwelling on the injustices experienced by America's indigenous peoples despite being told that this would hurt his presidential campaign. The text also makes us aware that the dark shadows cast by his brother's death pushed Bobby Kennedy, in his last years, to adopt and extend JFK's presidential agenda, including an apparent resolve to end the Vietnam War, and to part from and repudiate Lyndon Johnson's presidential leadership. Paupp's lucid essays chart Kennedy's extraordinary intellectual and political journey that was itself inspired by such deep wellsprings of thought as Albert Camus and the Greek tragedian Aeschylus.

The invocation of Greek tragedy as a source of guidance in addressing the tribulations confronting Kennedy might also be connected in some subconscious way to a wider drama that enveloped Kennedy's own life. It was the Kennedy brothers who were implicated in the Vietnam assassinations of the Nhu brothers in South Vietnam; the Nhus were seen as not prosecuting the war against North Vietnam and the National Liberation Front in the South in a satisfactory manner from an American counterinsurgency point of view. I have always felt that, in some haunting way, there was a connection between these ghastly murders, the Nhu brothers being the betrayed co-conspirators of America's lethal global projection of its power. Perhaps these parallel sets of siblings, both casualties of their country's troubles, need to be joined in our collective memory of what went wrong in the fateful decade of the 1960s.

In the end, Bobby Kennedy, despite the compromises associated with power and its pursuit, came to embody Gandhi's injunction to us all: "You must become the change you want to see in the world." Kennedy himself manifested this change when talking in South Africa in 1966: "Each time a man stands up for an ideal, or acts to improve the lot of others, or strikes out against injustice, he sends forth a tiny ripple of hope." It is fitting that these are the words found inscribed at Kennedy's memorial gravesite in Arlington National Cemetery.

And for me, and I believe for anyone fortunate enough to read *Robert Kennedy in the Stream of History*, the textual retelling of the Kennedy saga itself "sends forth a ripple of hope."

Preface

This is a book about the statesmanship, principles, and policies of Robert F. Kennedy. It is not intended to be a strictly conventional historical rendition of the man or his times. So, this book does not follow the traditional guidelines of historians who usually value chronological assessment without reference to the larger context of history. Therefore, this book places RFK in the stream of history so as to assess what came before his time in power, what happened during his time in power, and what happened to his legacy in the aftermath of his assassination in 1968. I have not written a conventional history or biography of RFK. Rather, the chapters of this book seek to fill a gap in the literature on RFK by taking an interdisciplinary approach to the themes and issues that he confronted, to which he responded, and which provided his often-visionary solutions. In that sense, my treatment of RFK and the quality of his policies and leadership is admittedly a work that praises and commemorates his legacy. As a result, some might say that this book is not academic, even though it contains a rather large bibliography of references to support the analysis and interpretations of events presented herein. Also, some might say that my treatment of RFK's legacy is counterfactual because I compare and contrast events, trends, and policy choices that he made with those people and events that came after his assassination. Yet, despite these anticipated criticisms, I think that by examining Kennedy through his own words and providing the reader with a history of the ideological and political battles in which he was engaged, this book effectively addresses the enduring meaning of the man and his legacy.

In order to explicate the before, during, and after periods of RFK's life and legacy, each chapter is dedicated to addressing these three periods in the stream of history. By reexamining RFK in the stream of history, it becomes possible to place RFK's interpretations and responses to the issues of his day in a context that offers a more comprehensive, yet partisan appreciation of the man and the ideals he was fighting to realize. For example, in his recovery from the despair of JFK's assassination, RFK learned that finding solutions to America's social problems, not expanding its power on the world stage, should be the most important goal of government. In particular, it was this perspective that allowed RFK to argue that the United States should commit itself to a pledge of "no more Vietnams" (Kennedy 1968b) in its foreign policy. Correspondingly, in America's domestic life, he believed that the nation should commit itself to altering the socioeconomic dynamic of domestic policies so that a national community could emerge that would be more inclusive, humane, and egalitarian. This was a perspective that allowed RFK to adopt a more communitarian vision of what the United States *should be*—as opposed to what it was. In making this commitment, he shared a common vision for America with Dr. Martin Luther King, Jr.

When understood in this way, it becomes evident that Kennedy's statesmanship in the arenas of both domestic and foreign policy was in opposition to the central bankers (the Rockefeller and J. P. Morgan Wall Street alliance), the World Bank, the International Monetary Fund, the military-industrial complex (Pentagon and CIA), racist structures and practices, and corporate interests that promoted profit over the protection of environment and the peoples of the earth. The recognition of these various injustices transformed him into a leader who was a dissenter—for he dissented from an unjust status quo of hierarchy, racism, privilege, and unaccountable power. Kennedy identified with the victims of these structures and the injustices they produced. Hence, RFK became a man who was personally acquainted with a world of pain and suffering. In so doing, he transformed himself and the country, thereby becoming what Arthur Schlesinger, Jr. (1978) called the "tribune of the underclass." It was in the evolution of his character and views that RFK himself was transformed and sought to transform both his nation and world. His last book on these subjects was *To Seek a Newer World*. In undertaking the quest to move toward a newer world, Kennedy sought to give more power directly to the people as a whole—not to vested financial interests or to bureaucracies. In that critical respect, RFK remains contemporary, relevant, and vital in our own times.

This book discusses the historical trends, personalities, and crisis that came before Robert Kennedy's rise to power. Therefore, I chronicle the influence of FDR's legacy as a vital prologue to the New Frontier and Great Society. Roosevelt's New Deal coalition was shattered by the late 1960s. With this history in mind, FDR's political principles, policies, and programs are discussed in reference to RFK's own efforts to build a new political coalition in the late 1960s. During Kennedy's time in power—both in his brother's administration and on his own in the US Senate—RFK struggled with striking the right balance between power and purpose. He believed that power and purpose should be united. So, while there were the practical concerns and considerations associated with electoral politics, there was, at the same time, a broader and inherently more idealistic purpose in RFK's work and message that transcended votes and coalitions. From his perspective, the national community was only viable when the rights of every person were protected and adequately advanced. In the philosophical tradition of Immanuel Kant, his message was one that increasingly spoke about the importance of the quality of life and the dignity of the individual.

Yet this was not a narrowly tailored concern to concentrate on narrow self-interest or the pursuit of wealth to the exclusion of people's needs. Rather, RFK's message was one that linked the dignity of the individual to the fate of the larger community in which a person lives. In so doing, Kennedy was concerned about the well-being, dignity, and purpose of individuals in reference to larger communities, both national and international. RFK promoted an expansive view of civil and human rights. His view transcended the boundaries of religion, race, class, and nationality. Kennedy cared about American Indians on reservations, migrant workers in the fields, and the young. In his foreign policy speeches, Kennedy spoke with equal fervor about racial apartheid in South Africa as an affront to human dignity and the viability of the human community when such practices are allowed to go unchecked. With respect to Latin America, he spoke of the need to break up large estates through land-reform measures so that peasant farmers and the socially marginalized could ultimately be incorporated into more just and egalitarian political, economic, and social orders. What truly distinguished RFK was the fact that he was not beholden to corporate business interests who were content to leave social reform to the dictatorships of the region. To the chagrin of David and Nelson Rockefeller, the historical record reveals that RFK was supportive of nationalization when the people's resources were being exploited.

In the years after RFK's assassination, his emphasis on the need to unite power and purpose, national and international concerns, ideals with practice, has been purposefully ignored and denigrated by what C. Wright Mills (1956) called "the power elite." President Nixon illegally expanded the Vietnam War into Laos and Thailand while conspiring with a Chilean military junta to overthrow the democratically elected government of Salvador Allende. President Reagan illegally funded the Contra "freedom fighters" in Nicaragua while illegally selling arms to Iran. President Bill Clinton endorsed a draconian version of welfare reform at home just as easily as he supported the North American Free Trade Agreement (NAFTA), allowing labor-law rights and land reform in Mexico to be destroyed along with the integrity of the environment. President George W. Bush illegally invaded Iraq on the basis false claims, in violation of the United Nations Security Council, and expanded the power of the federal government at home to curtail and violate constitutionally guaranteed civil rights and liberties in the name of fighting terrorism—as has President Obama. Since the 1970s, economic inequality within the United States has increased to such a degree that the middle-class is virtually extinct, poverty and incarceration have been rising, and a neoliberal economic doctrine/model/creed has justified privatization and deregulation in the North Atlantic democracies as well as throughout the Global South.

Throughout his life and career, Kennedy was preoccupied with human dignity issues—what would later be termed by Martha Nussbaum and Amaryta Sen (2011) as the "human capabilities approach." This approach to development centralizes human rights and dignity with respect to issues of governance, economics, and social and political policies. For RFK, these concerns were often addressed through his emphasis on the need for communitarian solutions to address the problems inherent in the failures of representative democracy to truly "represent" all classes and peoples within the national polity. He adopted communitarian considerations to effectuate the expansion of democratic citizenship, such as the rights to decent jobs, housing, and education. By the time he became a United States Senator, his views on poverty could be radically differentiated from those of both the Democratic and Republican parties. Despite his call for local control, Kennedy's unique concept of federalism was not based on state or city government. Instead, it hinged on the need to establish a direct relationship between the federal government and an imagined community of those in need who were kept from power at the grassroots level. He truly wanted to give power to the people. And so, there emerged what could be called the concept of "Kennedy federalism" on the problem of poverty. RFK sought to bypass the conventional machinery of entrenched social institutions that continued to render the poor powerless. His approach had radical implications. One key manifestation of his approach was evident in the introduction of his Bedford-Stuyvesant Program in New York. It was bold and imaginative, particularly in its pointed reluctance to depend on the federal government. Kennedy often spoke of the need to build self-sufficiency and self-determination within the African American community. He believed that this new emphasis was essential so that what is too often an undifferentiated mass might be helped to form a coherent and cohesive community. RFK viewed this as necessary to break the back of poverty itself, which he saw as a vicious cycle of reinforcing disabilities—unemployment, inferior education, discrimination, poor health, lack of motivation, unstable life, and other factors—all of which serve to render victims incapable of competing within the larger society.

In assessing RFK's statesmanship, this book examines his commitment to human and civil rights on both the national and international stage. This allows a linking of common themes and ideals from the civil and human rights struggles of his times within the United States itself to those struggles taking place against South Africa's system of racial apartheid. In the case of Latin America, RFK continued to advocate for social justice concerns by advancing and promoting the policies and social reform elements that were the hallmark of JFK's Alliance for Progress. In so doing, RFK's choice of themes, statements, and policy prescriptions for change left an indelible mark in the global consciousness of the world's peoples. However, RFK's assassination abruptly ended the forward thrust and direction of these transformative ideas and policies as forces for progressive change. After his death in 1968, the implementation of RFK's legacy has been eroded, betrayed, undermined, and supplanted by the administrations of Presidents Nixon, Ford, Carter, Reagan, Bush I and II, Clinton, and Obama. Regardless of which major party has been in control of the White House and/or the Congress, the America of post-1968 has increasingly experienced a leadership void. This historical trend makes the loss of RFK even more painful today. Decade after passing decade, it has become ever more evident what was lost with the death of RFK.

It is also true that international relations are not the same as in the 1960s. The era of European imperialism that was starting to end with the close of WWII in 1945 continued on into the 1960s with decolonization. The Bandung Conference of 1958 united many countries throughout the Third World under the banner of nonalignment. The Non-Aligned Movement sought not only national independence through sovereignty and self-determination, but also a developmental path that would take nations' futures out of the hands of the two Cold War superpowers: the US and the USSR. Despite the collapse of the Soviet Union in 1989—thereby signaling the formal end of the Cold War era—the ensuing post-Cold War world with one superpower has not resulted in a more peaceful world. As Richard Barnett noted in his 1972 book, *Roots of War: The Men and Institutions behind U.S. Foreign Policy*:

> The terrible problem for policy planners in mid-century America was that they did not and could not know what their long term interests really were. To be sure, they used the code word "national interest" to sanctify policies they perceived to be in their own class interests, i.e., the ever increasing capitalist system from which they, their friends and employers had amassed great wealth. But within a generation it had become clear that they lacked a sufficiently coherent understanding of the world and a sufficiently flexible strategy to realize their parochial definition of the "national interest." The world was moving too fast. (67)

Both JFK and RFK already understood this problem in the 1960s. That is why Kennedy offered his "no more Vietnams" speech in his 1968 presidential campaign. RFK realized during the course of the Vietnam War—which actually began in 1965 under LBJ—that U.S. military intervention was rarely a viable answer to problems, and usually the source of new problems. The US policy in Vietnam contributed greatly to profits within the military-industrial complex, but it wasted national treasure even as it squandered the social programs and "human capabilities" of millions of Americans. Hence, RFK and Martin Luther King, Jr., both criticized the Johnson administration for continuing to invest in the Vietnam War and the faulty logic of the "domino theory." RFK urged President Johnson to seek a viable political solution in Vietnam and to pursue serious negotiations, and even advocated a coalition government in Saigon. In other words, the so-called "national interest" could not be advanced under the rubric of militarization, corporate profits, and endless interventions throughout the Third World.

What RFK's message and legacy present is an understanding about the fuller nature of power and purpose, both nationally and internationally. He was an exemplary leader because he sought to make Americans more aware of the fact that beyond a limited and narrow conception of the "national interest," there existed a larger "human interest." In other words, the United States should not isolate its purpose, role, and mission in the world from the global problems of poverty, war, suffering, and social injustice.

Amidst the tumult and horror of 1968 came a fleeting reminder of the dawn of the New Frontier. Speaking in Portland, Oregon, in mid-April of that year, RFK harked back to his brother's policies of engagement with the non-aligned nations of the Third World, and decried the diminished moral authority of the United States in the world. Citing recent surveys and alluding to the Declaration of Independence, he said: "By the unilateral exercise of our overwhelming power, we isolated ourselves. To many of our traditional allies and neutral friends, we behaved as a superpower, ignoring our own historical commitment to 'a decent respect for the opinion of mankind.'" The phrase, "a decent respect to the opinions of mankind," appears in the preamble of the Declaration of Independence. Both the phrase and the idealism behind it were, in large part, a casualty of the 1960s. The hubris of American hegemony combined with an increasingly unilateral foreign policy would be responsible for a neoconservative and neoliberal endorsement of the idea of dream of making the twenty-first century into another "American century." In this regard, RFK's legacy of "no more Vietnams" and engagement with the Global South have been discarded by the American primacy coalition. Yet, by ignoring the RFK legacy, this bipartisan alliance in the American primacy coalition has financially bankrupted the nation. As it seeks to maintain more than 760 military bases around the world, continues to invest more than one trillion dollars a year in the Pentagon/CIA budgets and those of military contractors, and continues to engage in deficit spending and borrowing from China to pay the costs associated with such an enterprise, the American empire is experiencing financial collapse from within and suffering from what historian Paul Kennedy (1987) has called "imperial overstretch" abroad.

On the night of Martin Luther King, Jr.'s assassination, RFK quoted from the wisdom of the ancient Greeks and said, like them, it should be our purpose "to tame the savageness of man and make gentle the life of the world" (Newfield 1969, 281). This was the essential vision and purpose that informed and shaped Robert Kennedy's own unique conception of what constituted community at the local, state, federal, and international levels. It was the expression of this vision that made him more than an ordinary politician. It was a vision that transformed him into a statesman of his own time and for all time. It was for this reason that the RFK legacy has endured into the twenty-first century as a transformative call, reminding us that "we can do better." In all of the various arenas of human endeavor that he touched and addressed, this commitment to taming the savagery of humankind was Robert Kennedy's most basic and guiding principle. As such, this guiding principle serves as an enduring commitment at the dawn of the twenty-first century to creating the "newer world" (Kennedy 1967) to which he committed his career and for which he sacrificed his life. In fact, it is a commitment that endures as a beacon of light in dark times and still remains our greatest collective need on this planet.

Acknowledgments

Writing a book about Robert Francis Kennedy is both a challenge and a privilege. RFK became a transformative figure and leader in an era of global transformation. It is for that reason that I have focused my assessment of his legacy and significance upon his statesmanship—both nationally and internationally. Hence, it should be clear that the influence of RFK on my life, professional work, and involvements as a scholar, author, and progressive activist has been truly enormous. I came of age during the presidency of John F. Kennedy. In JFK's legendary "thousand days," Robert F. Kennedy served as the Attorney General of the United States. After the tragedy of JFK's assassination, RFK became a senator and also a candidate for the presidency. Together, they served as models that broke with the history of a violent century that had experienced two world wars, was emerging from an age of both imperialism and colonialism, and was confronted with a choice between the pursuit of peace (through cooperation and détente with the Soviet Union) or, if the Joint Chiefs and CIA had their way, engaging in a nuclear "first strike" to advance the illusion of global hegemony through military might.

The culture of the Cold War era was in flux. JFK was the first United States president to be born in the twentieth century. While the military hardliners and rightwing viewed the world in terms of confrontation and a refusal to negotiate, compromise, or even consider peaceful alternatives to the status quo, the Kennedy brothers and Martin Luther King, Jr. inspired and articulated a new direction—one that moved the trajectory of history closer to social, economic, and political justice. Their perspectives on peace and building functional communities were a radical proposition in the 1960s—and remain so even in the first decades of the twenty-first century. Therefore, I have dedicated this book to all three of these idealistic leaders.

Today, instead of fighting communism, we are told that the world is engaged in a "war without end" against terrorism—a term and a concept that refers more to a strategy of war than to an ideology. Yet, as the Kennedy brothers and Dr. King would remind us, humanity faces one vital, predominant, and critical choice: the choice between chaos and community. This book addresses that choice and the options associated with building a national and international community dedicated to civil and human rights as its primary source of meaning and practice, rather than the mindless terrorism of building and maintaining nuclear weapons, of seeking security in a denial of civil liberties, and of the need to emphasize human security for all peoples and nations. In short, the legacy of RFK embodies a commitment to the unequivocal advancement of a genuinely humane, sustainable, and liberating set of approaches to political life and community-building through dialogue, a sense of common purpose, and the resolution of differences through cooperation, empathy, and understanding.

My own thinking and scholarly evolution on these subjects and this history has been largely forged by Professor Richard Falk (Emeritus, Princeton University) who has supplied a moving and thoughtful foreword to this book. As a mentor, colleague, and friend, I have benefited greatly from Richard's commitment to human rights, his ideas about "humane governance" as opposed to the path of traditional notions of governance based on narrow geopolitical considerations, and his belief in the need to bring about creative solutions to the challenges which confront every nation and our international environment as a global community. So, my intellectual debt to him is beyond measure, but it is truly reflected in all of my publications—from books and articles, to chapters, lectures, and speeches.

My work has also benefited from my association with Professor Marcus Raskin. Along with Richard Barnett, he was a co-founder of the Institute for Policy Studies, Washington, DC. As a member of the National Security Council during the JFK years, he witnessed the dangers of nuclear war and the battles that the Kennedy brothers fought against the hawks in the Joint Chiefs of Staff and the CIA.

Just before earning my Juris-Doctor Degree at the University of San Diego School of Law, I had the good fortune to have Willard Wirtz as my labor law professor. He was US Secretary of Labor under both Presidents Kennedy and Johnson. Also, he was a close friend and ally of Robert F. Kennedy. In my personal conversations with Wirtz, he always emphasized what the historical record of his tenure in the Kennedy-Johnson years has effectively proven, with regard to advancing civil rights and socioeconomic rights, the vital importance of "jobs, jobs, and jobs." Hence, that particular emphasis of Wirtz in relation to the legacy of RFK comes through this entire book. It is especially poignant when addressing the crisis of the ghetto, the failures of the criminal justice system, the limits of the US labor market, and what needs to be done to advance the well-being of African-Americans in the context of the intertwined challenges of race and class. Additionally, I want to express my appreciation to Larry Birns, the Director of the Council on Hemispheric Affairs (COHA), Washington, DC. I have had the privilege of working with Larry since 1984 as a research associate and since 1996 as a senior research associate. My initial involvement with COHA came about because of its focus on the political, economic, and human rights conditions in Latin America.

Further, I want to acknowledge the important role and friendship I have enjoyed with Professor Lawrence Edward Carter, Sr., the distinguished Dean of the Martin Luther King, Jr. International Chapel, at Morehouse College. From 2001–2004, I served as National Chancellor of the United States for an NGO called the International Association of Educators for World Peace (IAEWP). As both a professor of religion at Morehouse College and IAEWP State Chancellor for Georgia, Dean Carter played an essential role in hosting an IAEWP national conference at the college in April of 2004. As early as 2003, he was instrumental in introducing me to the Toda Institute for Global Peace and Policy Research—as well as the thought and work of Daisaku Ikeda.

Since 2003, I have had the privilege of working with the Toda Institute's original director, Majid Tehranian. In subsequent years, the Toda Institute has provided me with two grants to write books on peace and human rights. This network of people has allowed me to further reflect upon and refer to the legacy of Robert F. Kennedy as a voice for peace in the area of nuclear abolition and the creation of Nuclear Weapon Free Zones (NWFZs)—as exemplified by the members of the Association of Southeast Asian Nations (ASEAN), as well as some Latin American nations. The work of ASEAN and the Toda Institute—in addition to the work of Daisaku Ikeda—inspired me to write a book entitled, *Beyond Global Crisis: Remedies and Road Maps by Daisaku Ikeda and his Contemporaries* (2012).

Finally, I want to express my appreciation to the editors at Transaction Publishers. My association with Dr. Irving Louis Horowitz was a true inspiration to me in writing this book. Today, I am grateful to Mary Curtis, the president of Transaction Publishers, who has made possible the publication of this book on the legacy, policies, and enduring importance of RFK from the twentieth to the twenty-first century.

Introduction

Robert Francis Kennedy's positive world vision for the advancement of peace, justice, equality, and responsibility continues to capture the world's imagination decades after his 1968 assassination. Following in the footsteps of his slain brother, President John Fitzgerald Kennedy, Robert renounced the unworkable dogmas that held both Russia and the United States in seemingly intractable positions—even to the point of engaging in nuclear war. Robert embraced peaceful coexistence in an era of militarism. Like his brother, Robert was receptive to a standing-down from armed rivalry with Russia. During the thousand-day presidency of John F. Kennedy, it can be said that the president and Robert together shared the presidency. They both sought to change the status quo in just about every arena of human activity. From reducing Cold War tensions to advancing the cause of human and civil rights at home and around the globe, they were visionaries. After the president's assassination in 1963, Robert Kennedy was more fully on his own. In his post-1963 role, Robert sought to expand his brother's legacy. In so doing, he made it his own.

As visionaries, John and Robert stood for ideals that were not confined to a nationalistic ethos of American exceptionalism and a self-righteous attachment to military solutions. Their vision transcended a narrowly conceived national loyalty and embraced the aspirations of the entire human family. Neither of them was satisfied with the way things were when so many people, both in the United States and around the world, were excluded from full citizenship in their own societies, their own communities, and their own nations. Neither of the brothers would remain content with the fact that political, social, and economic exclusion defined the political realities and limited the possibilities for so many other humans on the planet. This preoccupation with social justice, human rights, and genuine human security was the central quality that set John and Robert Kennedy apart from the conventions and establishment of their day, and defines what separates their legacy from the establishment of our day. Robert Kennedy's legacy still resonates on the themes that have come to redefine America's domestic debates in the Nixon/Carter/Reagan/Clinton/Bush/Obama years about the purpose, need, and direction of government in public affairs. As Attorney General of the United States in the early 1960s, Robert had many opportunities to address this theme. In a 1965 collection of some of his key speeches entitled *The Pursuit of Justice*, Robert Kennedy declared: *"I believe that, as long as there is plenty, poverty is evil. Government belongs wherever evil needs an adversary and there are people in distress who cannot help themselves"* (Ross 1968, 135, italics added).

Because of the traditional jurisdiction of the Justice Department, as well as the historical pressures of the early 1960s, Robert Kennedy's position as attorney general provided him with many avenues through which to confront the problems of poverty in America, and to expand his awareness of the depth and breadth of its challenge to the nation's future. On this matter, historian Edward Schmitt has astutely observed of this period that: "Kennedy's experience as attorney general would be pivotal to both his preliminary diagnosis of the problem and his nascent commitment to the issue. His interests and his initiatives at the Justice Department elevated the prominence of poverty in the administration's policy debates, with consequences that would extend beyond his brother's presidency" (Schmitt 2010, 67). Kennedy's involvement with the problems of poverty, social exclusion, and the injustices stemming from structural injustices and civil rights abuses placed his efforts on behalf of American Indians on a special trajectory. In late 1963, the attorney general was discussing the issue of poverty with particular attention to American Indians. Kennedy took the lead in promoting a National Service Corps and enabling its passage through a recalcitrant Congress. It was at this moment that "the domestic Peace Corps initiative alerted Robert Kennedy to the real depth of suffering among American Indians, and it was important to his emerging relationship with them" (Schmitt 2010, 85).

In the stream of history, Kennedy would confront the legacy of a centuries-long series of human rights abuses of American Indians by foreign settlers, beginning with the founding of the American Republic. This record reveals that "after the Revolutionary War, the United States became the successor nation to the European colonialist states. In 1787, the young United States adopted its constitution and formalized its relationship with Indian tribes and Indian people through treaty making. . . . The continuing diplomatic encounter resulted in more than 350 treaties—many of which were subsequently broken or disregarded" (Pommersheim 2009, 3). Legal scholars have increasingly come to classify these multiple encounters through the lenses of four primary themes, namely: (1) commerce and land acquisition, (2) diplomacy and war, (3) cultural difference, and (4) physical separation. In response to these early interactions, both Congress and the Executive branch were engaged in enacting a legal regime relative to trade and settlement. As this history progressed, "presumably, the Supreme Court reviewed all of these efforts to ensure they were constitutionally permissible and within the legitimate authority of Congress and the Executive Branch. This expectation of careful review—especially vaunted in our constitutional democracy—was largely unattended to and unfulfilled in the field of Indian law" (Pommersheim 2009, 3–4). As a result, one legal scholar has concluded: "What is truly unexpected is that in the course of the ensuing 200-plus years, there has been very little scholarly or sustained political attention to this constitutional drift. . . . Tribes (and tribal people), originally outside and on the margins of the new republic, were increasingly absorbed geographically, socially, politically, and 'legally' (but without their consent) into the republic without the slightest constitutional ripple. This is remarkable. If it took constitutional amendments to bring African Americans and women fully into the domain of dignity and equity within the Constitution, isn't an equivalent effort needed to guarantee enduring tribal sovereignty and full equality to Native people and nations?" (Pommersheim 2009, 5).

These were the conditions that made Robert Kennedy's efforts on behalf of American Indians so significant and, at the same time, so fraught with difficulty. As attorney general, Kennedy had special responsibility over matters of great concern to American Indians under the Lands Division of the Justice Department, which oversaw the Indian Claims Commission (ICC). The ICC was established at the end of World War II to adjudicate the compensatory territorial claims of Native peoples. In this task, "Kennedy departed from the course set by the Eisenhower Justice Department to urge more rapid settlement of claims, increasing the number of panels processing the disputes, and successfully pressing for the creation of a loan fund for tribes to secure adequate legal counsel to argue their cases" (Schmitt 2010, 80). Yet the process was hampered by the reality that the process of settling claims was tedious, beset by the difficulty of agreeing on land values, the profiteering of some self-interested lawyers for American Indian claims (who benefited from endless negotiations), and a Congress resistant to any settlement of payments (Schmitt 2010, 80). What connected the legal and political struggle of the American Indians with those of African Americans, as well as the emerging Mexican American community, was that all three groups would fit into "a distinctive new model of federalism with regard to poverty that Kennedy would come to idealize throughout the rest of his career" (Schmitt 2010, 83–84). What separated the legal and political struggle of American Indians from that of African Americans or Mexican Americans was the unresolved nature of tribal sovereignty, which would ultimately require major constitutional reforms and amendment; the issues of treaty obligations and diplomacy; the development of a partnership between American Indians and the US Government that would be respectful and protective of human rights claims under international law; and constitutional re-envisioning concerning the status of tribal sovereignty.

From Robert Kennedy's own moral, social, and political perspective, it became evident that what finally and ultimately united all of these groups was their common need to establish a new relationship with the government of the United States—a relationship in which their grassroots rights and claims would have to be given greater credence, strength, and respect under a new Kennedy-inspired brand of federalism. Such a new brand of federalism seemed necessary because of what Robert Kennedy had consistently and repeatedly discovered throughout his career, which was this reality:

> Bureaucratic ossification and the inertia of existing local power structures were stifling opportunity for true grassroots leadership; the federal government needed to coordinate its own activities to help directly those leaders most representative of the poor. The federal government would . . . have to share power with the poor for progress to be made, or else top-down welfarism—what Kennedy and his allies identified as the legacy of the New Deal—would only strengthen local reactionary forces. Instead, the grassroots power in communities could gain access to power in the form of federal recognition and resources, and their bottom-up pressures would make local structures more representative and responsive. (Schmitt 2010, 84)

In the stream of history, African Americans had experienced an "Age of Neo-Slavery" from the aftermath of the Civil War through the dawn of World War II (Blackmon 2008). It was a world in which, under laws enacted specifically to intimidate blacks, tens of thousands of African-Americans were arbitrarily arrested, hit with outrageous fines, and charged for the costs of their own arrests. With no means to pay these ostensible "debts," these prisoners were sold as forced laborers to coal mines, lumber camps, brickyards, railroads, quarries, and farm plantations. Government officials outsourced falsely imprisoned blacks to small-town entrepreneurs, provincial farmers, and dozens of corporations—including US Steel—looking for cheap and abundant labor. In this world, armies of "free" black men labored without compensation, were repeatedly bought and sold, and were forced, through beatings and physical torture, to do the bidding of white masters for decades after the official abolition of slavery (Blackmon 2008). This was not fully resolved by the Civil War because the practice was embedded in America's history at the foundation of the American republic, when the US Constitution helped to mold and shape slavery into the texture of its origin—thereby making it the nation's "original sin" (Goldstone 2005). It was never fully rectified by the Civil War because of the betrayal of equal rights by the Supreme Court from 1865–1903. In so doing, recent historians have demonstrated how the US Supreme Court subverted the cause of justice and served to empower the Jim Crow era (Goldstone 2011). As Professor Jack Balkin has noted, "What makes a constitution legitimate is not that it settles everything in advance in a way that is currently fair and just to the people who live under it. . . . Rather, what makes an imperfect constitutional system democratically legitimate is that people have the ability to persuade their fellow citizens about the right way to interpret the Constitution and to continue the constitutional project. What makes this legitimacy democratic is that constitutional redemption is not the product of isolated individuals but the work of the entire public" (2011, 9–10). The unjust conditions that African Americans had inherited had—in Robert Kennedy's view—both justified and necessitated the creation of a new social contract, a new federalism, and significant constitutional revision and amendment. The exact same thing can be said of what will eventually be required for the final realization of the human rights of American Indian as well as a more humane approach to immigration issues for Mexican-Americans. This insight does not even begin to address needed changes for enlarging the protections provided by US labor law.

Robert Kennedy would begin progressive efforts in the 1960s, but it would be left to others in succeeding decades to advance, advocate, and struggle to realize the emblematic motto of the "newer world" (not "new world order") that Kennedy constantly referenced. On this point, Professor Frank Pommersheim, in his comments on the need for constitutional revision and amendment, writes:

> The *yes* to constitutional reform and amendment is not a *yes* of assimilative condescension or residual colonialism, but a *yes* that builds on the treaty diplomacy of the past, a *yes* that seeks to change the landscape of (dominant) history, and a *yes* that seeks to translate the promises of the past into permanent guarantees for the future. This *yes* is grounded in partnership, dignity, and respect—not an easy *yes* but the *yes* of hard work and dialogue—and a *yes* that brings (constitutional) sunlight where there has only been shadow. A *yes* whose very contours will (hopefully) emerge from sustained discussion and engagement. A *yes* that also realizes the need for much doctrinal change and political reform as a necessary prelude to an constitutional revision concerning the status of tribal sovereignty. And finally, it is a *yes* committed to developing a constitutional architecture that is fully inclusive yet respectful of differences within the weave of historical and cultural pluralism" (Pommersheim 2009, 6, italics in original).

Robert Kennedy had already begun to make the first essential steps toward political reform as a necessary prelude to these changes. He was the first leader of national stature, vision, and commitment to say "yes." Yet, in the aftermath of Kennedy's tragic assassination, there has been no leader of national stature or commitment to fill the gap left by his untimely removal from the stage of history. So, many of these problems and injustices still remain with us at the dawn of the twenty-first century. Still, we have his legacy and his example as a template from which we can undertake the much-needed task to remake the world in a more humane form, to push the boundaries of possibility in a more expansive and hopeful direction—a more justice-oriented direction, a more inclusive and more compassionate and more transformative direction.

This was the world that Robert Kennedy inherited and whose wrongs he sought to rectify, remove, and reverse. Robert's very personal dissent from many structural and institutional features of American life placed him into conflict with a host of social, cultural, political, and economic elites (including those in organized crime), as well their bureaucratic protectors within the Federal Bureau of Investigation. His battles against white racism were evident not only on the domestic stage of American electoral politics and governance, but also on the international stage as a world citizen who opposed a racist war against the people of Vietnam. Robert's 1968 speeches declaring that there should be "no more Vietnams" for American foreign policy placed him into conflict with the Pentagon and the Central Intelligence Agency. His sympathy and commitment to the principles of the civil rights movement within the United States also served to place him into an automatic alliance with those social movements in South Africa that sought an end to a regime of racial segregation under the doctrine of apartheid. This same empathy placed him in alliance with social movements for land reform and social justice in Latin America that sought to throw off the bondage of local and national dictators—many of whom had previously enjoyed the support of the US government and its allies in corporate America: the US Chamber of Commerce, and Wall Street bankers and financiers allied with Rockefeller and Morgan interests. A review of this record demonstrates that Robert's empathy for the suffering of the poor, his loyal and continuous association with the disadvantaged and the socially excluded, all served to place him in conflict with the greedy economics and culture of a profit-driven corporate America and Wall Street, as well as a long history of American racism and the doctrine of white supremacy.

In short, Robert Kennedy sought to bring about an end to the human and civil rights abuses of American society and the entire American establishment—whether financial, governmental, or bureaucratic. He wanted power to become responsive to the people, to *all* citizens regardless of their race, or creed, or community. In this regard, Robert Kennedy was a strong advocate for inclusive governance. This book is a unique testament to that legacy, for it presents the reader with an examination of RFK's actual statesmanship. In so doing, this book does not focus on electoral politics, but upon the broad themes that defined his career and infused his speeches. In other words, this book is primarily about the statesmanship of Robert Francis Kennedy. It is also about his evolution as a visionary leader in the stream of history.

1

A Transformative Era

The Kennedy years constitute a transformative era in both American and world history. The choices that both JFK and RFK jointly made and the policies that they embraced during JFK's thousand-day presidency were significant. Both John and Robert worked together to further advance the agenda and claims of the civil rights movement as well as those of the Alliance for Progress in Latin America. The diplomacy in which they engaged to avoid nuclear war with the Soviet Union over the presence of Russian missiles in Cuba came during the most threatening moment of the entire Cold War. Because they were able to resist the pressures to launch a military action against Cuba, John and Robert Kennedy saved the world from what could have become a global nuclear war in October 1962. Their success in resolving the Cuban missile crisis of 1962 led to the beginnings of détente and resulted in the signing of the Nuclear Test Ban Treaty with Russia in the fall of 1963. In the tragic aftermath of the Dallas assassination of JFK in November 1963, Robert Kennedy struggled to move the United States toward a negotiated settlement of the Vietnam War in the hope that such an agreement would lead to a complete withdrawal.

In Latin American affairs, Robert sought to continue the legacy of land reform and social justice that was inaugurated in 1961 with the Alliance for Progress. In 1966, Robert made an historic journey to South Africa to speak out against the racial policies of a white-dominated apartheid government. Robert often spoke of the need to support and to pursue genuine land reform throughout the Third World, and to advance social progress in the fields of education, employment, and health care. In all of these efforts that Robert Kennedy undertook, the principles and ideals that he advanced can be seen as a thematically coherent effort to establish a "new politics," both in the United States and throughout the world. Robert Kennedy's various contributions in all of these fields of human endeavor can best be appreciated when viewed from the perspective that they all involved a call to action: a call to citizen involvement and participation in the life of one's own community, and in the world community at large. Robert Kennedy's legacy can be seen as embodying involvement in a host of struggles for justice that would ultimately combine to create a climate of change that would alter the course of world history at a pivotal historical moment.

In the ensuing pages of this book, I shall provide evidence and arguments to support the central thesis of this collection of interpretations and photos, which is this: Robert Kennedy rerouted the stream of history. In this sense, this book stands as a tribute to him as a man of conscience and action, as well as testimony to his success as a leader and visionary at a critical moment in both the life of his country and the life of his world. Therefore, this book seeks to bring a fresh perspective to his time and his personality, and to reflect on the broad nature and scope of his contributions to changing the course of human history and human thought about what is possible. His tenure in power was not merely a transitional moment. It was transformative time and, in so many ways, he was at the vital center of that transformation.

Robert Kennedy's speeches reflect this transformative outlook; selections from them are quoted at length throughout the essays in this book. The policies that Robert Kennedy embraced continue to serve as a guiding beacon in our own time. His words and legacy remain significant in our own time because they constitute a visionary path that can serve as a way to chart a course out of our present darkness. In large measure, Robert Kennedy's legacy has the capacity to chart a course out of the darkness of the early twenty-first century because he was a statesman and a champion of human rights in the preceding century. Many of the challenges that existed in his time have persisted into our own day and generation. We can see this reality in the traumas and tragedies of the wars of the early twenty-first century in Iraq and Afghanistan. Since the US financial crisis of 2008, the evidence of America's continuing economic and political corruption is evident in the crimes. conspiracies, and corruption that have become manifestly apparent in the linkages connecting Wall Street, Congress, and the White House. Now, more than forty years after his assassination, Robert Kennedy's political enemies—from Wall Street to the CIA, from the military-industrial complex to various hidden, non-transparent, unaccountable, and anti-democratic centers of private power—remain in power as the political enemies of the majority of people in the world today.

It is for these reasons—and many others—that the legacy of Robert Kennedy remains as a seminal force for change and not merely a repository of historical memory. As the nation's top banks and investment firms continue a policy of massive home foreclosures on millions of Americans, under the motto of "Too Big To Fail," it has become evident since 2008 that they are also apparently "Too Big To Jail." Presidents George Bush and Barack Obama have refused to allow the US Department of Justice to prosecute the known individuals and parties responsible for the theft and corruption associated with the home mortgage crisis, illegal lending practices, and the catastrophic destruction of the financial lives of so many millions of innocent American citizens. In these circumstances, it is not hard to imagine how different the response would have been from Robert Kennedy—who took on organized crime, Jimmy Hoffa and the Teamsters Union, the abuses of the CIA, and the racist policies of the Jim Crow era in both the North and the South. Instead, the first decades of the twenty-first century have revealed an America adrift, in crisis, and virtually lacking moral leadership. Both political parties remain hostages to their Wall Street contributors; the Pentagon and CIA have continued to operate illegal wars in the Middle East; and all the while. the jobless rate and unemployment picture on the American home front continue to mirror a seemingly hopeless decline for the middle-class and those already trapped in poverty. Robert Kennedy was different. In his time, Kennedy played the role of protector of the vulnerable while prosecuting their predators. His approach to issues of war and peace, the challenges posed by political corruption and accountability, the needs and aspirations of the poor, the working class, and the excluded are all part of an enduring legacy of what a vibrant and progressive alternative to the status quo would look like in the twenty-first century.

2

The Past Is Prologue

While the Kennedy brothers emerged in the era of the late 1940s from one of the wealthiest families in America, they were still attuned to the suffering and needs of the poor, the disenfranchised, the elderly, and the young—all those vulnerable to the vagaries and injustices of life. In other words, they overcame the dichotomy between the experience of having enjoyed great personal privilege, on the one hand, and their political commitment to extend freedom, opportunity, and basic human rights to all people on the other. Their philosophy, core values, and beliefs were not premised on having achieved great wealth, nor on a desire to exclude others from achieving basic human rights and human security. Rather, we discover in the political statements and public service of both JFK and RFK a shared commitment to a more universal and ecumenical concept of "justice."

In part, their Catholic faith supplied them with a moral grounding, for their conception of social justice differentiated them from many on Wall Street who inherited their social views from a wealthy Protestant establishment that was largely guided by a single-minded drive for profit, aptly described by what the German sociologist Max Weber identified as the "Protestant ethic and spirit of capitalism"(Diggins 1996). It also was—and is—an establishment deeply addicted to a particular version of the market economy and the centrality of corporate power that has depleted American democracy throughout the post-1945 decades, leaving in its wake a growing "democratic deficit," greater wealth inequalities, and an erosion of America's financial and moral foundations. During the 1940s and 1950s, and culminating in the 1960s, the United States was coming of age as an emerging global superpower. By 1961, the United States was on its way to becoming an empire that, by the late 1990s, would amass an armada of more than 750 military bases around the world. America's establishment was increasingly becoming represented in the government by what C. Wright Mills would call "the power elite." Yet John and Robert Kennedy did not share many of the assumptions and claims to privilege that this elite sought to exercise in the 1960s. As Attorney General of the United States, Robert found himself fighting the steel industry titans in 1962, who had violated an accord that had previously been worked out with labor and President Kennedy regarding the question of whether they could raise the price of steel by some six dollars a ton, thereby breaking a tripartite accord worked out by labor, the steel industry, and the executive branch.

The affinity that John and Robert shared with regard to labor, workers, the poor, and America's expanding middle-class, was a genuine reflection of their own family's struggle as immigrants from Ireland in the nineteenth century. This sensitivity to the struggles of immigrants, workers, and the poor also influenced their approach to the conduct of US foreign policy. In this sense, both JFK and RFK benefited from the influence of the historical experience of their family as Irish immigrants, insofar as it served to make them more sensitive to and aware of the struggles of oppressed peoples, and wary of the demands and claims of the European empires, beginning in the eighteenth century, progressing throughout the course of the nineteenth century, and culminating in the mid-twentieth century. By refusing to adopt the Anglo-American establishment's self-imposed and manufactured version of the "white man's burden," the Kennedy brothers refuted and rejected the geopolitical logic of colonialism, imperialism, and the claims of empire. Instead of embracing the idea of empire and all of the policies that would accompany the support of such an enterprise, they took an alternative course in the stream of history. To the chagrin of the traditional Anglo-American establishment, the Kennedy brothers' more humane and inclusive vision of global governance became evident in the early 1960s, when they purposefully sought to join in common cause with the struggles and aspirations of Third World peoples and nations to end colonial rule and imperial domination. The more humane instincts, policies, and programs adopted by John and Robert Kennedy would place them at odds with powerful bankers on Wall Street and powerful leaders in the corporate-financial world of commerce, dominated by the Rockefeller interests, J. P. Morgan interests, oil companies, the military-industrial complex, and the CIA.

In the aftermath of European imperialism, the United States had to create a new geopolitical vision for itself and for the rest of the world that would allow it to more effectively navigate the waters of the Cold War era. A new type of international politics was emerging as John F. Kennedy entered the presidency, and he would be the first of a succession of presidents who would be forced to confront this challenge. From a purely economic perspective, the early 1960s would become an era remembered for the ways in which various theories of modernization would be proposed for the Third World, relative to Western powers and corporate-driven interests. Since that time, the discipline of an emergent developmental economics came into vogue, along with such terms as "nation-building," "humanitarian relief," and "foreign aid." But this aspect of the 1960s and the decades to follow is usually remembered as a period in which the West engaged in an on-going intellectual effort and enterprise that comes under the more general and all-encompassing rubric of "development" (Cullather 2010, ix). According to historian Nick Cullather, this era is often remembered as one where:

> The domestic consensus behind development had always rested on a jury-rigged alliance of self-interest, strategic anxiety, and faith in the unique capacity of the United States to engineer progress. . . . The US standard of living, whose rise once validated Washington's mastery of the arts of growth, staggered and then fell back under the pressure of war-induced inflation and unemployment, while the annual festival of urban rioting offered a recurring disproof of America's claim to social advancement. . . . Startling revelations of the severity of domestic poverty even discredited US claims to competence in the area of basic needs. Leading a delegation to Mississippi in early 1968 to investigate segregation, Senator Robert Kennedy found himself instead answering appeals for food. Witnesses, who had come to testify on rights violations, admitted they were living on a diet of turnips. A subsequent nationwide investigation uncovered the extent of "*acute hunger and malnutrition*" in the world's best-fed country. . . . *There was no need to go to Asia to find disturbing images of starvation, one report observed; "if you will go look you will find America is a shocking place."* (Cullather 2010, 253, italics added)

In addressing the plight of American Indians on reservations, Mexican-American migrant workers in the fields of Delano and various other migrant worker camps around the nation, and African American ghetto residents trapped in chronic poverty within the various confines of America's urban centers, Robert Kennedy found himself responding as an empathetic, compassionate national leader and global statesman who constantly sought avenues to use his leadership positions—as Attorney General of the US, US Senator from New York, and as a presidential candidate in 1968—to expose the sufferings of the excluded, the dispossessed, the marginalized. Robert Kennedy was the embodiment of a principled leader who acted out of his moral core, idealism, and a sense of commitment to the cause of human justice and humane governance at home and abroad. This is what makes his brand of statesmanship radically different from those definitions that confine the meaning of statesmanship to striking a compromise or a bargain between contending political parties and interest groups. Robert Kennedy was different. Contrary to the conventional wisdom of the media and various biographical and historical accounts of the 1960s, the fact is that John and Robert Kennedy—not Lyndon Johnson—were responsible for setting a new direction for political and economic priorities and for hitting the reset button on the US national agenda. As historian Edward Schmitt has astutely noted of Robert Kennedy's legacy: "Ultimately his most concerted antipoverty efforts in the Senate were his attempts to save or augment funding for Johnson's existing poverty programs (*most of which had their genesis in the Kennedy administration*), to learn how those programs were or were not working, and to build public pressure to sustain the waning national will for the War on Poverty" (Schmitt 2010, 225, italics added). In this environment of national change, transition, and transformation, we discover that what RFK accomplished was singularly unique and remains so, right up to the present time. Again, according to historian Edward Schmitt: "By the time he ran for president, Kennedy had achieved a political rarity—an honest dialogue with racial minorities and the poor in America. What Robert Kennedy would have continued to offer, which few national politicians since have conveyed, was a sense of outrage at '*poverty in the midst of plenty*' that would not have been easily branded a class warfare, radical, or left-wing vision" (Schmitt 2010, 228, italics added).

3

"No More Vietnams"

As students of history, JFK and RFK had formed their own opinions about British rule and abuses in Ireland, India, Africa, and Asia. They condemned French colonial policy in Algeria and the folly of France's imperial designs on Vietnam and the rest of Indochina. When Robert Kennedy decided to give his first speech before a large audience following his brother's assassination, it was to the Sons of St. Patrick in Scranton, Pennsylvania, on March 17, 1964. In his remarks, he directly connected Ireland's painful history to the issue of US policy toward colonies and the struggles of the underdeveloped nations. He specifically made a linkage between an appreciation for Ireland's historical difficulties to America's obligation to foster economic and political independence. In doing so, he referenced the fact that everything had been changed by World War II, insofar as "the frontiers of our national security became the frontiers of the world. We found ourselves obliged to deal with the harsh facts of existence on a global basis." He then proceeded to admit that "for the sake of our own security, we found our destiny to be closely linked with that of nations that maintained large colonial empires on which they felt their ultimate security depended. In some of the underdeveloped countries we have found our destiny linked with ruling powers or classes which hold the vast majority of their people in economic or military subjugation" (Gibson 1994, 39; Ross 1968, 430).

Having identified the Cold War fallacy of America choosing to be aligned with dictators while espousing its fidelity to human freedom and human rights, Robert proceeded to observe: "It is easy for us to believe that the imperialism of the West was infinitely preferable to the tyranny of communism. But the sullen hostility of the African and Asian colonial nations has shown us that not all hold the same view. The bloody struggles for liberty in the sands of Algeria to the steaming jungles of Indonesia and Vietnam proved that others would make the same sacrifices to throw off the yoke of imperialism today that the Irish did more than a half-century ago" (Gibson 1994, 39; Ross 1968, 430). In the speech, RFK also indicated his views on the British establishment by noting that Queen Victoria's response to mass starvation in Ireland in 1847 had been to offer five pounds to the Society for Irish Relief. Robert also made it clear that his view had been his brother's view as well.

In retrospect, it seems that John Kennedy's opposition to colonialist policies may have originated in a strong identification with Ireland's long subjugation to England. As a senator, John Kennedy was no more lenient on the French than on the English with respect to colonial policies in the Third World. One month before the fall of Dien Bien Phu, on April 6, 1954, Senator John Kennedy delivered a major address in the US Senate that condemned French actions in Vietnam—referred to in the 1950s as French Indochina—and specifically addressed the question of whether the US should act unilaterally. He said no. Kennedy indicated that he would not "pour money, material and men into the jungles of Indochina without at least a remote prospect of victory" (Siff 1999, 73). Again, in 1957, JFK invited the ire of the French government when, on the floor of the US Senate, he thoroughly condemned France's colonial policies and imperial rule in Algeria (Parmet 1980, 399–408). It was a harbinger of Kennedy's recalcitrance to allow the introduction of US combat troops into Vietnam, and his plans in late 1963 to complete effectuating a total US withdrawal from Vietnam by early 1965 (Newman 1992; Kaiser 2000; Porter 2005; Jones 2003; Siff 1999, 70–78).

The historical record demonstrates that JFK had planned and signaled a total withdrawal from Vietnam, as evidenced by his directive of October 11, 1963, as well as in the context of National Security Action Memoranda 263 (NSAM 263). After undertaking a review of the entire spectrum of events that made up Kennedy decision-making on Vietnam in October 1963, historian Howard Jones concluded that "on October 2, 1963, President Kennedy made the final decision to withdraw the first contingent of US military forces from Vietnam, the initial step toward a major disengagement" (Jones 2003, 377–406. *See also* Scott 1993, 24–37; Lane 1991, 102–103; Douglass 2008, 119–122, 186–190; Prouty 1973 and 1992; Kaiser 2000, 261–262; Newman 1992; Logevall 1999, 55; Dallek 2003, 678–680). This particular decision was extremely significant insofar as "Kennedy's decision to withdraw was unconditional, for he approved a calendar of events that did not necessitate a victory" (Jones 2003, 377). All of these plans were immediately changed after his assassination in Dallas on November 22, 1963. John F. Kennedy's orders for a withdrawal from Vietnam were reversed by Lyndon Johnson only four days after the assassination, in NSAM 273 (Scott 1993; Prouty 1973; Prouty, 1992; Siff 1999, 70–78). The change in policy was abrupt. Of this immediate post-assassination timeframe, Arthur Schlesinger notes: "On November 24 the new president convened a small group to meet with Lodge, just in from Saigon. Robert Kennedy was not invited. Johnson told them, 'I am not going to lose Vietnam. I am not going to be the President who saw Southeast Asia go the way that China went'" (Schlesinger 1978, 726). Schlesinger proceeded to make clear the gravity of the change in Vietnam policy after the assassination, when he wrote: "While renouncing the December troop withdrawal, NSAM 273 also emphasized that American military programs 'should be maintained at levels as high as those in the time of the Diem regime.' *This nullified Kennedy's extrication intent*" (Schlesinger 1978, 726, italics added).

By 1968, it would fall to Robert Kennedy to not only call for an end to the Vietnam War, but also demand an end to US military interventions throughout the Third World in his "No More Vietnams" speeches that were delivered throughout the course of the 1968 presidential campaign. In a reflective and insightful speech at the University of Indiana on April 24, 1968, Robert began his remarks by noting that:

> Long ago it was said, "the time for taking a lesson from history is ever at hand for those that are wise." The war in Vietnam is not yet fully consigned to history. The fighting and bloodshed continue. The bombing of North Vietnam is restricted; but that too continues. And the negotiations, toward which we have taken the most tentative and still far from certain steps—these have not yet begun. Still in one sense the war may be passing into history; and that is in the thinking of the American people. There has been settled, in the year 1968, one simple proposition; the American people—scholars and officials, soldiers and citizens, students and parents—are determined that there must not be another Vietnam. What we must now debate and come to understand is what it is about—the war in Vietnam that we are determined not to repeat; what effect this determination will have on our other policies and goals; what it means to live our own lives and to the future of our nation. *What does it mean to say, no more Vietnams?*

In proceeding to answer the question, Robert discussed other insurgencies around the world that existed beyond Southeast Asia and extended into Latin America, Africa, Japan, India and Pakistan.

He then concluded his assessment of all these illustrations of Vietnam-like insurgencies by debunking the logic that lay behind Washington's official explanation for the war: the "domino theory." Robert explained that "all this is not to say that Vietnam is the last challenge we will face abroad. That would be nonsense. It is to say that *Vietnam is only Vietnam—that it will not settle the fate of Asia or of America, much less the fate of the world*" (Kennedy, April 24, 1968, italics added).

Like his brother, Robert Kennedy expressed his recognition of the force of nationalism throughout the Third World and what implications it presented for the way in which the United States would formulate its response through a more enlightened foreign policy. No conviction was more basic to John F. Kennedy's foreign policy than his belief that America had to recognize the historic sweep of Third World nationalism (Logevall 2012, 703; Rakove 2013). It was regarding Africa—one of the key crisis areas of the early 1960s—that Kennedy used the full powers of his presidency to influence the course of self-determination (Mahoney 1983). This view of John Kennedy's approach to nationalism, and his affinity with and courtship of African leaders, has been confirmed and reconfirmed by historians from the early 1980s on into the early decades of the twenty-first century (Muehlenbeck 2012). President Kennedy's leadership and approach to Third World nationalism, and his embrace of anti-colonial struggles in an age of decolonization, set him apart from the more common pattern of American disinterest in the lands between the Mediterranean and the Cape of Good Hope. It was a perspective translated into policy and leadership that also came to characterize the views of Robert Kennedy. Like his brother, Robert Kennedy exhibited a statesmanship attitude toward the emerging nations of the Third World, an attitude that took their aspirations and hopes for the future seriously. He sought to bring a more enlightened view of these issues to the attention of the American people and a larger global audience. Robert Kennedy noted that:

> Even within the nations once ruled by Moscow, the forces of national independence and personal freedom are steadily eroding the Soviets' once unquestioned position. That force can be our strongest ally in the world, if we respect and honor it. It can also be our nemesis, if we continue to ignore it. The worst thing we could do would be to take as our mission the suppression or disorder and internal upheaval everywhere it appears. This is even more true if the means for this policeman's role is to be the indiscriminate introduction of American troops into the internal struggles of other nations. (Kennedy, April 24, 1968)

Unfortunately, those American presidents who came after 1968 failed to heed Robert's warning and cautionary analysis. While Kennedy's 1968 campaign called for no more Vietnams, the elite rightwing elements of the US establishment called for the resurrection of an idea from the Truman years that has been termed "containment militarism" (Sanders 1983). The idea of containment militarism envisioned not only an anti-communist crusade, but also a political and economic path of imposing an Ameri-centric notion of world order on all other nations—in other words, the domination of the world and the ordering of it through corporate capitalist interests working under the rubric of American hegemony (Sanders 1983; Paupp 2007; Paupp 2009; Paupp 2012). The roots of this doctrine can be traced to the post-World War II era in which the post-1945 world of US foreign policy makers produced NSC-68. In NSC-68 lies the Cold War doctrine of the US as both a superpower and an empire. NSC-68 was the doctrinal endorsement for the pursuit and maintenance of a Pax Americana, designed to be enforced on the world through American weapons of war. These were the foundational premises of an ideology that sought to buttress America's nuclear superiority in international relations even as it justified interventions everywhere in the Third World.

In the 1970s, one such leading pro-interventionist group was formed, calling itself the Committee on the Present Danger (CPD). Its leading proponents were Eugene V. Rostow, co-founder and chairman for the CPD, and Paul H. Nitze, co-founder and chairman of Policy Studies for the CPD. Eugene's brother, Walt Rostow, had been an influential foreign policy adviser to both JFK and LBJ. He was the first to advise JFK to send combat troops to Vietnam, which Kennedy rejected. Likewise, the national security adviser to Presidents Kennedy and Johnson, McGeorge Bundy, urged that combat troops should be introduced into Vietnam (Goldstein 2008, 29–30; Bird 1998). Whether being urged by McGeorge Bundy or the Joint Chiefs of Staff, the introduction of US combat troops into Vietnam was a suggestion that John Kennedy would reject until the day he died. After Kennedy's death in Dallas, Walt Rostow framed a policy of military escalation for Johnson and strongly advised LBJ against pursuing a compromise peace with North Vietnam (Milne 2008). Walt Rostow was a true ideologue who opposed Robert Kennedy's cautionary warning about the need to follow a no-more-Vietnams approach to US foreign policy. Rostow believed that it was beholden upon the United States to democratize other nations, no matter what the cost. Even after the American defeat in Vietnam and forced withdrawal in 1974, the CPD began an ideological campaign to resurrect an interventionist US foreign policy. It did so throughout the presidential term of Jimmy Carter by presenting the idea that the Carter administration suffered from what the CPD called the "Vietnam Syndrome."

The CPD alleged that the Vietnam Syndrome represented a "failure of nerve" in US leadership and reflected an aversion by the American public at large to repeat another Vietnam-like experience (Sanders 1983). President Reagan's response to the message of the CPD was to appoint its leadership to top policy posts in his administration. The ideological successor to the CPD was the Project for the New American Century (PNAC). After assuming the presidency in early 2001, President George W. Bush repeated what Reagan had done with the membership and views of the CPD when he appointed leading hawks from the PNAC to the top policy positions of his administration. The result was the Iraq War and the Afghanistan War, which, as of 2008, have cost more than $3 trillion (Stiglitz 2008). By 2011, the actual costs of these wars had swelled to more than $5 trillion.

Tragically, Robert Kennedy's warning and proposed foreign policy regarding the implementation of a no-more-Vietnams principle was ignored and dismissed after his assassination in 1968. The old guard returned to power in Washington with a vengeance. As a consequence of this failure to learn from the lessons of history, Nixon would mindlessly and needlessly extend the length of the Vietnam War for another six years. Reagan would needlessly embroil the nation in military actions and covert CIA operations throughout Central America in the 1980s, leaving El Salvador and Nicaragua worse off in terms of human rights and socioeconomic progress than before. This ideological direction was a pattern that Reagan would repeat by engaging the US with illegal interventions in Lebanon and Grenada (Paupp 1987). Subsequently, George H. Bush would illegally invade Panama and engage the US in the first of two Gulf Wars against Iraq. Subsequently, Clinton would violate international law and usurp the US Constitution under the banner of "humanitarian intervention" as he brought both US and NATO troops into conflict in Kosovo. George W. Bush would follow Clinton's illegal Kosovo precedent by using the CIA to manufacture false claims about the alleged presence of weapons of mass destruction in Iraq, as well as dubious claims about terrorists in Afghanistan. Known sources of terrorism within Saudi Arabia and Pakistan were swept under the rug and routinely ignored. Under Barack

Obama, George W. Bush's policies were continued in these countries, thereby making Obama's first term a virtual third term for Bush.

Had each of these post-1968 US presidents taken the time to read and reflect upon the implications contained in Robert Kennedy's "No More Vietnams" speech, it is highly doubtful that the United States would have been brought into these intractable conflicts throughout the entire Middle East. This is especially the case when Kennedy concluded his speech by warning:

> The great danger is not from an external enemy. It is from ourselves. This is precisely the danger that in seeking universal peace, needlessly fearful of change and disorder, we will in fact embroil ourselves and the world in a whole series of Vietnams. But that danger can only be of our own making. The way to avoid it is to use our power always with restraint; to avoid over-commitment in rhetoric and action; above all to recognize that America's interest is not in the automatic use of military force in the attempt to preserve things they are elsewhere in the world. (Kennedy, April 24, 1968)

It would not be until three decades later that Robert McNamara, Secretary of Defense for both Presidents Kennedy and Johnson, would admit the errors associated with American intervention in Vietnam with the publication of his book, *In Retrospect: The Tragedy and Lessons of Vietnam* (McNamara 1995). Four years later, McNamara would follow this with another volume: *Argument Without End: In Search of Answers to the Vietnam Tragedy* (McNamara, Blight, and Brigham 1999). After mapping out crucial mistakes, the book comes to the irrefutable conclusion that the war could not have been won militarily by the United States without resorting to genocide or triggering a devastating war with China or the Soviet Union. Despite these very clear warnings, and despite the fact that Richard Cheney and Donald Rumsfeld served in the Ford administration during the time that US helicopters were desperately departing from the roof of the American embassy in Saigon, these rightwing ideologues of the George W. Bush administration still felt an enduring obligation to put a final end to the Vietnam Syndrome (Fitzgerald 2008, 30). By doing so, the administrations of Nixon, Ford, Reagan, Bush I and II, Clinton, and Obama have all left a legacy of "More Vietnams," with more tragic results for both America and the world at large.

What separates the Kennedy legacy from those that followed can be seen in the centrality that JFK and RFK gave to ensuring that the government of the United States, as well as the larger national society, honored and respected the human dignity of all people. In much the same way that Robert argued that the gap between the affluent and the poor in America could no longer be tolerated, so too he predicted an international disaster if the chasm between the have and have-not nations was not dramatically reduced in the near future. This view was a recurrent motif in his remarks about the lesser developed nations throughout his public career. As early as 1962, Robert delivered a speech in Bonn, Germany, in which he declared:

> It is in all our interests to narrow the frightening gap between the rich nations and the poor—between people living in affluence and comfort and people scratching to survive on less than one hundred dollars a year. A high standard of living cannot remain the exclusive possession of the West—and the sooner we can help other peoples to develop their resources, raise their living standards and strengthen their national independence, the safer the world will be for us all. As President Kennedy said in his inaugural address a year ago: "If a free society cannot help the many who are poor, it cannot save the few who are rich." (Ross 1968, 426–427)

By making human rights and civil rights their ultimate concern in formulating US policy at home and abroad, the Kennedy brothers demonstrated that American ideals need not be inconsistent with rational policies. It was this fundamental insight that became the guiding principle that served to define the essential core concerns of their policies, their ideals, and their message in all realms of political and economic affairs. On August 7, 1964, in a speech before the Fifth General Assembly, World Assembly of Youth, at the University of Massachusetts, Robert Kennedy declared:

> Two-thirds of the present world population—about two billion people—live in the so called "developing nations" of Asia, Africa and Latin America. The "developing" refers to technology, for, as we all know, many of these countries had advanced civilizations when people in Europe and America were living in caves. But these areas had fallen behind in the race for technological progress. Their problems today are the basic problems of population, and hunger and education, and it is these which demand and must receive worldwide attention and worldwide solution. I believe that we recognize now—perhaps for the first time—that the gap between the developing and the developed nations of the world must be closed. And for this reason the attention of the world is turning to the problems which may engage your energies and your leadership talents tomorrow. (Ross 1968, 427)

In the shared presidency of John and Robert Kennedy, their idealistic call to action had a practical component: to win the Cold War while, at the same time, advancing a moral and ethical claim to a more enlightened future for all of humanity. In turn, their concept of justice demanded that human rights be extended as far as possible so as to incorporate the needs of the disenfranchised, the excluded, and the dispossessed. In this fundamental respect, Robert Kennedy held a radically different perspective from most who occupied the top tiers of power in the American establishment. Men like McGeorge Bundy shared the establishment conviction that they knew what was right and what was wrong for the country. As Irving Bernstein noted of Bundy, he took a "hard-line attitude which was very much the product of the fifties and the Cold War, the ultra-realist view" that he taught his Harvard students (Bernstein 1996, 333). This was the exact opposite view of that held by Robert Kennedy. Kennedy looked at the moral implications of the war effort in Vietnam—something that most members of the establishment were either adverse to do or afraid to do.

In an interview on *Face the Nation,* November 26, 1967, Robert responded to Wicker's question: "In whose interest is this war?" with this:

> First we were making the effort there so that people would have their own right to decide their own future and could select their own form of government, and it wasn't going to be imposed on them by the North Vietnamese, and we had the support of the people of South Vietnam. I think that is why we were involved in that struggle. That is certainly the way I looked at it when I was in President Kennedy's administration and when I was with President Johnson. Now we turned, when we found that the South Vietnamese haven't given the support and are not making the effort; now we are saying we are going to fight there so that we don't have to fight in Thailand, so that we don't have to fight on the West Coast of the United States, so that they won't move across the Rockies. (Ross, 1968, 537).

By referring to these shifting arguments and the mounting ridiculousness of the rationales for the war that were being offered by the Johnson administration and leading members of the establishment, we find that Kennedy's remarks are laced with condescension.
Kennedy then continued:

> But do we—our whole moral position, it seems to me, changes tremendously. One, we're in there, we're helping people. We're working with them. We're fighting for their independence. Second we're—and

> we're killing the enemy and we're also killing many civilians, but we're doing it because they want it. Now we've changed and switched. Maybe they don't want it, but we want it. So we're going in there and we're killing South Vietnamese; we're killing children; we're killing women; we're killing innocent people because we don't want to have the war fought on American soil, or because they're twelve thousand miles away and they might get to be eleven thousand miles away.

At this point of Kennedy's answer he is clearly exposing, with moral indignation, his contempt for the rationales that have been promulgated by the Johnson administration and the establishment.

Without missing a beat, Kennedy continued: "Our whole moral position changes, it seems to me, tremendously. Do we have the right here in the United States to perform these acts because we want to protect ourselves, so that . . . it is not a great problem for us here in the United States? I very seriously question whether we have that right . . . I think other people are fighting it, other people are carrying the burden . . . but this is also our war." He was now bringing out the central theme of his message, which was to remind the American people of their moral obligation toward what was being done in their name in Vietnam and throughout Asia. Kennedy concluded with an appeal to conscience and with a strong reminder about the role of every citizen to work toward bringing the war to an end by remembering the fact that the costs involved had been not only economic, but also moral. Hence, on the theme of personal accountability, Kennedy unequivocally stated:

"Those of us who stay here in the United States, we must feel it when we use napalm, when a village is destroyed and civilians are killed. This is also our responsibility. This is a moral obligation for us here in the United States. And I think we have forgotten about that. And when we switched from one point of view to another, I think that we have forgotten about it. And I think that it should be discussed and all of us should examine our own conscience about what we are doing in South Vietnam. It is not just the fact that we are killing North Vietnamese soldiers or Vietcong; we are also responsible for tens and tens of thousands of innocent civilian casualties, and I think we are going to have a difficult time explaining this to ourselves" (Guthman and Allen 1993, 302–303).

In coming to this conclusion about the war, Robert identified with those who suffered the most from the abuses of the powerful, the tragedies of war, and the realities of racial discrimination and economic subordination—all of which were the direct consequences of the actions of the American Empire, not the American republic, which he dedicated himself to restoring. It was for the sake of the restoration of the American republic that Kennedy devoted his energies, his message, and his last campaign. His faith in the enduring promise of the American republic, as the potential embodiment of a community of liberty that honored individual dignity and worth, is what led him to evolve a unique and inclusive vision for his time—and for our time as well.

4

Seeking Social Justice at Home and Abroad

Both RFK and JFK were products of their time. Still, they learned to transcend the ideological, political, and dogmatic barriers of that time. They were caught between the promise of global justice, human rights, and social inclusion that came to define the post-World War II era and, at the same time, the inheritance of a nation and a world that still operated largely within historical, bureaucratic, and ideological constraints that reinforced barriers of social, political, and economic exclusion. In an electoral world of politics where votes mattered, they were under constant pressure to accommodate the prejudices and interests of these old enclaves of discrimination, subordination, and exclusion. It was only their political ideals and Catholic value structure that empowered them to jettison these tattered conventions and seek instead to raise the consciousness of a new generation, even as that new generation grasped at the possibilities for a better and more human world than the one that had been bequeathed to them. Hence, the Kennedy brothers were fully immersed in the social pressures of the early 1960s. To begin the process of fully actualizing the potential of the historical moment, as well as their campaign promises to advance civil and human rights, they had to deal with the practical challenge of developing programs and public policies that would be capable of advancing these interests, claims, and concerns.

January 1, 1963, marked the centennial of the Emancipation Proclamation. The first three months of 1963 were relatively quiet in the North. Early spring brought the first major rumblings of discontent as events in the South, especially in Birmingham, began to heat up. Alabama's George Wallace and Mississippi's Ross Barnett blocked school house doors to integration efforts by the Kennedy administration (Lesher 1994; Carter 1995; Black and Black 2002).

When Attorney General Robert Kennedy finally sat down with a group of influential northern blacks in his New York City apartment, "participants tried to explain to Kennedy that the 'festering of hostility in New York, Chicago, and Los Angeles—as well as Birmingham—is rooted not in segregation of public accommodations or even in segregation by neighborhoods, but in resentment at being so long and so hopelessly at the bottom" (Sugrue 2008, 295). Both President Kennedy and his Attorney General were driven by events to learn quickly and act decisively in response to the pressures of the "Negro Revolt" and worries about a national uprising in anger due to building resentments that were about to explode. On June 11, 1963, the president addressed the nation on the "fires of frustration and discord that are burning in every city, North and South, where legal remedies are not at hand. Redress is sought in the streets, in demonstrations, parades and protests which create tensions and threaten violence and threaten lives" (Kennedy 1963, 469). The Kennedy brothers had come to realize the non-sectional nature of the civil rights problem and issues such as black unemployment. The president concluded his remarks by stating that this was "a time of domestic crisis."

In an attempt to understand the Kennedy administration's efforts following this speech, one historian remarked: "Scrambling to put out the fires of frustration, the president also dispatched Secretary of Labor Willard Wirtz to conduct a hasty investigation of workplace discrimination in twenty cities—several of which Wirtz identified as 'danger spots,' most of them outside the South. Other Kennedy advisors prepared troubling reports on growing black discontent in northern cities" (Sugrue 2008, 296).

By early summer of 1963, the Kennedy brothers shared with Martin Luther King, Jr., a powerful passion and message for the need to confront the damaging effects of poverty, persistent racism, and class cleavages that resulted in huge socioeconomic disparities (Braun 1997; Winant 2001). At the international level and in the context of the Cold War, these interconnected challenges came in the form of nationalism, decolonization, and opposition to the imperial policies of European states. At the national level, these interrelated challenges appeared in the crises affecting America's cities, the lingering problems of racism as exemplified by a legal structure of racial subordination under the rubric of Jim Crow laws and restrictions, and in various forms of discrimination that ranged from employment and educational barriers to voting rights and housing abuses (Branch 1998). Between 1963 and 1968 were five years of astonishing transition, "as a large part of the American public moved from openness and embrace of the federal role as agent of social change to resentful anger and rejection" (Russell 2004, 91).

By the time of the 1968 presidential campaign, Robert Kennedy had largely come to agree with Dr. King's diagnosis of the nation's ills and what the potential remedy would have to entail. In this period:

King spoke of restructuring society, of rebuilding America's cities to benefit the poor, of nationalizing industries, and of a guaranteed annual wage. In his work in Chicago, Cleveland and Detroit he made demands for jobs, open housing, citizen review of police and housing boards, and economic boycotts of business. He spoke of creating a new coalition, of eliminating the barrier of racism to forge bonds of economic interest between black and poor whites. King's vision of the future rested on the "macroeconomics of total, direct, and immediate abolition of poverty." "Poverty is not new," he said. "What's new is that we have the techniques and tools to get rid of poverty. The real question is whether we have the will" (Russell 2004, 90).

On May 31, 1968, Kennedy announced his solution: "A Program for the Urban Crisis," which declared in its opening sentence that: "*The next administration will face no problem more serious than the crisis in America's cities*" (Kennedy, May 31, 1968, italics added). When Robert spoke of the crisis of America's cities, he was also talking about the intertwined issues of race and class. In so doing, he sought to make his program and message for national renewal an approach to human relations that bridged the gap between black and white. Robert Kennedy's thinking was so advanced in this period that he already grasped the reality that poverty was more significant than race itself as the issue that needed to be confronted and resolved within the United States. In 1968, he told journalist Jack Newfield, "*You know, I've come to the conclusion that poverty is closer to the root of the problem than color . . . We have to convince the Negroes and poor whites that they have common interests*" (Newfield 1969, 287, italics added). History would prove Kennedy right. Writing on the subject of affirmative action in 1996, attorney Richard Kahlenberg would observe: "After thirty years of race-based affirmative action, it may seem odd to rediscover that 1960s progressives proposed nonracial solutions to the problem of past racial discrimination" (Kahlenberg 1996, 12).

In the fall of 1964, while campaigning for the US Senate in Rochester, New York, Kennedy reminded the American people what they should stand for. It was the day after the Warren Report's release, but Robert came out of his depression at a press conference to define his foreign policy differences with his opponent, Kenneth Keating. On the issue of defense, Robert told the press that he stood for a strong military, but added the caveat that America's military strength should be united with "the inner strength and wisdom not to use that military strength precipitately or indiscriminately." Returning to the subject of social justice concerns that he saw linked at both the national and international levels, he said that communism would only be defeated "through progressive practical programs which wipe out the poverty, misery and discontent on which it thrives." In this effort, he suggested that genuine national security would come from strongly supporting the United Nations—"mankind's noblest experiment"—and helping to lift the world's two billion poor from their brutal fate. He then concluded his remarks by noting that America would only earn the world's respect if it practiced at home what it preached abroad. In concrete terms, this meant being faithful to democratic principles while moving toward greater racial equality. In this task, he made clear that "we cannot expect an African to believe that we are on the side of equality and human dignity when his own ambassadors are not served in our restaurants. We cannot expect countries with far lower standards of living to respect our belief in human dignity if their aged are venerated and ours are neglected. We cannot expect nations to join with us in combating poverty if in the midst of unprecedented wealth, six million families live in poverty" (Talbot 2007, 297).

In confronting these challenges, both JFK and RFK had actively started the process of embarking upon a transformative politics that would move the United States, and the world at large, toward the realization of a more inclusive, just, and humane social order. In the stream of history, Robert Kennedy personally came to realize in the 1960s what some scholars later came to acknowledge about the nature of the social order: "Power may be wielded in numerous ways. Historically, armed force has been a central pillar of power, as liberal theory rightly stresses. But the arsenal of domination goes beyond the gun. Control of the tools with which we produce our livelihoods and the words that give our lives and loyalties their meanings have been no less central to the exercise of power" (Bowles and Gintis 1986, 92). The clashes of the 1960s over poverty, racism, and social justice issues reveal the fact the historical trajectory of liberal-democratic-capitalist societies was not the product of a unified logic expressed in an economically determined set of laws in motion. Nor was the historical trajectory of liberal–democratic-capitalist societies to be ultimately understood as "a teleological movement of modernization pulled by the magnet of enlightenment, but rather as the result of contradictory possibilities of two conflicting tendencies, the expansion of personal rights and the expansion of property rights" (Bowles and Gintis 1986, 93).

By 1997, groundbreaking scholarship emerged with the publication of Rogers Smith's book, *Civic Ideals: Conflicting Views of Citizenship in US History*. In his sociopolitical history of America, Smith discovered that civic identity in the US was not predominantly defined by liberal, democratic political principles. Rather, US citizenship is the product of multiple traditions—not only liberalism and republicanism, but also white supremacy, Protestant supremacy, and male supremacy. From colonial times through the Progressive era, most adults were legally denied access to full citizenship. This exclusion was based on race, ethnicity, and gender. Basic conflicts over these denials have driven political development and defined US civic identity up to this day. Armed with the doctrine of racial Darwinism and the practices associated with European imperialism, as well as rising economic inequalities, "the nation's dominant groups found that they could best entrench and expand their support by portraying Americans as the world's greatest master race . . . And because most voters were still middle-class white men, most found reassuring the fact that this mission justified keeping the poorer classes, the nonwhite races, and women in subordinate places for the foreseeable future, even if it promised more freedom and equality eventually to those who proved worthy" (Smith 1997, 469). In the stream of history, Robert Kennedy focused his political, economic, and social critique of American society on the need to expand personal rights—and to do so by emphasizing the theme of participation. Those at the local level, at the grassroots level, at the community level, were supposed to have greater control of their own destiny.

Kennedy's views traversed the liberal-democratic continuum of the nation's political, social, and cultural evolution. Yet he was not a conventional "liberal" and he did not consign himself to the dictates of a political dogma. What made him unique and an exciting political leader is the fact that he was willing to break out of the boxes of social convention and political traditions. He was willing to do so to find real solutions to the problems faced by real people. To merely adopt the dogmas of the past and wrap them in ideological explanations was not sufficient in Kennedy's mind. To solve the problems of the country and to begin to understand the world at large, Kennedy believed that one had to grasp not only where we were, but also where we had been and where we intended to go as a country and as a people. In this context, within the stream of history, Robert Kennedy was the leading establishment figure of his time who did not want to reify and perpetuate the racial status quo by consigning black Americans "to a twilight zone where they are politically invisible" (Russell 2004, 132). Rather, RFK joined with the US Secretary of Labor, Willard Wirtz, to advance the idea that there was a genuine need for employment programs—especially for blacks. Both RFK and Wirtz understood that employment programs were generally superior as anti-poverty measures (Russell 2004, 132). It was this fundamental idea that most differentiated these two voices in Washington from the rest of the liberal policy makers in 1963–1964.

In Judith Russell's book on this period, *Economics, Bureaucracy, and Race: How Keynesians Misguided the War on Poverty*, she concludes:

> The case for jobs policies in 1963 was compelling, and a social opportunity was lost that has yet to recur. Jobs policies should have been the centerpiece of the War on Poverty . . . Yet the decisive influence of Walter Heller and the Council of Economic Advisors had the impact of cutting off a critical opportunity for the structural argument. The essential economic consensus need was not fully formed in government as of 1963 because of the prevalence of fiscal Keynesianism as the basis of economic policy . . . in part because of the belief that the problems of unemployment in the black community were not government responsibilities. (Russell 2004, 158)

Robert Kennedy held a different view about government's responsibilities toward black America's employment problem and the future of the cities, the role of government, and its capacity to address the problem of poverty in America. Like Wirtz, RFK clearly believed that:

> The crisis of unemployment . . . is significant far beyond its economic effects—devastating as those are. For it is both measure and cause of the extent to which the poor man lives apart—the extent to which he is alienated from the general community. More than segregation in housing and schools, more than the difference in attitudes or life style, it is unemployment which marks the urban poor off and apart from the rest of America. *Unemployment is having nothing to do—which means having nothing to do with the rest of us.* (Ross 1968, 141–142, italics added)

During his Senate campaign in the fall of 1964, he frequently spoke on jobs and unemployment: "One of the major problems of our time—in a sense, the cruelest problem—is unemployment. It is a problem that causes other problems—social as well as economic. *Unemployment causes delinquency, poverty, injustice . . . it damages our purchasing power and increases our relief rolls*" (Ross 1968, 142, italics added). As Kennedy's term in the Senate progressed, he found himself more embittered and angry about the inability and unwillingness of the federal government to guarantee equality for people of color, or to revitalize America's decaying cities. In a speech on October 8, 1966, delivered at the Democratic State Committee Dinner in Columbus, Ohio, Robert declared:

The War on Poverty authorization just passed by the Congress, as a beginning, is totally inadequate—nowhere close to meeting the needs of all our people for jobs, and training, and health, and self-sufficiency and respect. It is all very well to support civil rights bills, and open-housing bills; but it is far more ***right and relevant*** to assure all our people decent and dignified conditions where they live now. But this cannot be done if we are unwilling to make the effort, to spend the money, to help people help themselves, to once and for all end debilitating and demeaning welfare programs and instead insure that every family has the means to support itself (Ross 1968, 145, bold, italics added).

5

Seeking to Do What Is "Right and Relevant" for the People

Robert Kennedy remained loyal to the basically humane commitments of liberalism as a tradition and the institutionalization of those commitments. He did not like all "liberal politics" or all liberals, but he did remain true to values that reinforced and protected the human rights and dignity of the person—whatever political label one might ascribe to those values. This was particularly the case in the life and career of Robert Kennedy because he was primarily a man of conscience and conviction. It is in this significant sense that he differs so radically from those who came after him and have effectively denigrated the term "politician." For Kennedy, politics was "an honorable profession" because, if properly undertaken and pursued, it was the most effective avenue through which to advance the broad public interest, to enshrine communitarian values in the public discourse and, in so doing, ennoble both the spirit of individuals and the spirit of the communities they inhabit. Thus it can be argued that:

> With all their limitations, liberal democratic policies promoting personal and collective freedom still offer more potential than any alternative to provide paths to greater human material prosperity, personal security and happiness, domestic and international peace, and intellectual and spiritual progress. And even if liberalism is not hegemonic in America, its finest commitments remain deeply enough embedded in the traditions and institutions of the US, as well as many other societies, to make feasible the project of crafting national identities in fuller accord with it. (Smith 1997, 489)

In 1968, Robert Kennedy was in the midst of not only an electoral contest for the presidency of his nation, but also in the midst of crafting a new national identity with a progressive coalition that he was attempting to assemble. It was a coalition of labor, the young, minorities, women, the progressive left, workers, and average citizens who sought true social justice. It was a more egalitarian and inclusive vision of justice than those versions that allowed for authoritarian and bureaucratic tendencies, which, in turn, had allowed the status quo to remain in place, virtually unaltered. Kennedy, like the antiwar movement and radicals of his day, wanted fundamental change. In 2001, Peter Edelman, a former aide to Robert Kennedy, wrote a book about the RFK he knew and explained how Kennedy's policies differed so much from those of Bill Clinton. Edelman observed that "Robert Kennedy was uncomfortable when anyone called him a liberal—in fact, when anyone tried to put any label on him. Yet his politics did not resemble the abdication of responsibility and commitment that characterizes too many of today's 'new Democrats.' There could be no doubt of his passion for justice. This, combined with a commitment to results and a highly original mind, produced a view of government and of remedies for powerless people different from that of Bill Clinton" (Edelman 2001, 7).

In August 1996, President Bill Clinton signed an historic bill ending "welfare as we know it." Reflecting on the bill and its failures, Edelman noted: "the bill that President Clinton signed is not welfare reform. It does not promote work effectively, and it will hurt millions of poor children by the time it is fully implemented" (Edelman 1997, 43). Edelman's indictment of Clinton and his welfare bill was the cover story of the March 1997 issue of *The Atlantic Monthly*. His article was entitled "The Worst Thing Bill Clinton Has Done." In signing the welfare bill, Clinton had quoted a line from Robert Kennedy: "Work is the meaning of what this country is all about. We need it as individuals, we need to sense it in our fellow citizens, and we need it as a society and as a people." Edelman was outraged that Clinton had invoked Robert Kennedy's words to justify legislation that Kennedy would most likely have deplored. Clinton signed the bill, originally formulated in large measure by Newt Gingrich and the House Republicans, mainly to insure his own political survival in the November 1996 campaign.

Shortly thereafter, to Edelman's credit, he decided to resign his administration position as the assistant secretary for planning and evaluation at the Department of Health and Human Services in protest. In the *Atlantic* article, Edelman stated: "I am amazed at how many people have bought the line that the welfare bill was a little set of adjustments that could easily be done away with. *Congress and the President have dynamited a structure that was in place for six decades*" (Edelman 1997, 44–45, italics added). Further, Edelman noted, "this was *the* major milestone in the political race to the bottom. The

President had said he was willing to sign legislation that would end a sixty-year commitment to provide assistance to all needy families with children who met the federal eligibility requirements. In the floor debate Senator Edward Kennedy, who voted against the bill, described it as 'legislative child abuse'" (Edelman 1997, 45, italics in original). In the closing paragraph of his article, Edelman articulated the spirit of Robert Kennedy in response to what had transpired when he writes: "To do what needs to be done is going to take a lot of work—organizing, engaging in public education, broadening the base of people who believe that real action to reduce poverty and promote self-sufficiency in America is important and possible. . . . *The best thing that can be said about this terrible legislation is that perhaps we will learn from it and eventually arrive at a better approach. I am afraid, though, that along the way we will do some serious injury to American children, who should not have had to suffer from our national backlash*" (Edelman, 1997, 58, italics added).

In Robert Kennedy's view, the lives of too many American citizens had been hollowed out by the bigness of uncaring corporations, the insensitivity of Washington's bureaucracies, and the malaise inherent in a consumer culture devoid of a larger civic commitment that would be more attuned to the needs, aspirations, and suffering of one's fellow citizens. Kennedy saw that their freedom had been turned into the unfree life of consumers, no longer citizens. Their freedom of choice had been turned into life under the thumb of both a corporate and bureaucratic prison, unresponsive to either their needs or aspirations. Robert Kennedy wanted the voices of those at the bottom of the well to be heard. He wanted to create a socioeconomic and sociopolitical climate in which the fullest expression of the rights and dignity of the poor and dispossessed could finally be realized as empowered citizens. The welfare system, he said, should give recipients "a voice in shaping the program which is their sole sustenance" (Schmitt 2010, 185).

Historian Edward Schmitt, commenting on this debate over the expansion of personal rights, had noted that:

Despite the fact that the Community Action Program, and its legislative clause requiring maximum feasible participation by the community, was coming under increasingly heavy attack, Kennedy publicly defended the provision more vigorously in 1967 than ever before . . . According to Adam Yarmolinsky, the original intention of the participation clause was not that the poor should be involved in policymaking but that they should be helping to administer programs.

Kennedy disagreed. ***'The intention,' he said, 'was to give them power'"*** (Schmitt 2010, 185, italics and bold added).

In 2002, Peter Edelman echoed Robert Kennedy's commitment to give power to the powerless when he wrote: "The traditional liberal position has been marginalized. If we are going to revive the Left, those of us on the progressive side have a responsibility to redefine our stance. We need to speak for fairness, and for children and families. *We need an inclusive politics that invites everyone's involvement in pursuing a better public policy and in helping people directly*. This new progressivism insists on an important role for both government and community" (Edelman 2001, 180, italics added).

In the struggles of the mid-1960s over the meaning and direction of human welfare, human agency, and the empowerment of the individual, Robert Kennedy sought to give power back to the individual person—especially the poor, the disenfranchised, and the excluded. He purposefully guided his political career and efforts through the dynamics of unresolved issues of racial justice, the role of the courts, the integrity of the laws, and the struggle between contending and contradictory worldviews about social order and human dignity. Robert Kennedy spoke in 1967 of the dangers to community development and national purpose—dangers that have, in the year 2011, metastasized into a full-blown crisis in America's civil culture and political life. Speaking at a dinner in honor of ex-Senator Paul Douglas, in Chicago, Illinois, on October 23, 1967, Kennedy lamented this fact:

> Most dangerous of all, millions of American—who can say how many?—have lost confidence in each other and in their ability to shape their own fat, their community's development, or their nation's course . . . We are losing many of our most active and committed young to extreme movements or public indifference . . . The Minutemen and the Revolutionary Action Movement agree only on one thing—that they have the right to use guns and violence against fellow citizens with whom they disagree. More and more, debate is not an interchange of views but a dialogue of the deaf, often serving to demonstrate differences but not to reconcile them. (Ross 1968, 343)

With respect to the plight of the African American community and the claims of the growing black power movement, Kennedy made a series of statements in late 1966 at the University of California at Berkeley, in which he sought to address the problem of race and racial justice:

> Some among us say the Negro has made great progress—which is true—and that he should be satisfied and patient—which is neither

> true nor realistic . . . We have unveiled the prospect of full participation in American society, while television, radio and newspapers bring to every Negro home the knowledge of how rewarding such participation can be. With so bountiful a promise how much greater must be the frustration and the fury of the Negro . . . who desperately wanting to believe, and half-believing, finds himself confined in the slums, unable to get an education and a job, confronted by the open prejudice and subtle hostilities of a white world, and seemingly powerless to change his condition or shape his future. (Ross 1968, 90–91)

Kennedy was a strong and ardent advocate for jobs, decent employment, and developing new avenues for grassroots participation in the life of one's own community. In his view, this was the only way to effectively dismantle the ghetto, restore dignity to the lives of excluded African Americans, and begin the task of building a truly just and democratic society. In order to dismantle the ghetto, Kennedy understood that entrenched barriers of segregation would have to be overcome. As William Julius Wilson, Professor of Social Policy at Harvard University, has noted:

> If large segments of the African-American population had not been historically segregated in inner city ghettos, we would not be talking about the new urban poverty. The segregated ghetto is not the result of voluntary or positive decisions on the part of the residents who live there . . . the segregated ghetto is the product of systematic racial practices such as restrictive covenants, redlining by banks and insurance companies, zoning, panic peddling by real estate agents, and the creation of massive public housing projects in low-income areas. (Wilson 1996, 23–24)

If employment and jobs were to become available to the residents of the ghetto, then Kennedy understood that the traditional forms of segregation had to be removed and demolished. This would also mean having to take on the challenge of entrenched social institutions. This was essential because Kennedy recognized in the late 1960s what sociologists in the 1990s had only to confirm—the reality that:

> Segregated ghettos are less conducive to employment and employment preparation than are other areas of the city. Segregation in ghettos exacerbates employment problems because it leads to weak informal employment networks and contributes to the social isolation of individuals and families, thereby reducing their chances of acquiring the human capital skills, including adequate educational training, that facilitate mobility in a society. Since no other group in

> society experiences the degree of segregation, isolation, and poverty concentration as do African-Americans, they are far more likely to be disadvantaged when they have to compete with other groups in society, including other despised groups, for resources and privileges. (Wilson 1996, 24)

While Kennedy was often focused on his primary initiatives—such as hunger, community development corporations, and tax incentives to industry for investing in poverty-stricken areas—it is also true that these more conservative themes were counterbalanced by liberal and even radical signals (Schmitt 2010, 208). Specifically, the historical record demonstrates this about Robert's approach to the problems of the poor and disadvantaged:

> Despite his call for local control, Kennedy's unique notion of federalism was not based on state or city government. Instead it hinged on the vitality of a direct relationship between the federal government and an imagined community of those in need who were kept from power at the grassroots level. "*Kennedy federalism*" on the problem of poverty thus sought to bypass the conventional machinery of representative democracy (*and other entrenched social institutions*) that continued to render the poor powerless. While other elements of Kennedy's approach to poverty had traditional roots, this conception of federalism had truly radical implications. (Schmitt 2010, 186, italics added)

The radical implications of Kennedy's approach grew out of his knowledge of a dysfunctional social system that negatively impacted those at the bottom of the American social and economic hierarchy. He understood what many others involved in social welfare issues came to recognize in his own time: "The structural position and sub-societal behavior patterns of the poor stem from historical and contemporary sources which generally involved multiple factors, including lack of access to the political and economic systems, systematic racial discrimination, and ineffective social institutions which prohibit rather than facilitate full participation in the larger society" (Rose 1970, 97). In addressing these problems, Robert initiated what amounted to a private Kennedy war on poverty with the introduction of his Bedford-Stuyvesant Program. It was bold and imaginative in many of its approaches—particularly in its pointed reluctance to depend on the federal government. In this most radical respect, Robert Kennedy was prepared to test many of the assumptions and ideas that he frequently mentioned in his various speeches and legislative proposals designed to combat poverty. On December 9, 1966, Kennedy formally launched the program. At its core was its most central and foundational principle; in Kennedy's words: "The plan begins with a perspective: that questions of technical or surface integration are far less important now than is the building of self-sufficiency and self-determination within the Negro community; in fact, that what is too often an undifferentiated mass must be helped to form a coherent and cohesive community" (Ross 1968, 151). From these statements, it appears that it was clear in Kennedy's mind that government could not create a "coherent and cohesive community," for only the people themselves could do that. Yet, what is implicit in Kennedy's program is the view that poverty is a vicious cycle of reinforcing disabilities—unemployment, inferior education, discrimination, poor health, lack of motivation, unstable family life, and other factors—all of which serve to render its victims incapable of competing within the larger society.

Speaking before the NAACP Legal Defense Fund Banquet in New York on May 18, 1966, Kennedy declared that: "Government is an institution too often set in ways accepted in the past—but the old answers have failed, and ***we need new institutions to shape new solutions***. Most importantly, reliance on government is dependence—and what the people of our ghettos need is not greater dependence, but full independence; not the charity and favor of their fellow citizens, but equal claims of right and equal power to enforce those claims" (Ross 1968, 154, italics and bold added. At the end of that year, in a statement to the Subcommittee on Executive Reorganization of the Senate Committee on Government Operations on December 10, 1966, Robert Kennedy proposed the creation of Community Development Corporations to insure the active participation of inner-city residents in the program, and to help foster a great sense of community among the poor. With this purpose in mind, Kennedy declared: "The measure of the success of this or any other program will be the extent to which it helps the ghetto to become a community—a functioning unit, its people acting together on matters of mutual concern, with the power and resources to affect the conditions of their own lives. Therefore, the heart of the program, I believe, should be the creation of Community Development Corporations, which would carry out the work of construction, the hiring and training of workers, the provision of services, the encouragement of associated enterprises" (Ross 1968, 152).

In the decades following his assassination, however, the nation began embarking on a rightward drift. Instead of decent employment combined with decent wages and new avenues for democratic civic engagement, there was an expanding emphasis on building prisons and warehousing minorities, with accompanying draconian shifts in the Federal Sentencing Guidelines that installed the "three strikes" law, mandatory minimums, and other harsh penalties that were largely aimed at suppressing people of color. These were the trends embraced by presidents of both parties. They were almost indistinguishable trends that were reinforced by the policies of Reagan, Bush, and Clinton. Take, for example, the fact that by 1997 the state of California alone was responsible for the incarceration of 200,000 Californians, thereby earning it the name of "Singapore West" (Koetting and Schiraldi 1997, 40–53). By 2010, California could boast of having built more than thirty-six prisons (Bacon 2010, 16–20).

In her book entitled *Golden Gulag: Prisons, Surplus, Crisis, and Opposition in Globalizing California*, Ruth Gilmore, professor of geography at the University of Southern California, noted that: "The California state prisoner population grew nearly 500 percent between 1982 and 2000, even though the crime rate peaked in 1980 and declined, unevenly but decisively, thereafter . . . African Americans and Latinos comprise two-thirds of the state's 160,000 prisoners . . . Most prisoners come from the state's urban cores—particularly Los Angeles and the surrounding southern counties. More than half the prisoners had steady employment before arrest, while upwards of 80 percent were, at some time in their case, represented by state-appointed lawyers for the indigent. In short, as a class, convicts are de-industrialized cities' working or working poor" (Gilmore 2007, 7). A perfect storm had taken place across America's socioeconomic landscape in the aftermath of the Robert Kennedy era.

Throughout the 1970s and cresting in the 1980s, corporations began to initiate a policy of unrestrained deindustrialization, which was the precursor to globalization. With the ascendancy of Ronald Reagan to the presidency, the welfare state was dismantled in conjunction with a host of corporate mergers, jobs sent overseas, and workers laid off with no safety net in place as corporations went looking for cheap, low-wage workers abroad. At home, the unresolved problems of the ghetto, racial segregation, and a new "war on the poor" came into focus (Block, Cloward, Ehrenreich, and Piven 1987).

Part of the reason for this war on the poor can be explained by the new economic realities of the 1970s, a decade in which "faltering profits in the 1970s led American business interests to try to reduce uncertainty and shore up profits through a series of changes in public policy. In part the business mobilization was simply an effort to shift the distributional effects of government taxation and spending by reducing business taxes, increasing spending on military contracts, and slashing programs that distribute income and services to the poor and working class" (Piven and Cloward 1987, 89). The other reason for the war on the poor: "Countries with top-heavy corporate bureaucracies tend to lock a lot of people behind bars. Indeed, looking more closely at the numbers, the countries that seem most clearly to feature conflictual labor relations on the Stick Strategy [are] . . . the United States, Canada, and the United Kingdom. And there are those that build their labor relations upon substantially more cooperative foundations—[such as] . . . Belgium, Denmark, Finland, Germany, Japan, the Netherlands, and Sweden" (Gordon 1996, 142). These factors combined to create the modern prison-industrial complex in the United States (Rosenblatt 1996; Cole 1999; Zimring, Hawkins, Kamin 2001; Dyer, 2000; Alexander 2010; Donziger, et al, 1996; Mauer 1999; Tonry 2004; Tonry 1995; Tonry 1996; Miller 1996). Also helping to drive the forces of mass incarceration and the expansion of the prison-industrial complex was an ideological shift from a war on poverty to a "war on crime" that was accented by an attendant "war on drugs" (Reinarman and Levine, 1997; Bertam, Blachman, Sharpe, and Andreas, 1996; Miller 1996).

Kennedy's words of compassion for the plight of African Americans had been effectively drowned out by the time the Reagan years arrived in the 1980s. Commenting on these trends, Loic Wacquant, professor of sociology at the University of California, Berkeley, noted that:

> In the 1980s, the United States added an average of 20,000 African-Americans to its total prisoner stock *every year* (over one-third the total carceral stock of France). And, for the first time in the twentieth century, the country's penitentiaries held more blacks than whites: African-Americans made up 12 percent of the national population but supplied 53 percent of the prison inmates in 1995, as against 38 percent a quarter-century earlier. The rate of incarceration for blacks *tripled in only a dozen years* to reach 1,895 per 100,000 in 1993—amounting to nearly seven times the rate for whites (293 per 100,000) and twenty times the rates recorded in the main European countries at that time. (Wacquant 2009, 61, italics in original)

The above-cited statistics show that only twelve years after Robert Kennedy's assassination in 1968, the growing incarceration rate for blacks had escalated dramatically. Kennedy's message, policies, and identification with black Americans had been replaced by the callous indifference and outright hostility of an American public that had been taught by the social and political culture to fear "the Other."

In many ways, it could be said that the post-Robert Kennedy era was a time that reflected the criminalization of poverty and the resurgent tides of racism, all tied to the emerging economic doctrine of neoliberalism. This is what Wacquant has called "the Neoliberal government of social insecurity" (Wacquant 2004). It is a theme that has been taken up by a host of other scholars who have studied the Reagan-Bush-Clinton era. As the Clinton years came to a close in 1999, crimes rates had been in steady decline for the previous twenty-five years. Yet despite this fact, continued and massive investments in the prison-industrial complex escalated, thereby depleting and diverting funds that could have gone to other social services, such as education, health care, and social welfare (Chambliss 1999). In place of the communitarian vision, in pursuit of which Robert Kennedy had dedicated his life, there were now hundreds of gated communities that sprawled out from urban centers. The collapse of the New Deal approach in the closing years of the 1960s had sent political leaders searching for a new model of governance. They found it in the war on crime, which had the effect of turning the average citizen into little more than a crime victim—a victim whose vulnerabilities opened the door to further forms of government intervention.

By the 1980s and through the 1990s, a transformation of the core powers of government had occurred in all of the institutions that govern daily life (Simon 2007). In so doing, this trend has distorted the fundamental building blocks of a democratic society. The net effect was to remove the scaffolding of a "free society" and to destroy social trust. The unraveling was set into motion with dramatic speed on June 4, 1968, when Robert Kennedy was assassinated, for his violent death—and the death of the promise that he embodied—was to mark the end of hope in a social-justice approach to governance and the beginning of the age of "law and order" (Flamm 2005, 153). In the aftermath of Kennedy's assassination, the nation lurched from Lyndon Johnson's crime commission to three-strikes laws and mandatory minimums in sentencing (Gest 2001). The right-wing drift was further accelerated and complemented by a host of right-wing US Supreme Court appointments that eventually led to a right-wing effort to remake the entire federal courts system (Schwartz 2004). By 2008, the US Supreme phalanx of right-wing judicial extremists had been consummated in a new right-wing bloc, led by Antonio Scalia, Clarence Thomas, John Roberts, and Samuel Alito (Dworkin 2008). The trend toward right-wing judicial extremism had been in the making ever since Robert Kennedy's death (Keck 2004). The trend began in earnest with Nixon's appointment of William Rehnquist as Chief Justice of the Supreme Court. The rights of prisoners were significantly curtailed, capital punishment procedures were accelerated, and a states'- rights assault on federal authority was given new impetus (Schwartz 2002). By 2001 to 2008, the Bush II presidency enjoyed the full-throttle support of a court that largely endorsed the imperial presidency, accelerated the dismantling of the wall separating church and state, endorsed the erosion of civil and individual liberties, and made it easier to buy an assault rifle than to obtain an abortion (Chemerinsky 2010).

In many respects it is the embrace of the neoliberal economic model, coupled with draconian criminal laws, that has created a new set of Jim Crow laws and sentencing practices that has turned the criminal justice system into a modern prison-industrial complex. It has been supported by the legal apparatus of the nation from the top down. It is a reality that returns us to a reconsideration of the place of race in American politics and law. It also returns us to question the "what-if" possibilities of Robert Kennedy's legacy and the meaning of that legacy in the stream of history. To raise this question is not to embark upon a counterfactual expedition through history. Rather, to raise this question is to take history even more seriously, insofar as the assassination of Robert Kennedy was also the assassination of his mission and message to remake America and its promise into a more justice-oriented national community, and *not* to transform it into a purely profit-oriented carnival of individual egos who gamble at the Wall Street casino of deregulated capitalism. It seems clear now that Robert Kennedy's death and the suppression of his legacy, mission, and message can be seen as a calculated rebuke of an historical trend toward greater equality and justice for all Americans. Insofar as Kennedy identified his politics not only with the civil rights movement at home, but also the human rights movement abroad, it can be historically argued that Kennedy's statesmanship remains a transcendent legacy that can be accessed even now, at the dawn of the twenty-first century.

Robert Kennedy's life and career paralleled tectonic shifts in the stream of history in the decades of the 1950s and 1960s. Those shifts served to place his career and the course of nations on a trajectory that was invariably headed in the directions that he spoke of in his speeches and that he identified in his proposals and policies for "a newer world." Take, for example, the global phenomenon of decolonization in the 1950s and early 1960s. It was a time of movements for liberation from imperialism, colonialism, and the dogmatic confines of Cold War ideologies. Of this period, Michael Klarman, the James Monroe Distinguished Professor of Law and History at the University of Virginia, has noted:

> The decolonization of Africa may also help to explain why direct-action protest broke out in the 1960s rather than a few years earlier. In 1957, Ghana became the first black African nation to win its independence from colonial rule. Within a half-dozen years, more than thirty other African countries had followed suit, seventeen of them in 1960 alone. American civil rights leaders identified the African independence movements as an important motivation for their own. They saw American civil rights protests as "part of the revolt of the colored peoples of the world against old ideas and practices of white supremacy." African freedom movements demonstrated to American blacks the feasibility of racial change through collective action, while heightening their frustrations with the domestic status quo. As James Baldwin explained, American blacks who observed African independence movements lamented that "all of Africa will be free before we can get a lousy cup of coffee." In 1960, Roy Wilkins observed that Africans were electing prime ministers and sending delegates to the United Nations, while Mississippi blacks still could not vote. The decolonization of Africa possibly provided the spark that was necessary to detonate a social protest movement that was already to explode. (Klarman 2004, 376)

From the perspective of American history, world history, and the academic field of sociology, Professor Howard Winant, writing about how the idea of race has affected and influenced perceptions on a global and national level, has addressed the shaping power of race in human affairs and concludes: "Race has been a constitutive element as an organizing principle, a *praxis* and structure that has constructed and reconstructed world society since the emergence of modernity, the enormous historical shift represented by the rise of Europe, the founding of modern nation-states and empire, the conquista, the onset of African enslavement, and the subjugation of much of Asia" (Winant 2001, 20).

On this matter, it can also be argued that the issue of race cannot and should not be divorced from considerations of empire, notions of sovereignty, constitutional law, and the practice of international relations. This argument can be specifically supported by recognizing that "insofar as colonialism was associated with ideas of innate and therefore permanent racial superiority, it plainly impinged upon the conceptions of human equality and human dignity which underlie the belief in human rights" (Simpson 2001, 300).

To understand and appreciate the full scope of this global reality, as well as the nature of imperialism in the post-1945 world, it is important to note that "in the immediate post-war period, during which the international human rights movement produced the Universal Declaration (1948), the European Covenant (1950), and the early drafts of the United Nations Covenant, Britain remained a major colonial power. Indeed in 1944 some 263, 722,000 people lived in dependencies of one kind or another, under the control of such powers: Britain, Denmark, South Africa, Australia, New Zealand, France, the Netherlands, Japan, the USA, Belgium, Portugal, Italy, or Spain" (Simpson 2001 276). In the stream of history, the decolonization process of the late 1950s and early 1960s was not the first global manifestation of a human rights campaign against the abuses of white supremacy. The movement for the abolition of slavery was its antecedent. What the global abolition of slavery movement, the global decolonization movement, and the global campaign in the 1980s against apartheid in South Africa all share is the fact that they all exhibited a moral indictment of a political, social, and economic structure that emerged over the course of many decades. Each one of these victories for the cause of human rights—the abolition of slavery and the end of apartheid in South Africa—was predicated upon the accumulated work of human rights advocates who agitated, worked, and spoke out for change. In the stream of history, all of these events, people, and movements leading toward provisional victories and final victories in the struggle for human rights had to confront the fortress of white supremacy. Hence, human rights struggles and victories can be best understood within the context of converging social movements and forces advocating for human rights that ultimately resulted in the forging of a new human rights consciousness, which was itself the product of a dramatic "sea-change in sensibility" (Blackburn 2011, 337).

However, the sea-change in sensibility had not yet reached into the depths of the US domestic political consciousness at the end of the Second World War. Rather, the United States in the 1950s was not host to an enlightened political or favorable social climate for the enunciation of human rights. The proposed United Nations Covenant on Civil and Political Rights, as well as social and economic rights, was feared by many in the United States because of its potential legal power to make international law protections of human rights applicable throughout all of the domestic jurisdictions and forums of the United States, without recognizing a Congressional power to implement such a covenant or treaty by legislation. As early as 1949, it had become apparent that there was inevitably going to be "serious opposition in the Senate to the ratification of any human rights instrument" (Simpson 2001, 819). The opposition came into full and threatening prominence when "in 1951, Senator John Bricker of Ohio proposed to the Senate that the USA should take no further part in negotiating the covenant. Between 1952 and 1957 his name was associated with a succession of attempts to amend the US Constitution, with the intention of ensuring that the ratification of a treaty would not confer on the Congress a power to implement the treaty domestically by legislation unless Congress would have possessed the relevant legislative power in the absence of a treaty" (Simpson 2001, 819–820).

Why was this action undertaken by Senator Bricker and his supporters? The primary explanation and the fundamental reason for Senator Bricker's action reveals the lingering challenges posed by racism, the structure of white supremacy, the Jim Crow laws of the American South, and the ideological scope of the doctrine of "states rights." To place these elements in a broader historical context, it is important to appreciate the lingering effects of racial slavery. In his book, *White Supremacy: A Comparative Study in American and South African History*, George M. Fredrickson, professor of American History at Northwestern University, notes:

> Before segregation laws and suffrage restrictions had apparently put southern blacks "in their place," anxieties about how to maintain total dominance over a group that persisted in asserting its claim to civil and political equality helped provoke an epidemic of lynchings and pogrom-type "race riots" in the South. Even after the full array of discriminatory legislation was off the books, extralegal violence, or the threat of it, continued to play an important role as a device for intimidating blacks and shoring up the color line. Besides being symptomatic of pathological negrophobia, these brutal vigilante tactics also reflected a persistent insecurity about the effectiveness of white dominance and a lack of faith in the full adequacy of legal or institutional control over blacks. (Fredrickson 1981, 251)

As far as Senator Bricker and his support-base was concerned, the record demonstrates: "They wanted to protect 'states rights' from being whittled away through the use of the treaty making power, some in order to maintain the discrimination regime existing in the southern states . . . Integral to this scheme was a provision which ensured that treaties were not self-executing, so as to ensure that legislation was always essential for them to have domestic effect" (Simpson 2001, 820). Ultimately, the Constitution was not amended. Even if it had been, this action may not have restricted the progressive enlargement of congressional power (Simpson 2001, 821). At the same time, while Senator Simpson and his constituency were seeking to hold onto the institutions of white supremacy, there was a radical-national movement advancing the cause of civil rights from 1919–1950.

The civil rights movement that looms over the 1950s and 1960s was the tip of the iceberg, the visible legal and political outgrowth of a far-reaching American movement for social justice that flourished from the 1920s through the 1940s. In her book, *Defying Dixie: The Radical Roots of Civil Rights, 1919–1950,* Glenda Gilmore, Professor of History at Yale University, introduces her study by noting that: "*Defying Dixie* begins at the radical edges of a human rights movement after World War I, with Communists who promoted and practiced racial equality and considered the South crucial to their success in elevating labor and overthrowing the capitalist system. They were joined in the late 1930s by a radical left to form a southern Popular Front that sought to overturn Jim Crow, elevate the working class, and promote civil rights and civil liberties. During and after World War II a growing number of grassroots activist protested directly against white supremacy and imagined it poised to fall of its own weight. They gave it a shove" (Gilmore 2008, 4). Giving white supremacy a shove is precisely what was transpiring throughout the nation's civil rights struggles from 1919 to the 1960s.

A persistent and continuous effort undertaken by civil rights advocates was evident at the local, regional, and national levels. Opposition to the associated doctrines and ideology of white supremacy was being pursued on a regular basis, as evidenced by a series of state and federal statutes prohibiting discrimination in public accommodations, voting, and education. However, these statutes were enacted only after a series of Supreme Court decisions during the 1940s and 1950s (Hill 1977, 39). Despite advances in these areas, federal action in the arena of labor relations lagged seriously behind. The Supreme Court decision that established "fair representation" as a possible means of redress was *Steele vs. Louisville & Nashville R.R. Co.* In that case, black railway workers raised the issue of discriminatory labor unions operating under the mantle of governmental authority. In the aftermath of these events, the historical record reveals that: "Application of the fair representation doctrine resulted in several important court decisions, but the doctrine itself was sharply limited because it did not deal with such essential questions as union membership for black workers and segregated locals. In addition, for many years the National Labor Relations Board did not apply the duty of fair representation in the area of racial discrimination" (Hill 1977, 40, italics added). And, just as the application of the fair representation doctrine did not proceed beyond a certain legal threshold until further legal developments in the 1960s, so, too, it can be said that the full application of the Fourteenth Amendment's promise of equal protection did not proceed very far in desegregating the doors to America's schools until the 1954 case of *Brown v. Board of Education.* It took the added legal, political, and social pressure of the NAACP and its army of lawyers, litigating for decades as dedicated "*crusaders in the courts*," before the exclusionary doctrine of "*separate but equal*" could be challenged and defeated (Greenberg 1994, italics added).

What the judicial evolution of civil rights through the courts reveals is that reliance on legal precedent may be a necessary but not sufficient basis on which to reach what some legal scholars have termed "constitutional clarity." Neither the scope of legal doctrines nor the nature of judicial rulings can ever escape the personal values of the interpreter, or the social and political context in which legal constructs exist. That is because, as Michael Klarman reminds us:

> Constitutional clarity is itself an ambiguous concept. Whether the traditional sources of constitutional law are thought to plainly forbid a particular practice depends on the personal values of the interpreter and on the social and political context . . . Because constitutional clarity lies in the eye of the beholder, no judicial interpretation can ever be a result simply of the legal axis; rather, all such interpretations are inevitably a product of the intersection of both axes. *Brown* illustrates the same point. To the justices who were most committed to traditional legal sources, such as text, original intent, precedent, and custom, *Brown* should have been an easy case—for *sustaining* school segregation. Jackson candidly conceded that barring segregation could be defended only in political, not legal terms. Thus, the legal axis alone can never determine a constitutional interpretation, as judges always have to choose whether to adhere to that axis. When

> their preferences are strong, the judges may reject even relatively determinate law, because they are unable to tolerate the result it indicates. In 1954, most of the justices considered racial segregation the doctrine that Hitler had preached—to be evil, and they were determined to forbid it, regardless of whether conventional legal sources sanctioned that result. (Klarman 2004, 447, italics in original)

In the 1950s and 1960s, Robert Kennedy was a witness to and a participant in such a massive sea-change of sensibility. He became a leader who was able to play a transformative role because he aligned himself with forces for social change that had been operating within the wider political and social context. Robert Kennedy's evolution as a civil rights leader in the stream of history began at the moment he was sworn in as Attorney General of the United States, January 1961. Reflecting on that period, he later admitted: "I won't say I stayed awake nights worrying about civil rights before I became Attorney General" (Ross, 1968, 49). By 1966, in the aftermath of his trip to South Africa, he wrote an article for *Look* magazine in which he asked his readers to consider a new question: "But suppose God is black? What if we go to heaven and we, all our lives, have treated the Negro as an inferior, and God is there and we look up and he is not white? What then is our response?" (Ross 1968, 49). These two statements serve to bookend Robert Kennedy's evolution as not just an Attorney General of the United States and his role as a Senator from New York, but his transformation into a statesman with a global consciousness. Kennedy clearly understood that a massive global revolution in values, economics, and political demands was taking place in the 1960s that required immediate choices and actions that transcended the conventional and traditional. Hence, the case should be made that Robert Kennedy's legacy should be viewed through the lens of his national and global statesmanship. His words, policies, message, meaning, and legacy are bound up with the freedom and human rights struggles of his time.

Like other progressive leaders, social movements, and principled actors on the progressive side of history, Robert Kennedy can be best understood as a statesman who came to possess an alternative conception of the uses of power. Noted historian James Hilty concluded, "With the burial of JFK, Robert Kennedy's trial by existence had passed. Now he faced another trial, this time on his own. In his depression, however, he found within a spiritual intensity and a sense of invincibility that he could channel simultaneously toward achieving social change, preserving his brother's legacy, and seeking the presidential nomination. His fundamental instincts, basic temperament, and innate character remained the same. What changed were his public and family roles and his belief in his own political and historic destiny. JFK's death and his own intimate involvement in the civil rights revolution had deepened Robert Kennedy's concerns for social inequities, until finally he became champion of the outcasts, the Jeremiah of the sixties" (Hilty 1997, 498). Because of his own inner transformation and change of consciousness about the meaning and proper role of power in human affairs, he felt the need to radically alter the social structures of his day that denied human dignity and rights to millions, both within the United States and around the globe. This perspective brings us to an insight born out of the experience of the 1960s, which is that *with* "an alternative conception of power, social structure, and history" *we can* "make better sense of the historical clash of rights in liberal democratic capitalism and the political nature of the economy" (Bowles and Gintis 1986, 94).

From the standpoint of progressive scholarship in economics, Samuel Bowles and Herbert Gintis have proposed that we need to reexamine our ideas about power so as to develop alternative conceptions of it, rather than to just uncritically accept the status quo as immutable. Therefore professors Bowles and Gintis urge us to consider the insight and implications that emerge from an examination of the following five propositions:

> First, power is heterogeneous, wielding a variety of weapons, yielding to a host of counter-pressures, and obeying no single logic . . . Second, power is not an amorphous constraint on action but rather a structure of rules empowering and restraining actors in varying degrees . . . Third, the perpetuation of any power structure is generally problematic . . . Fourth, distinct structures of power—be they the liberal democratic state, the patriarchal family, the capitalist economy, or other—are not merely juxtaposed, they are bound together in a common process of social reproduction. Each one may contribute to the survival of another; or they may foster mutually corrosive and subversive impulses. And fifth, because people's lives are generally governed by more than one distinct power structures . . . we experience power as heterogeneous, and are often able to bring the experiences within one system of power to bear in the pursuit of our projects within another. (Bowles and Gintis 1986, 94)

Any critical, objective, and relevant examination of the nature of the US power structure in the late 1960s should have to eventually recognize the objective accuracy and relevance of these five propositions. Robert Kennedy was one of the few voices in the late 1960s who had demonstrated an awareness of the importance of these insights. It was evident in his speeches throughout his career as a senator from New York. If the events between 1965 and 1968 reflected any general truth about the nature of the times, it was that the nation was unraveling from within. The counterpressures of pro-war and antiwar groups had struck a national nerve. The counterpressures of the civil rights movement collided against the segregationist walls of Jim Crow laws, the lingering presence of ingrained bigotry, the growth and spread of rightwing extremism, and the enduring forces of racial prejudice (Lopez 1996; Berry 1994; Muhammad 2010).

The Jim Crow system was a structure of rules, laws, and social mores that had been in place since the Reconstruction era. To deal with this lingering challenge to the Fourteenth Amendment's promise of equal protection, newly empowered federal courts were provided with a mandate from the US Supreme Court to undo and eliminate the vestiges of the old doctrine of "separate but equal." Yet the legal battles would not always result in a principled resolution of the problem, or produce a progressive outcome. Specifically, it is a matter of historical record that the Supreme Court itself proved to be recalcitrant in extending welfare rights and/or socioeconomic rights into traditional enclaves of a white power structure that stubbornly clung to a juridical set of interpretations that implied that inequalities spawned in the market economy are constitutionally irrelevant outside the delineated sphere of protected property rights. The court had decided to relegate the objective problems of poverty, racism, and economic inequality to the status of little more than subjective interpretation. This view became evident in the *Shapiro* opinion of 1967, in which an obdurate and unmoved Chief Justice Earl Warren stated: "Poverty has pricked the nation's conscience in recent years . . . To the extent that appellees have attempted to show that durational residence requirements impose handicaps upon the poor of the nation, they appeal to the right instincts of all men. *However, instinct cannot be our guide*" (Draft opinion, June 3, 1968, filed in the Earl Warren Papers, Library of Congress, container number 566, italics added). Commenting on this ruling, Elizabeth Bussiere, professor of political science at the University of Massachusetts, sardonically observed that "acting on the basis of 'right instincts,' Chief Justice Warren admonished, would be tantamount to acting subjectively" (Brussiere 1997, 111).

Acting subjectively may not have been the judicial style of Earl Warren, but it was the driving force behind Robert Kennedy's empathy and advocacy for the poor and his approach to issues involving poverty and the burdens it placed on its victims. Hence, what we see in the record of the times is that Kennedy's existential "new politics" was not limited by his knowledge of legal precedent, but was largely influenced and inspired by his sensitivity to human suffering as well as by the passions and ideals of the time. In Kennedy's term of public service from 1961–1968, he was moving in the stream of history at a time of gathering social movements, of new visions about what America could become, and of a gathering hope that the nation could finally move collectively and inclusively toward realizing the ideals embodied in the Declaration that proclaimed that "all men are created equal." The Supreme Court has struggled with this issue many times since its passage in the aftermath of the American Civil War (Perry 1999).

Given the practical constraints of politics, American culture, history, and the law itself, it was clear to both Chief Justice Warren and Robert Kennedy that the perpetuation of the power structure was problematic. Where they parted company was on the question of *whether the content of rights should be divorced from the capacity to exercise them.* Having rights without remedies was a prescription for disaster. To articulate rights claims was one thing, but to actualize those claims and provide concrete avenues for their realization was another matter. The Warren Court remained caught in the legal quandary of being unable to apply a different constitutional standard to welfare regulation as opposed to traditional business regulation. Having failed to advance the meaning and application of the Equal Protection doctrines in the economic domain of distributive politics, the judicial record of the Warren Court reveals the justices' difficulty in addressing the "paradox of poverty amidst plenty" (Brussiere 1997, 111). However, for Robert Kennedy, there was no such difficulty. He called the paradox of poverty amidst plenty immoral. Unwilling to endorse or tolerate a blind adherence to such a system and its further retrenchment and its historical legacy of seemingly intractable institutionalization, Kennedy incessantly called for immediate action to remove the glaring inequalities, the perpetual deprivations, and the needless sufferings of the dispossessed throughout society. These deprivations and injustices were constantly being engendered, promoted, and even justified by the maintenance of social structures dedicated to an exclusionary social, economic, and political status quo.

In the decades after Kennedy's assassination, some scholars have come to see the problem of poverty as centered within the capitalist market system itself. Charles E. Lindblom, professor of political science at Yale University, has concluded that "*market systems imprison policy. Those of us who live in those market oriented systems that are called liberal democratic exercise significantly less control over policy than we have thought. And we are also less free than we may have thought. Such are the inevitable consequences of imprisonment*" (Lindblom 1984, 11, italics added). Similarly, Loic Wacquant, professor of sociology, University of California, Berkeley, notes that "blacks had entered the Fordist industrial economy, to which they contributed a vital source of abundant and cheap labor willing to ride along its cycles of boom and bust. Yet they remained locked in a precarious position of structural economic marginality and consigned to a secluded and dependent microcosm, complete within its own internal division of labor, social stratification, and agencies of collective voice and symbolic representation: a '*city within the city*.'" (Wacquant 2009, 202, italics added).

Thus the practical problem for Kennedy was deciding how to construct an urban program that went beyond the "maximum feasible participation of the poor" language, which was the ambiguous phrase in the Poverty Act. To take on the problem of market failures and democratic failures, it would be necessary to ask for, in Kennedy's words, the "full and dominant participation by the residents of the community concerned" (vanden Heuvel and Gwirtzman 1970, 90). Kennedy's answer was to support a device called the "community development corporation." According to two of his legislative assistants, "more than any other institution or government program, these corporations, Kennedy hoped, would transform ghettos from vast, undifferentiated masses into real communities, in which residents would have a sense of control over their lives, and feel, for the first time, part of the American experience of self-determination" (vanden Heuvel and Gwirtzman 1970, 91).

6

Confronting Poverty with a New Conception of Democratic Order

To meet the challenge of eliminating poverty and confronting the limitations of both the market economy and the social pathologies of ghetto life, Kennedy sought to bring about the innovation of new economic incentives for the market economy itself. The community development corporation perhaps could achieve, in combination with the market, that which the market by itself could not hope to achieve. Kennedy recognized that contemporary governments in market societies find themselves practicing planning, whether they admit it or not. And he also knew that by providing new incentives for the market system that were attuned to governmental priorities and planning for the general welfare, it would be possible to transform the market, the society, and governmental practice in such a way that human rights could finally be realized in a more democratic, fair, and equal society.

Those who worked with him and knew of his approach to these problems have revealed:

> *Kennedy knew the work of these corporations would be far too costly for government.* Mayor Lindsay estimated in the 1966 Rubicoff hearings that $50 billion in federal funds would be needed over a ten-year period for the physical rebuilding of New York City alone, a federal share Kennedy called "totally unrealistic." *He sought, therefore, to bring private resources into the process.* Even they could not furnish all the money that was needed, but given the fiscal limitations caused by the war in Vietnam and public reluctance to pay for major new ghetto programs, they could do much more than government alone to meet the urgent needs and they could do it in ways that made money. *This, rather than the production of goods and services for the affluent, could be the new frontier of the free enterprise system in the building of America.* (vanden Heuvel and Gwirtzman 1970, 91, italics added)

This idea was the basis of Robert Kennedy's experimental model in Bedford-Stuyvesant, New York.

What Kennedy was seeking to actualize in the model of Bedford-Stuyvesant was a marriage between government planning for social welfare to the mechanisms that govern the economic sphere of market-system societies. Commenting on this strategy, Professor Charles Lindblom observed:

> Models of pure market system aside, all real-world market-system societies practice a great deal of central planning of production, whether it is called that or not. Despite the ascendance of the market system as the twenty-first century opens, national planning of production is not dead either as an idea or practice, anathema as the word is in some circles. I mean by national planning those procedures through which a society or its rulers make efforts toward informed and thoughtful governmental choices about both the near and distant future. Whether or not one likes it, all societies make such efforts. Planning, so defined, has never been absent. (Lindblom 2001, 267)

From 1966 through 1968, Robert Kennedy was practicing what Lindblom later preached. Kennedy sensed that the free market system should be rerouted from serving the affluent to meeting the needs of the broader society. By so doing, Kennedy was identifying the shape of what he considered to be a preferred political order. In this task, he was proposing nothing less than a revolution in values and the economy—a revolution that would have dramatic repercussions in the lives of the poor, regardless of race. Hence it appears that Kennedy was proposing nothing less than a marriage between governmental planning and the investment of the managers and business leaders of the nation's free-enterprise system: a coupling designed to wipe out the ghettos and erase poverty. Kennedy's true genius is that he sought to activate a comprehensive approach to the problems of poverty and the ghetto, while at the same time taking into account the structural constraints of capitalism and seeking ways to mitigate and overcome those constraints. Writing thirty years after Kennedy's assassination, Professor Michael K. Brown examined federal social policy from Roosevelt to Reagan in his book, *Race, Money, and the American Welfare State*, in which he concluded: "Any real account of social policies which ignores the limits to state autonomy—the structural constraints of capitalism—is insufficient. Though the importance of investor and taxpayer resistance varies with the circumstances, no policymaker, especially none intent on adding new social policies, can escape the necessity of balancing the claims of entrepreneurs and taxpayers against the beneficiaries of new policies" (Brown 1999, 361). To his credit, Robert Kennedy did not ignore the competing claims of entrepreneurs, taxpayers, or the residents of the ghetto and the poor as a class. Rather, as a champion and as an advocate of community-based development corporations, Kennedy was uniquely attuned to the demands and aspirations of all three of these constituencies. Unfortunately, Johnson's advisers were hostile to the idea of investing in the ghetto, and Kennedy's plan was regarded as a failure (Brown 1999, 285).

By mapping out this strategy of social action and social reform, Kennedy was acting as an apostle of change who courageously challenged his countrymen to begin to make democratic ideals correspond to economic practices, thereby strengthening both the civil society and the general economy at the same time. Given this interpretation, I will submit that Kennedy's policy proposals for the ghetto in particular and the economy at large were proposals that complemented one another. His proposals were particularly salient with regard to establishing a more clear formulation of the democratic conception of society, because it is a conception of a *political* order. To understand this point is to understand the heart of the Robert Kennedy legacy: the centrality he gave to the importance of a democratic conception of society in both theory and in practice. In defining what is constitutive of a democratic conception of society, Joshua Cohen and Joel Rogers have suggested that:

> It is a conception of a social system in which public debate over the direction of social life would not only be expected, but would in fact be publicly encouraged. Implicit in this conception is the conviction that the removal of familiar barriers to free deliberation would not eliminate all grounds for political disagreement. Thus the task of the democratic conception is not to describe a social order in which all disputes would be trivial, or indicative of a failure to realize the principles of the order. *The democratic conception is not a utopian conception, dedicated to the ideal of perfectly harmonious community, and the burden of the conception is not to outline a political order in which such an ideal is realized. The burden rather is to outline a political order in which disagreements over the direction of that order could be socially addressed through free deliberation.* (Cohen and Rogers 1983, 148–149, italics added)

On April 5, 1968, the day after Dr. King's assassination, Kennedy delivered a speech on violence in America and spoke of "schools without books" and "homes without heat in the winter." He spoke of the way in which the human spirit was broken under the weight of social injustice. Kennedy believed that if only Americans could finally come to understand the burdens under which the poor and people of color were forced to live and labor, then there might be a possibility for national renewal. Therefore, he called for a renewed recognition of common brotherhood and common human needs of all citizens, regardless of the color of their skin. Even in this moment of national grief over King's death, Kennedy was outlining a *democratic conception of society* that would honor King's memory and the cause to which he gave his life. On April 4, 1968, the day of King's assassination, Kennedy called for an end to both racial and economic divisions so that Americans could "become brothers and countrymen once again" (Newfield, 1969, 284). He had come to understand that there were structural forces in the economy and the larger society that reinforced poverty, unemployment, and exclusion for people of color. It was a situation that constituted "unfinished democracy" and to finish it would require a new approach. This was especially the case because: "While the New Deal had excluded African-Americans, the War on Poverty would favor them" (Quadango 1994, 31). It was in light of this basic recognition that he called for a whole new approach to both poverty and discrimination so that violence born of social exclusion could be eliminated and, in its place, a set of national policies developed that would make possible the evolution of a more socially just and democratic society.

In the stream of history, an optimistic version of the War-on-Poverty years would make the case that "while the New Deal had conspired with southern elites to deny political and social rights to African Americans, the War on Poverty would integrate them into local politics, local job markets, and local housing markets . . . The War on Poverty would do more than eliminate impediments. It would extend equal opportunity to African Americans and complete the task of fully democratizing American society" (Quadagno 1994, 31; *see also* Katznelson 2013, 133–316). Still, despite its many achievements, a much more pessimistic view of the War on Poverty can also be set forth—even by one of the leading civil rights leaders of era. The fact is that "Martin Luther King Jr. regarded the Great Society as a failure, but for substantially different reasons than today's critics. The Great Society was unequal to the task of significantly diminishing the numbers of white and black poor, he thought; it failed on its own terms. *Many whites have failed to understand Martin Luther King's insight that class and racial inequality are fundamentally linked and cannot be severed*" (Brown 1999,

362–363, italics added). Part of the problem with the Johnson administration's handling of the War on Poverty is that it failed to grasp the intertwined nature of class inequality and racial inequality. Yet Robert Kennedy's approach differed from that of the Johnson administration insofar as his brand of political advocacy for change was not limited to racial issues in isolation from the larger challenges posed by class and poverty. A comprehensive review of Kennedy's record demonstrates that "Kennedy's call for programs and provisions such as a negative income tax, family and children allowances, income supplements, and a guaranteed annual income, sought to move beyond race-specific federal antipoverty programs. He seriously discussed solution to the problem of urban poverty that would cost the federal government $100 billion. Throughout 1967, he moved steadily toward class-based solutions to poverty designed to give people the opportunity to work, while maintaining a floor below which the poor of all races could not fall" (Palermo 2001, 170).

By 1968 Kennedy had brought his proposals on these matters into even sharper focus. In this respect, the goals and practices of his 1968 presidential campaign were the polar opposite of what came to be referred to as Nixon's "Southern strategy" (Palermo 2001, 170). Kennedy was trying to effectuate a reconciliation of races and classes through a social-justice approach. On the other hand, Nixon used the campaign slogan of "law and order," minus the social justice component, in order to fuel white backlash tendencies, especially in places where blacks and whites lived together in relatively close proximity due to similar economic class conditions (Palermo 2001, 170). Robert Kennedy's campaign strategy, which also had clear political implications for race relations, was premised upon the ties he had built over the years by cultivating his alliances with African American civil rights leaders who, like him, remained committed to the principles of equality, integration, and racial solidarity. He was also able to mobilize civic and church groups, peace and civil rights activists, students, farm workers, progressive labor unionists, Latinos, working-class whites, and New Leftists.

In short, by the time of Kennedy's California primary victory, he possessed the unique ability to inspire diverse groups of people from very different backgrounds to work together for peace and justice. It can be surmised that, within the stream of history, "Kennedy's abrupt and cruel removal from the national political scene decapitated the emergent Democratic coalition he had labored so hard to build" (Palermo 2001, 553). Kennedy's death was also the death of a way out of the failures of the Great Society. Michael Brown has observed: "Passage of the 1964 Civil Rights Act diminished labor-market discrimination and thus one basis for racially stratified social policies. But the Great Society failed to dismantle the ghetto, the other axis of America's system of racial stratification, and in this context Lyndon Johnson's social policies reproduced the color line in federal social policy" (Brown 1999, 364). So, while Robert Kennedy was in the midst of addressing the problem of the ghetto and starting the process of transcending the structural forces that reproduced America's system of racial stratification, he was assassinated—and so was the last political hope of fulfilling the promises of the New Frontier and the Great Society.

Had Kennedy not been assassinated, it is clearly evident that what was to become "Nixon's America" would never have seen the light of day. Had Robert Kennedy lived to become president, there would have been an earlier end to the Vietnam War, no Watergate, and no Kent State massacre. Instead, the national and global situation without Robert Kennedy's leadership and statesmanship resulted in a deepening racial divide, a continuation of the corrosive effects of the Vietnam War, and a deepening fiscal crisis that would leave America and the world worse off. By 1968, Robert Kennedy—along with large segments of his fellow citizens and citizens of the world—had come to recognize just how massively the corrosive and subversive impulses of many corporate institutions and right-wing ideologues had mercilessly and needlessly sacrificed human rights and human dignity in the name of profit and private interests. It is beyond question that Robert Kennedy's worldview and policies were radically different from the establishment norm. Kennedy had been transformed by his reading of the ancient Greeks and their vision of a viable community. Further, his own Catholic upbringing had supplied him with a moral and political lens through which he could revise and re-envision the course of American society so that social justice concerns and human rights issues would gain greater prominence, and, as a direct consequence, enjoy greater ascendancy in the priorities of the body politic. In response to these powerful corporate and right-wing interests, as well as the various problems and injustices that they continued to generate, he set out a vision that was reflective of a more communitarian worldview.

Specifically, Kennedy was seeking "to assess issues on the basis of potential threats or benefits to community, with particular attention to the most vulnerable. The American political spectrum has been strongly reinforced by a wide variety of powerful cultural, social, and economic impulses, including laissez-faire economic liberalism, nineteenth century romanticism, and an evangelical Christian emphasis on the salvation of the individual" (Schmitt 2010, 17). Robert's focus was on the needs of the vulnerable, the poor, and the excluded throughout American society; here he drives the point home:

> [He] told an audience of young CEOs that *"the blight of American poverty"* was the most pressing domestic problem in a century . . . and contended that the time had come to end the *"gap between private and public crisis."* The New York senator cautioned against a desire to merely punish the rioters of the previous summer. *"We must give encouragement to those who still believe progress is possible within our democratic system,"* Kennedy pleaded. *"We cannot denounce those extremists who reject it if we do not prove that our society is capable of helping people lead a better life—in our urban ghettoes, in our areas of rural poverty, and on our Indian reservations as well."* (Schmitt 2010, 192, italics added)

What remains important and relevant about Robert Kennedy's message in the twenty-first century is the fact that he was addressing the challenge of how to build and construct an inclusionary democracy for the United States. He understood that by neglecting and even actively excluding the poor, a nation produces greater inequalities and thereby greater social injustice. Such a path would also have disastrous economic and political results. Robert Kennedy had been seeking a "middle way" between the extremes of central planning on the one hand, and the welfare state on the other. Within the broad sweep of history, we can frame Kennedy's efforts within the larger matrix of the times. Richard Pomfret, professor of economics at the University of Adelaide, has chronicled the events of this era, noting that "during the 1960s there was much talk of systematic convergence: capitalist economies would have more intervention in the name of equality, while communist economies would admit a larger role to the market in the name of efficiency . . . After 1968 there was a retreat from the middle way, and the division between planned economies and market economies became wider. In the market economies, Nixon in 1968, de Gaulle in 1969, and Heath in 1970 each won closely fought elections in the United States, France, and the United Kingdom, respectively, by arguing against the center and in favor of less-regulated market forces" (Pomfret 2011, 9–10).

Just ten years after Kennedy's death, the record shows that "by the end of the 1970s . . . as the racial and class backlash against the democratic advances won by the social movements of the preceding decade got into full swing, the prison abruptly returned to the forefront of American society and was offered as the universal and simplex solution to all manners of urgent social problems by politicians eager to reestablish state authority while rolling back state support for the poor" (Wacquant 2009, 206). Robert Kennedy's campaign of compassion for those who suffered, his campaign of reconciliation between races, and his campaign to create a more equal and just society had all been forsaken by the new political and financial power barons. By the time of the 1980s, Reagan and Thatcher had "pursued ideological attacks on the modification of capitalism by government regulation, public ownership, and the welfare state. The lasting legacy of this conservative reaction was to demonstrate the merits of the market in allocating resources and the potential costs of distorting the process through excessive regulations or state ownership" (Pomfret 2011, 10). Just a decade after this conservative tide had set into motion a global wave of market-mania under the guise of the neoliberal economic model, the Clinton administration took up the cause where the Reagan-Bush years left off. Once again, Robert Kennedy's constituency of the poor, minorities, the excluded, and the dispossessed would bear the brunt of the neoliberal assault on economic equality, human rights, and human dignity.

The congressional crime debate of 1993 and 1994, coupled with the failure of the Clinton administration to offer policy options outside the narrow ideological spectrum of *"get tough"* measures, served to underscore the limited scope of criminal justice policy in the 1990s (Poveda 1994, 79, italics added). Even though a Democrat was in the White House, the ideological drift of the nation had turned so far right that it dragged Clinton along with the trend, thereby erasing the last vestiges of Kennedy's legacy. Commenting on these trends, Marc Mauer noted:

> The political landscape at the moment is defined by the legacy of years of government inaction and disinterest in issues of poverty and economic justice, along with widening racial polarization. We are faced with the twin problems of worsening conditions of life for many people of color in urban areas in particular, along with their growing marginalization from mainstream America. A defining feature of political life today is that, in contrast to periods such as the 1930s or the 1960s, there is little compassion for the poor. Thus, we

> see pervasive anti-immigrant sentiment, proposals to curtail welfare benefits, and in criminal justice, myriad variations on the theme of locking them up and throwing away the key. (Mauer 1994, 27)

It has become clear that these new realities of the 1980s and the 1990s represented a complete reversal of the message, policies, and leadership direction that was supplied by Robert Kennedy.

The reversal of Kennedy's policies continued in earnest throughout the presidency of George W. Bush. In the immediate aftermath of the Bush II presidency, there was an opportunity to review the damage done since Kennedy's death in 1968. Professor Frank Stricker offers a rather comprehensive assessment in his book, *Why America Lost the War on Poverty—And How to Win It.* After reviewing the many failures of Lyndon Johnson's handling of the War on Poverty, as well as assessing various theories about the culture of poverty, the underclass, the effects of Reaganomics, and Clinton's 1996 welfare reform, Sticker concluded, as did Robert Kennedy, that most antipoverty efforts are futile in the absence of a serious effort to actively create more good jobs. In his final assessment of these trends and their enduring legacy, Stricker provides a rather comprehensive list of seventeen proposals that are designed for the purpose of overcoming poverty through viable and effective social programs. Most of his proposals reflect the essence, purpose, and spirit of Robert Kennedy's own policy proposals: (1) use government tools to stimulate job creation; (2) create good government jobs; (3) lift the low-wage job market; (4) avoid scapegoating immigrants; (5) do more to support the unemployed; (6) strengthen social security; (7) expand the earned income tax credit; (8) rethink poverty lines; (10) enforce equal opportunity for good jobs and income for women and minorities; (11) protect affordable education; (12) move toward a more progressive tax system; (13) start planning for an American minimum wage; (14) increase pay rates so that people can work less; (15) scrap our current welfare program, Temporary Assistance for Needy Families (TANF); (16) do more to support affordable housing; (17) challenge conservatives on unions and the working poor (Stricker 2007, 235–243).

Robert Kennedy's communitarian focus remains the best antidote to the "market mentality," which can be radically individualizing. On this matter, history professor , Michael B. Katz notes: "Market argument are . . . used to justify the limitations of the welfare state. . . . Opponents of the welfare state often deploy the idea of scarcity as an excuse to draw the boundaries of exclusion more tightly, reduce public spending, and privatize public responsibilities. In the name of fairness and economy, they promote the marketization of citizenship. In the process, they redefine not only the welfare state, but American democracy itself. That is because market models recast democracy as consumer choice—a definition that accentuates inequalities and excludes the poor" (Katz 2008, 356). This is not what Kennedy wanted or envisioned for the United States.

On March 29, 1965, in any address in Binghamton, New York, Kennedy declared: "We are our brother's keepers. As long as the benefits of prosperity are denied to one-fifth of our number, there can be no complacency—there can be no stopping—there can be no pride of place or quarreling over labels. Until poverty is eliminated; until education is truly universal; until the least among us is secure in freedom and opportunity, in the inalienable rights for which this country was established, none of us can rest content" (Ross 1968, 147–148). Now contrast Kennedy's 1965 statements on poverty to the July 1999 "New Markets" poverty tour of President Bill Clinton. On that tour:

> Clinton argued that America's depressed rural areas, Indian reservations, and inner cities deserved private investment because they represented huge untapped markets . . . The poor deserved help not because they are citizens entitled "to live the life of a civilized being according to the standards prevailing in the society," but because of their cash value. America could solve the problem of poverty by turning the poor into commodities and selling them, albeit with the price subsidized by government . . . As he jettisoned the big government strategies of the War on Poverty and Great Society era, Clinton also tossed overboard its language of deprivation, pathology, and culture of poverty. (Katz 2008, 358)

Similarly, William F. Pepper, an English barrister and American lawyer who worked in Kennedy's 1964 campaign for the US Senate seat from New York, observed:

> In 1967 to 1968, the last year of his life after he had announced for the presidency, *Robert Kennedy went into the south to see for himself how the poor lived.* When he saw the squalor, he cried . . . *In 1999, President Clinton visited impoverished areas of the United States which included Indian reservations and ghetto neighborhoods. His trip was referred to as a "new markets initiative." He did not go to see how the poor were living.* Those folks lived in ghetto areas neatly named "new markets." We have effectively made the masses of poor people more invisible than ever. (Pepper 2003, 265–266, italics added)

In comparing and contrasting Robert Kennedy with Bill Clinton—both man and message—one is tempted to ask: "What communion does light have with darkness?" Kennedy's heartfelt identification with the poor and their suffering remains an enduring memory, while Clinton's quest for a "new market's initiative" simply collapses into the financially induced mania of the "roaring 1990s" led by the lobbyists on Wall Street and the executives at Goldman Sachs.

Ever since the presidency of Ronald Reagan, Democrats have avoided talking too much about social programs for the poor, fearing that the middle-class would withdraw their support from any candidate who gave their hard-earned money to "welfare moms." Yet recent history is testimony to the reality that "neither the nation's vaunted economic growth nor its breathtaking rise in productivity had dented the concentrated poverty of America's racially segregated cities, where second-class citizenship found vivid spatial expression" (Katz 2008, 361). Nothing had changed for the better after the death of Robert Kennedy. His assassination left a gaping wound in American society and body politic from which it has never recovered. Rather, Americans have been left with a legacy of worsening poverty, a privatized and growing "prison-industrial complex," a declining middle class after the 2008 financial crisis, and growing wealth disparities between the super-rich 1 percent and the rest of the country (Smiley and West 2012).

None of this was inevitable. Had Robert Kennedy's message and legislative record in the United States Senate remained in place beyond 1968, a whole new set of economic, political, and social policy initiatives could have reformed and changed the way that business was done in the United States so that it would not have been business as usual. Take, for example, Kennedy's introduction of Senate Bill 2088 on July 12, 1967. It was designed to provide federal tax credits, accelerated depreciation schedules, and job-training programs as incentives for businessmen to locate industry in poverty centers, thus creating jobs for the unemployed. Like its companion measure, Senate Bill 2100, which proposed similar devices to stimulate the building of low-cost housing in poverty areas, Senate Bill 2088 was notable for its replacement of the federal government with private enterprise as the principal institution in the fight against the slums and poverty (Ross 1968, 155–156). In his speech on the floor of the US Senate, July 12, 1967, Kennedy explained the purpose and operation of his plan with a warning: "By failing to involve the private sector, we have not only ignored the potential contribution of millions of talented and energetic Americans in tens of thousands of productive enterprises. More dangerously, *we have created for the poor a separate nation: a second-rate system of welfare handouts, a screen of government agencies keeping the poor apart from the rest of us. That system—ineffective, inefficient, and degrading—must be changed*" (Ross 1968, 154, italics added). Kennedy had issued the clarion call for change—and he was its most eloquent apostle.

The situation that Robert Kennedy was forced to confront was one in which, "as Martin and Malcolm and the activists of SNCC all argued, it was unsupportable to claim that the United States was 'fighting for freedom' in Vietnam and elsewhere when the rights of US citizens were systematically denied at home" (Winant 2001, 173). In the stream of history, in the historical nexus of the 1960s, Robert Kennedy found himself having to address the problems of race, class, and the cities simultaneously. To be in Robert Kennedy's shoes meant that it was now a requirement to address the issues of class, race, and the crisis of the cities in conjunction with the core values of United States politics and culture: individualism, equality, competition, opportunity, the accessibility of the American dream, and the like.

In his 1998 study, *Making Race and Nation: A Comparison of the United States, South Africa, and Brazil,* which assessed the complexity and roots of the task of nation-building and the core political, cultural, and economic values that invariably accompany the enterprise, we find an explanation of the dilemma in which Kennedy found himself. Professor Anthony Marx wrote: "Citizenship is a key institutional mechanism for establishing boundaries of inclusion or exclusion in the nation-state. It selectively allocates distinct civil, political, and economic rights, reinforcing a sense of commonality and loyalty among those included. But by specifying to whom citizenship applies, states also define those outside of the community of citizens, who then live within the state as objects of domination. Even in formal democracies, some are not included nor have their interests served . . . Gradual expansion of citizenship is then gained through protracted contestation" (Marx 1998, 5).

In the historical course of this national contestation, the poor were placed at a major disadvantage at the outset. Commenting on this set of circumstances in a paper prepared for the community organization staff at Mobilization for Youth in 1963, Frances Fox Piven observed: "Lower-class people have not developed large-scale formal organizations to advance their interests. The reasons are not mysterious. To be poor means to command none of the resources ordinarily considered requisites for organization: money, organizational skill and professional expertise, and personal relations with officials. *The instability of lower-class life and the character of lower-class beliefs also discourage the poor from organizational participation*" (Cloward and Piven 1972, 80, italics added). Recognizing the existence of these barriers, it can be said that Robert Kennedy dedicated his life and political career to dealing with the obstacles that the poor faced and exposing these obstacles and mass injustices to public view. Kennedy undertook this path so that the poor would become politically, socially, economically, and culturally empowered to exercise their personal power in order to finally claim their human dignity and human rights.

Most of Kennedy's policy proposals throughout 1964 and 1965 centered on expanding federal public works programs to create more jobs, more effective job-placement services in the slums, and increases in the minimum wage to improve the lot of the employed poor. In a campaign statement that was issued on October 19, 1964, Kennedy said: "I advocate a standby Public Works Bill authorizing the President to provide additional funds, up to one billion dollars, to bolster the economy and increase jobs. This bill would provide for public works such as federal buildings, water and sewage systems, and port facilities which are needed and which the federal government would help construct in any event" (Ross 1968, 148–149). In an address to the International Ladies' Garment Workers Union Convention in Miami, Florida, on May 18, 1965, Kennedy declared:

> The present minimum wage of $1.25 an hour amounts to $2,600 a year—$400 less than the Congress has declared to be the poverty line, the absolute minimum income for health and safety. *You know how little can be bought for $3,000 a year; yet millions of American workers do not even earn that much. This country can afford better wages than that—and we cannot afford not to pay better wages.* I support an immediate rise in the minimum wage to $1.50 an hour—and further increases compatible with our competitive position and our advancing standards of decent living. This nation has declared a war on poverty (Ross 1968, 149, italics added).

This was the world that Robert Kennedy inherited. His response to it was to find ways to advance a consciousness of inclusion, of the need to identify with the suffering of others, and to begin the task of reconciliation through the path of compassion, empathy, and love for one's fellow human beings. These qualities were all specified by

Kennedy the night that he spoke in Indiana, April 4, 1968, as news of the assassination of Dr. Martin King was breaking. These qualities had been a part of Kennedy's civic ideal and his mode of governance long before that night. And these were the qualities Kennedy called upon the nation to embrace, right up through the night of his own assassination.

7

"Power to the People"

In Robert Kennedy's own words, his intention was to help the poor and that meant "to give them power" (Schmitt 2010, 185). Kennedy's proposal was radical in that it struck at the heart of the economic establishment of his day and the class interests that benefited from unjust arrangements that not only left the ghetto in place, but produced it in the first place. This statement is not just some kind of radical accusation out of thin air. Rather, it is actually one of the major findings of a 1968 report that was produced by a US government commission: *The National Advisory Commission on Civil Disorders*, commonly known as the Kerner Commission Report. The Kerner Report is significant primarily because it saw the problems of black people in American society as a result of the white-controlled social structure. On page two of the report, the commission declared that "segregation and poverty have created in the racial ghetto a destructive environment totally unknown to most white Americans. What white Americans have never fully understood—but what the Negro can never forget—is that white society is deeply implicated in the ghetto. *White institutions created it, white institutions maintain it, and white society condones it*" (*Report of the National Advisory Commission on Civil Disorders* 1968, 2, italics added).

Robert Kennedy agreed with the commission's findings and said so when announcing his candidacy for the presidency on March 4, 1968. Kennedy's agreement with the findings of the Kerner Report explains why he understood that the best way to help the poor meant "to give them power." What passes for permanent states of being among the poor is, in fact, a continued effort to adjust to an unjust social order. Therefore, as Stephan Rose noted in his dissertation on community action programs: "In order for poverty to be eliminated, two changes have to be brought about simultaneously: Alterations of the social structure to ensure open access to economic opportunity, and increased power for the poor vis-à-vis the institutions which affect their lives" (Rose 1970, 102). This approach is precisely the approach advocated by Robert Kennedy from 1964 onward. This was a proposal that posed a direct challenge to traditional capitalist rule because capitalism "combines private ownership, remuneration for property, power, and to a degree, output, corporate divisions of labor, and markets in ways primarily benefiting the capitalist class" (Albert 2010, 61).

It was clear that Kennedy wanted to help the residents of the ghetto and to give them power through a new brand of economics. In twenty-first century parlance, it is referred to as "participatory economics." It also was clear to Kennedy that a new approach was needed. Michael Sandel, professor of government at Harvard University, noted:

> [Kennedy] observed that by the mid-1960s the federal government had largely fulfilled the agenda of liberal reform: "The inheritance of the New Deal is fulfilled. There is not a problem for which there is not a program. There is not a problem for which money is not being spent. There is not a problem or a program on which hundreds or thousands of bureaucrats are not earnestly at work." But despite the success of the liberal project, and perhaps partly because of it, Americans found themselves the victims of large, impersonal forces beyond their control. Kennedy linked this loss of agency to the erosion of self-government and the sense of community that sustains it. *Kennedy sought to redress the loss of agency by decentralizing political power. This marked a departure from the liberalism of his day.* (Sandel 1996, 300, italics added)

This is what made RFK unique and innovative. Yet Kennedy's call for decentralization should not be conflated with those of George Wallace or Barry Goldwater, both of whom opposed social and economic entitlements while waving the banner of states' rights and opposing federal policies that they disliked. We discover something far more progressive in Kennedy's views from those of Goldwater and Wallace, and certainly far different from the views of either Ronald Reagan or Bill Clinton. We clearly find that "Robert Kennedy's case for decentralization was different. Since he was an advocate of civil rights and federal spending to help the poor, his worry about federal power did not spring from opposition to the ends it served. Rather, it reflected the insight that even a realized welfare state cannot secure the part of freedom bound up with sharing in self-rule; it cannot provide, and may even erode, the civic capacities and communal resources necessary to self-government. *In the mounting discontents of American public life,*

Kennedy glimpsed the failure of liberal politics to attend to the civic dimension of freedom" (Sandel 1996, 300, italics added).

Robert Kennedy was preoccupied with individuals having a chance to experience self-sufficiency and participation in the life of the community. In order to effectuate the realization of those essential qualities for citizenship in a democracy, Kennedy proposed bringing jobs to the inner city. This proposal reflected his broader aim of restoring a political economy of citizenship (Sandel 1996, 303). In this critical respect, Kennedy did not propose to rely on market forces alone. Rather, he specifically proposed the creation of Community Development Corporations, community-run institutions that would direct development in accordance with local needs (Sandel 1996, 303). The logic behind this approach was grounded on the assumption that "in contemporary American society, the most likely source for those changes necessary to eliminate poverty is in the organization of the poor to exercise political power, to participate in the planning and administration of relevant programs, and in increasing control by the poor over the institutions which are instrumental in their lives" (Rose 1970, 105).

In the period of 1963–1964, the Task Force on Urban Areas was assigned the job of delineating the legislative specifications and attendant administrative regulations that would emerge as the Community Action program of the Office of Economic Opportunity. In short, the Task Force had an undefined concept to begin the process of a attempting to "operationalize" this institutional and governmental effort. In his role as Attorney General of the United States, Robert Kennedy gave testimony before a Senate Committee on this matter, wherein he said: "The institutions which affect the poor—education, welfare, recreation, business, labor—are huge, complex structures, operating from outside their control. They plan programs for the poor, not with them. Part of the sense of helplessness and futility comes from the feeling of powerlessness to affect the operation of these organizations. The community action programs must basically change these organizations by building into the program real representation for the poor. This bill calls for maximum feasible participation of residents. This means the involvement of the poor in planning and implementing programs: giving them a real voice in their institutions" (Donovan 1967, 35). The net effect of this empowerment would solve the class problem by: (1) identifying the key classes; and (2) accomplishing economic functions without incurring class division and class rule. The central features that are most important in solving the class problem are: (a) seeing that economies produce people and social relations, not simply outputs; (b) understanding that not only ownership relations, but also conditions under which people work and the things they do impact both their collective motives and their operational means (Albert 2010, 61).

Kennedy's declaration that his understanding of the role of Community Action Programs for the poor was "to give them power" signaled his strong and unwavering commitment that the poor must have a voice and, for their voice to be heard, they must have the opportunity to engage in "maximum feasible participation." In making this argument, Kennedy was endorsing what has come to be referred to in the post-1968 years as "participatory economics" (Albert 2010, 61). According to Michael Albert, what has been called "participatory economics" involves the following elements, insofar as it "combines social ownership, self-managing workers and consumers councils . . . and participatory planning where workers and consumers cooperatively negotiate outcomes with no class divisions," and therefore "it transcends capitalism and also market and centrally planned socialism by establishing core institutions that promote solidarity, equity of circumstance and income, diversity, participatory self-management, classlessness and efficiency in meeting human needs and developing human potentials" (Albert 2010, 61).

To undertake this new direction would require a new politics and a new set of definitions to go with it. Kennedy tried to transcend the delimiting vocabulary of the old politics and called for a "new politics." On May 21, 1968, Robert offered his own perspective on the failed politics of the past. He urged his audience to recognize in the face of these new circumstances and new challenges that "the new politics of 1968" now urgently called for "an end to some of the clichés and stereotypes of past political rhetoric." In response to the contradictions and conflict posed by a divided America, he noted that: "In too much of our political dialogue 'liberals' have been those who wanted to spend more money; while 'conservatives' have been those who wanted to pretend that all problems should solve themselves." He then quoted Emerson, who wrote that: "conservatism makes no poetry, breathes no prayer, has no invention; it is all memory," while reform, he asserted, "has no gratitude, no prudence, no husbandry." Given this diagnosis, Kennedy concluded that, in 1968, "the times are too difficult, our needs are too great, for such restricted visions. *There is nothing 'liberal' about constant expansion of the federal government, stripping citizens of their public power—the right to share in the government of affairs—that was the founding purpose of this nation. There is nothing 'conservative' about standing idle while millions of fellow citizens lose their lives and their hopes, while their frustration turns to fury that tears the fabric of society and freedom"* (Kennedy, May 21, 1968, italics added).

In 1963, the last year of his presidency, JFK had become more preoccupied with the problem of poverty—scribbling in his last notes during a meeting of his cabinet the word "poverty" and circling it many times over. Like RFK, President Kennedy had read Michael Harrington's 1962 book, *The Other America,* and he was beginning to calibrate a presidential response to it. It was left to RFK and the civil rights movement under the leadership of King to further that effort. This consciousness of the problem was revealed a few weeks after the Dallas assassination, when Robert Kennedy told Arthur Schlesinger, Jr.: *"My brother barely had a chance to get started—and there is so much now to be done—for the Negroes and the unemployed and the school kids and everyone else who is not getting a decent break in our society. . . . The new fellow doesn't get this. He knows all about politics and nothing about human beings"* (Lemann 1989, 55, italics added).

By 1966, LBJ had launched the Model Cities program, which was designed to spend billions on the rehabilitation of the ghettos. Robert's response to this initiative: "It's too little, it's nothing . . . we have to do twenty times as much" (Lemann 1989, 55). By 1968, in the final stages of Johnson's presidency, "the idea of large-scale government programs for the ghettos had become so bound up in his mind with liberal opposition to him that Johnson became positively hostile toward them. He was deeply suspicious of the Kerner Commission, which he had appointed after the terrible Newark and Detroit riots of 1967 to determine how future riots could be avoided" (Lemann 1989, 55). From Kennedy's point of view, the enduring political recalcitrance of Johnson to deal with the central issues of the crisis had robbed the country of a chance to deal with the real issues confronting the nation. Therefore, Robert believed that it was incumbent upon him to move against Johnson and reclaim the promise of the New Frontier. Robert sought to unite that promise with the demands of Dr. King and the civil rights movement for a more just and inclusive socioeconomic order within the United States (Jackson 2007, 308–358).

Concern for the excluded, the poor, the unemployed, the dispossessed, was the preeminent focus of both Robert Kennedy and Dr. King. Capturing the spirit of the era, their visionary call for the recognition of human rights in conjunction with a complete socioeconomic overhaul of the US economy was essential. It was an evolving view that became increasingly evident and clearly articulated in the speeches, writings, and private conversations of RFK and King (1964–1968). We discover Dr. King addressing this challenge not only on a national basis, but also from an international perspective. In Dr. King's last book, *Where Do We Go from Here: Chaos or Community?,* he wrote:

> The time has come for an all-out world war against poverty. The rich nations must use their vast resources of wealth to develop the underdeveloped, school the unschooled and feed the unfed. The well-off and the secure have too often become indifferent and oblivious to the poverty and deprivation in their midst. The poor in our countries have been shut out of our minds, and driven from the mainstream of our societies, because we have allowed them to become invisible. Ultimately a great nation is a compassionate nation. No individual or nation can be great if it does not have a concern for "the least of these." (King 1967, 178)

For Robert, the practical achievement of these human rights for the least of these preoccupied his thoughts. His concern for the achievement of these rights was often expressed in his speeches, as exemplified by his remarks in Spring Valley, New York, on August 18, 1965. In reflecting on the 1965 Watts riots, Kennedy noted: "And now—even after the crisis has come—we continue to be surprised by how difficult the problems are to solve. In the last four years, the Negro has made great progress; and the Civil Rights Act of 1964 and the Voting Rights Act of 1965 are rightfully regarded as achievements of which we can all be proud. But as we are learning now, it is one thing to assure a man the legal right to eat in a restaurant; it is another thing to assure that he can earn the money to eat there" (Guthman and Allen 1993, 161). It was a theme to which Kennedy would return time and again. A few months earlier on February 4, 1965, in an address to the Lexington Democratic Club of New York, New York, RFK had admitted:

> *Better laws cannot change this impotence which is the lot of the poor. Laws confer 'rights' only on those who can articulate a claim before some authority who will enforce it. But it is precisely this ability that the poor do not have. They do not know what claims to present—or to whom to present them—or how to do it. Pure food and drug laws, building codes, welfare and social security programs, schools, all are designed to create rights in all citizens—to clean food and fair measure, to dignified age and training in youth. None create rights in the poor.* (Ross, 1968, 140, italics added)

So the question becomes: "If the real purpose of laws in the American welfare state was not to create rights in the poor, then what was the real purpose of the laws?" In answer to the question, Frances Fox Piven and Richard Cloward concluded that the real purpose of the welfare state and its supportive structure of laws and rules was supposed to be nothing more and nothing less than the regulation of the poor. In this world, it was social regulation and control, not rights or human dignity, that ultimately mattered. They published their first edition of *Regulating the Poor* in 1971. In 1993, they noted: "In the Epilogue to the original edition, written in 1970, we said that the great expansion of relief beginning in the 1960s had, by the end of the decade, helped to mute protest and riots, and we predicted an imminent 'shift from regulating civil disorder to regulating labor'" (Piven and Cloward 1993, 343). In their view, the civil disturbances and riots of the 1960s were responsible for the liberalizing of poor relief. However, liberalization was short-lived because it was meant only to moderate disorder (Piven and Cloward 1993, 344). If this interpretation is accurate, then it helps to explain why Kennedy was correct in arguing that all of the laws on the books failed to "create rights in the poor," because if the effect of laws and public policies were to result in the effectuation of recognized rights in the poor—as a class of people—then there would be a change in the very nature of the social order, class structure, and the social hierarchy of privilege. This was, in fact, what both Robert Kennedy and Martin King were advocating at the time of their deaths. In order to effectuate the uplifting of both the poor and the working class, both Kennedy and King were making an appeal to lift wages, create jobs, and build more just communities. It was an agenda that conflicted with what most elites in the predominantly white establishment wanted to see happen. Rather, by 1970, there was evolving the "mounting of a campaign by business to solve its problems of profitability by forcing workers to take less" (Piven and Cloward 1993, 348).

Hence, beginning in the 1970s and continuing through the 1980s, 1990s, and on into the early twenty-first century, the American establishment engaged in the practices of disinvestment, speculation, and broad attack on social programs (Piven and Cloward 1993, 348). It was in this thirty-year period that the groundwork was laid for the financial crisis and collapse of 2008. In 1993, Piven and Cloward were rather prophetic about the trends in the 1970s and 1980s when they noted:

> In the United States, corporate and government elites coped differently. One way was to shore up profits by closing plants and moving capital out of the old high-wage industrial regions and into low-wage regions here and abroad. Another way was to turn to speculation—in real estate and in the financial markets, including mergers and leveraged buyouts of industrial assets. By the 1980s, speculation reached frenzied heights, and the rash of Wall Street "insider trading" scandals was one result, although the elaboration of entirely legal forms of paper speculation was more important. Predatory business practices in the multi-billion dollar defense-contracting sector escalated, and widespread fraud helped bring about the collapse of the savings and loan industry. (Piven and Cloward 1993, 349–350)

From this period forward, until 2008 and beyond, paper speculation morphed into "derivatives," thereby engulfing the entire real estate market and Wall Street strategies in general with a casino-mentality that, in turn, ruined the US economy and sent the global economy into near collapse.

The question then becomes: *Could the 2008 financial crisis been avoided by following the Kennedy/King prescription for America's social and economic renewal?* As early as 1984, political and economic commentator Robert Kuttner argued in his book, *The Economic Illusion: False Choices Between Prosperity and Social Justice*, that: "The difficulty of maintaining egalitarian policies against the steady thrust of the market system toward greater inequality is immense. Big money retains a potent hold on the limits of the possible. In a liberal democracy, conservative parties frequently govern; they usually can be counted upon to reintroduce policies that frustrate universalistic income distribution, weaken labor movements, separate the dependent poor from the working poor, and erode the political constituency for equality. *Egalitarianism never quite reaches escape velocity*" (Kuttner 1984, 267, italics added). Kuttner's analysis serves to identify with graphic precision what Robert Kennedy and Martin King had been up against when making their proposals for America's renewal by incorporating the poor and working classes into the controlling forces of America's economy, as well as the priorities enunciated in its social policies, wage structures, and legal regime of rights (Jones 1992; Jones 1998). Both Kennedy and King wanted a strengthened labor movement, but the establishment (business, Wall Street, Washington power-brokers) opposed it. Both Kennedy and King wanted to effectuate policies and programs that would result in uniting the rights and agenda of the dependent poor with the rights of the working poor, but the governing and predominantly conservative establishment opposed it. Both Kennedy and King sought to advance a more universalistic distribution of income, but a significant number of elites in the establishment opposed it.

For Robert Kennedy, the rights of citizens and his hope for building a more communitarian vision of community formed the focus of his proposals for US economic renewal and his commitment to the fuller realization of the human rights and dignity of individual persons—regardless of race, class, or gender. Kennedy understood how welfare states, particularly those of northern Europe, had gone a substantial way toward establishing need as a distributive criterion by providing for certain needs as entitlements of citizenship. Therefore Kennedy sought to advance support for medical care, education, jobs, and decent housing. He condemned policies that did not directly deal with these intertwined problems. In an address to the Day Care Council of New York, May 8, 1967, he stated: "We have created a welfare system which aids only a fourth of those who are poor, which forces men to leave their families so that public assistance can be obtained, which has created a dependence on their fellow citizens that is degrading and distasteful to giver and receiver alike. We have built vast, impersonal high-rise public housing projects—ghettos within ghettos—isolated from the outside world and devoid of any sense of humanity" (Ross 1968, 146).

As an antidote to these various public policy failures, Kennedy had become a strong advocate of Community Action, the Community Development Corporations (CDC), and the Model Cities program as the initial means to provide a vehicle for the poor, jobless, and disposed to reenter American society and become beneficiaries of a more egalitarian economy. Kennedy recognized that the expansion of human rights and entitlements to the basic human needs of people also reinforces community and a sense of shared destiny, solidarity, and citizenship with others—regardless of how great or small individual resources might be. On this matter, Robert Kuttner has noted: "*The idea is that universal entitlement to these basics is not only decent social policy, but serves to reinforce a sense of community and solidarity.* Being treated in the same medical clinic or sending one's children to the same day-care center or school—regardless of one's personal resources—is inherently egalitarian. *When the middle class shares basic public services with the poor, the middle class demands high quality and dignified treatment; the middle class is also reminded that poor people are human. Thus does universalism in public services cement the political constituency for egalitarian social policy*" (Kuttner 1984, 231, italics added).

However, to move from the principle of universal entitlement toward the practice and implementation of what that would actually look like is a path fraught with hazard. Kennedy and other advocates of the War on Poverty were faced with trying to determine the best approach as they sought to empower the poor in rather difficult political circumstances. The challenge of empowering the poor arose because "once the liberal programs were institutionalized in the middle ground, they were open to attack from both extremes. As the historian Allen Matusow succinctly summarizes, conservatives charged that they had inherent flaws—'violation of market logic, covert service to special interests, and perversion by bureaucrats'" (Zarefsky 1986, 204). In this context, it had become evident that "to define one's goals in the loftiest terms is to arouse expectations and to court disappointment when the tangible benefits of legislation fall short of its avowed goals, as inevitably they will . . . *The War on Poverty illustrates how the liberal's middle ground was eroded from both poles. Many sympathizers of the objective moved leftward, concluding that poverty was but a symptom of a more fundamental illness requiring redistribution of wealth and power. Because the War on Poverty could not countenance this admission that society was flawed, Matusow proclaims for it the epitaph, 'Declared but Never Fought'*" (Zarefsky 1986, 205, italics added).

Critiquing American society was a dangerous enterprise in the 1960s. That is why the twin examples of Robert Kennedy and Martin King are unique. Their words and message leave citizens of the twenty-first century with an enduring legacy of what still needs to be done to fight a successful war on poverty that benefits all Americans. Despite their efforts in the 1960s, the times and strategies were not fully conducive to a full and fair examination of their views. In the case of RFK, one historian records this: "Asked privately what he thought of Moynihan, Kennedy confided, 'He knows all the facts, and he's against all the solutions'" (Schmitt 2010, 186). Given this recalcitrance, Kennedy's own brand of federalism sought to bypass the conventional machinery of representative democracy because it operated in conjunction with other entrenched social institutions that continued to render the poor powerless (Schmitt 2010, 186). To find a work-around, Kennedy renewed his promotion of community action because he had lost faith in state or city government.

The same can be said of Martin Luther King. King maintained that "corrective legislation requires organization to bring it to life. ***Laws only declare rights; they do not deliver them. The oppressed must take***

hold of laws and transform them into effective mandates. Hence the absence of powerful organization has limited the degree of application and the extent of practical success" (King 1968, 158, italics and bold added). For RFK, the answer was—as he had stated to the graduating youth of South Africa in 1966—"to rely on youth." In Kennedy's estimation, the active participation of young people constituted a new constituency for progressive action. Because it was a uniquely engaged generation, it had the capacity to both quicken and lead the rights revolution, thereby becoming the powerful organization that King insisted was so critical to the success of both civil rights and a more broad-based economic justice for all Americans. If that were to happen, in Kennedy's view, then the youth would be the key to renewing the national community (Schmitt 2010, 229).

By the late 1990s, the problems of the poor, the ghetto, and workers were no longer just national—they had become global. William Julius Wilson, professor of social policy at Harvard University, has commented: "The problems of joblessness and social dislocation in the inner city are, in part, related to the processes in the global economy that have contributed to greater inequality and insecurity among American workers in general, and to the failure of US social policies to adjust to these processes. *It is therefore myopic to view the problems of jobless ghettos as if they were separate from those that plague the larger society*" (Wilson 1996, 220, italics added). In Wilson's opinion, the key to solving the problem is increasing the employment base. Not only would an employment program of this magnitude "have an enormous positive impact on the social organization of ghetto neighborhoods," but such a program would also provide effective solutions for the entire nation because "*the problems of jobless ghettos cannot be separated from those of the rest of the nation. Although these solutions have wide-ranging application and would alleviate the economic distress of many Americans, their impact on jobless ghettos would be profound*" (Wilson 1996, 238, italics added). Just three decades after Robert Kennedy's assassination, his solutions for the interrelated problems of poverty, class, and race have been revived as the most viable solutions for an entire nation plagued by deepening inequality, poverty, and despair.

8

Advances and Retreats (1960–2000)

As both Kennedy and King would acknowledge, what was needed to rectify the situation of the poor—as well as reclaim the promise of America as an idea and as a nation—was a revolution of values. Such a thorough and comprehensive revolution would have to encompass a reversal of a system of values that had made America a *thing-oriented* society and transform America into a *person-oriented* society. To accomplish this, Kennedy and King concurred that three problems had to be confronted: racism, materialism, and militarism. Such a revolution in values was necessary, as King warned: "A civilization can flounder as readily in the face of moral and spiritual bankruptcy as it can through financial bankruptcy" (King 1967, 186). Exactly forty years later, in September 2008, King's prediction came true. Largely due to America's failure to embark upon a revolution in civic values beginning in 1968, America found itself in a financial crisis in 2008 that was worse than that of the Great Depression of the 1930s. Largely brought about by criminal corruption and deregulation on Wall Street, coupled with a longstanding failure to confront and redress the socioeconomic injustices against which Kennedy and King had consistently warned, the America of late 2008 began its downward economic spiral as unemployment mounted and remained largely unabated throughout the first term of the Obama presidency. Taking into account all of the other relevant economic and social justice factors, such a result should have not come as a surprise. The unaddressed needs of the poor during three decades of rising income inequality; an economy increasingly built on credit; falling wages for the poor and middle class; greater deregulation for Wall Street; and greater regulation of the poor and minorities under the auspices of the prison-industrial complex: all these factors combined to destroy the very foundations of the American economy—not to mention American society itself (Rasmus 2010, 2012).

Addressing this history from the vantage point of 2010, Barry Lynn noted:

> The one battle that never ended was at home, against our own would-be economic lords, who repeatedly took advantage of the freedom we won for all to concentrate power sufficient to monopolize that freedom for themselves alone. Often they simply seized what they wanted. Their main tools were two forms of government—the business corporation and the bank. Other times they made us promises. They would deliver us a little more material wealth if we would but cede them a little more political control over our lives. For most of our history, confident in our ability to provide for ourselves, we resisted their power and resisted their lies. But twice our would-be lords succeeded in capturing the commanding heights. They would do so immediately after the Civil War, and they managed to hold that power until the early years of the New Deal. Then a generation or so they did so again. Franklin Roosevelt long ago warned that men flying the banner of "liberty" would seek to "regiment" the majority of Americans "into the service of the privileged few." And so it came to pass. (Lynn 2010, 244)

What came to pass in 2008 can ultimately be understood in light of the fact that "typically, a stock market boom does not translate into real economic benefits for most Americans. The richest 10 percent of Americans own about 80 percent of the stocks; the wealthiest 20 percent own 90 percent of the stocks. The remaining 80 percent of middle-class and working-class households own only 10 percent of stocks, either directly or indirectly" (Greenfield 2006, 156). The gross economic disparities of late twentieth century and early twenty-first century America can be further delineated by the fact that, according to professor Kent Greenfield: "The wealthiest 1 percent of the US population owns almost 40 percent of the nation's personal wealth. This is almost a third more than the poorest 90 percent combined." This reality is even more tragic than one might have anticipated: "Inequality is getting worse. Comparing the early 1980s with 2003, the richest 5 percent has seen their share of the wealth grow from about 81 percent to almost 85 percent, whereas the poorer four-fifths have seen their share fall from 18.7 percent to 15.6 percent. Income inequality is at its highest level since the Census Bureau began tracking these data in 1947" (Greenfield 2006, 157).

How this came about is a complicated story. However, there are some basic elements that can be articulated. For example, economic historian Michael Bernstein has argued that the economics profession in America ended up repudiating the state that nurtured it. As a result, in the aftermath of the 1960s, the profession ended up ignoring distributive justice and engaged in privileging private desires in the study of economic life. In lamenting this turn of events, Bernstein proceeds to castigate the economists of the "Reagan Revolution" for embarking upon a form of national policy-making that was intrinsically flawed and resulted in antidemocratic consequences (Bernstein 2001, 191). He further concludes that "*an enlightened citizenry*, mobilized in political debate and expression, the essential foundation of Progressivist designs for reform early in the twentieth century, has now become increasingly rare" (Bernstein 2001, 191–192, italics added).

The presence and power of such an enlightened citizenry was largely eclipsed from the American political landscape and consciousness with the assassinations of Robert Kennedy and Dr. King. Into the abyss of their political legacy came an army of economists more committed to corporate privilege, the defense of the warfare state, and the unregulated doctrines of laissez-faire and free market dogmas. As a result, Bernstein argues, "a smug confidence in the presumed superiority of 'free markets' and 'deregulated' economic environments cannot and does not substitute for a genuine grasp of the history that has framed particular policy outcome" (Bernstein 2001, 194). Given the nature of Bernstein's analysis, it may be concluded that "*this perilous progress*" has "*brought economics, and with it the very nature and quality of the public policy debate on which it has always subsisted and thrived, to the point of extinction*" (Bernstein 2001, 194, italics added). His conclusion is shared, in large measure, with an analysis of the period that has been undertaken by history professor Daniel Rodgers at Princeton University. In the course of Rodger's book, *Age of Fracture*, there is an explanation of how structures of power came to seem less important than market choice. In Rodger's critique of the economic situation, the argument is presented in terms of how the deep structures of the late-capitalist economy witnessed the birth and evolution of a new world where we discover that "corporatist compromises between labor and management unraveled; manufacturers went abroad in search of cheaper labor; corporations hollowed themselves out by outsourcing all but a few core activities; production of goods and services moved from an inventory to a just-in-time basis . . . In the 'cultural logic of late capitalism,' as Jameson termed it, the structuralist assumptions of post-World War II social thought shattered and dissolved" (Rodgers 2011, 8–9).

When viewed in combination, these developments under the rubric of corporatist compromises characterize the post-Kennedy and post-King era that began around 1970. Two years after their assassinations, both the mindset and economic categories that corporatists, government leaders, and the public-at-large began to inhabit as the dominant worldview of the time reflected a perspective held throughout American society. The nature of this transformation revealed that a major ideological shift had been set in motion in the aftermath of the Kennedy and Kind assassinations. For many Americans, their worldview had begun to be transformed from a 1960s focus on social justice, human rights, and human dignity into a 1970s world of markets and financial speculation. This shift reflected a slow but steady retreat from a communitarian preoccupation with the larger issues of social welfare and social justice that Kennedy and King had devoted their lives and political efforts toward achieving. The early 1970s was starting the slow turn toward an uncritical acceptance of the ideologies of individualism and self-preoccupation.

As described by Rodgers: "Where the instruments of finance came ever closer to most American's lives—in pension stock funds, balloon-rate mortgages, leveraged buyouts, corporate restructuring, and plant closings—it was not surprising that the language of market economics should travel with them, sweeping into new terrains of social imaginations" (Rodgers 2011, 9). Yet it would be a mistake to attribute this turn of events as rooted merely in "structures of exchange," because what counts just as fundamentally are "ideas, practices, norms, and conventions" (Rodgers 2011, 9). Hence, it is necessary to make an interpretative recalibration of the historical changes that took place between the era of Kennedy and King in the 1960s, and the ensuing decade of the 1970s governed by Nixon, Ford, and Carter. As Rodgers emphatically reminds us, it is crucial to acknowledge that "what precipitates breaks and interruptions in social argument are not raw changes in social experience, which never translate automatically into mind. What matters are the processes by which the flux and tensions of experience are shaped into mental frames and pictures that, in the end, come to see themselves natural and inevitable, ingrained in the very logic of things" (Rodgers 2011, 9–10).

When viewed in this light, the legacies of Robert Kennedy and Dr. King can probably be best understood as a mental framing of the importance of human rights and dignity for the entire enterprise of American society. Together, RFK and Dr. King had worked toward creating a human-rights discourse. In their speeches, actions, and policies—as well as in the social movements that they both shaped and led—Kennedy and King were leaders who had effectively conveyed the idea that human-rights discourse would be enriched by a greater focus on the conditions that are necessary for the fuller protection, development, and refinement of the human spirit (Jackson 2007; Dyson 2000). To this end, they advocated the view that there should be an immediate end to the Vietnam War and a commitment to a policy of no more Vietnams. At the same time, they sought to focus the attention of the entire American public on the plight of the poor, the revitalization of the inner cities, the ending of poverty, the advancement of job creation for all races and classes, and the birth of a national and global sense of collective unity framed under the rubric of human rights, human welfare, and human dignity and security (Pepper 2003).

Both RFK and Dr. King made it clear that the human spirit is the appropriate focus for human-rights concerns because it embodies the intrinsic value of the human person, provides the basis for the interdependence of humankind, and defines those very capacities of consciousness upon which the future of civilization depends. In this fundamental respect, just as Professor Rodgers's historical analysis stressed the vital importance of our collective "mental frames," which seem to be "ingrained in the very logic of things," so, too, Michael Penn and Aditi Malik have advanced the argument that:

> A significant discovery of the twentieth century is that our actions are governed not by reality, but by our inner model of reality. These inner models have been variously labeled, "theories of reality," "structures of meaning," or "worldviews." A worldview provides the lens through which we perceive and understand the human experience. It determines, to a significant degree, what we hope for, how we spend our time, and how we relate to the natural and social environment. Worldview provides the overarching conceptual matrix within which we come of age. It determines, to no small degree, the trajectory of our individual and collective development, and provides the visionary material out of which is formed the kind of human beings we aspire to become. (Penn and Malik 2010, 666)

One example of an operative worldview with the potential to shape the contours of both the political imagination and political action can be seen in the speeches, public service, and early career of Robert Kennedy in his brother's administration. As attorney general of the United States, Robert had the opportunity to address an annual meeting of the South Carolina Chapter of the American Association of University Professors. In his tenure in the US Department of Justice, while engaged primarily in the legal struggle to advance civil rights and to undo the burdens imposed by racial discrimination, Robert had become sensitized to and aware of the emerging socioeconomic and cultural aspects of the civil rights struggle. Therefore, on April 25, 1963, in Columbia, South Carolina, RFK emphatically declared:

> We must recognize, as responsible citizens and as responsible government officials, that the Negroes in this country cannot be expected indefinitely to tolerate the injustices which flow from official and private racial discrimination in the United States. The troubles we see now, agitation and even bloodshed, will not compare to what we will see a decade from now unless real progress is made. I am not speaking of the South alone, for these injustices are not a matter of region. As years pass, resentment increases. The only cure for resentment is progress. The only antidote to agitation is the effort which state, local, and Federal officials are making to deal both with discrimination itself and with its deep-seated economic and social effects. (Hopkins 1964, 153)

Throughout his career as both attorney general and as a senator from New York, Robert Kennedy put forth a vision for the country that changed people's worldviews as well as the nature of public discourse (Bernstein 1991; Brauer 1997). RFK presented the nation, the world, and the Democratic Party, with a principled vision on the nature and meaning of racial and class equality. It was a vision that had been virtually lost and ignored by the dominant players in the Democratic Party by the early 1990s, when Clinton assumed the presidency. Writing of this historic juncture of events and personalities in his book, *Faded Dreams: The Politics and Economics of Race in America*, professor Martin Carnoy noted: "Democrats will not do well in the 1990s unless they are able to develop a popular ideological vision and make it the everyday currency of public discourse . . . If the president does not do ideological battle around legislation and appointments—ideological battle specifically intended to shift the political ground under the conservatives . . . —Democrats should be pessimistic about their chances for reshaping politics in the 1990s. African-Americans should be just as pessimistic about their chances for greater economic equality" (Carnoy 1994, 238–239). This is the historical reality and worldview that effectively separates Robert Kennedy and his times from Bill Clinton and his times.

Kennedy fought for social justice, while Clinton abdicated. In fact, John Kenneth Galbraith, one of Robert Kennedy's friends and political allies, who had endured through the right-wing/conservative drift of the 1980s and the 1990s, was irate about the directions taken by government and the private sector in this new Gilded Age under Clinton. Galbraith was unambiguous in his dislike for the neoliberals who—by the time of Michael Dukakis and Bill Clinton—dominated the Democratic Party. In response to these trends and in his commentary upon their meaning, Galbraith produced a scathing indictment of the implications, policies, and worldview of these neoliberals in his book, *The Culture of Contentment.* Commenting on Galbraith's critique, Galbraith's biographer, Richard Parker, noted: "In *The Culture of Contentment's* final chapter, entitled simply 'Requiem,' he wondered openly what it would take for them to fight once again for greater economic equality and for the public goods he believed the nation required—stronger environmental limits, health care for 40 million uninsured Americans, better schools, better employment and welfare benefits, rehabilitation rather than incarceration for the addicted, and protection rather than privatization of Social Security" (Parker 2005, 627).

In this new 1990s Gilded Age, Galbraith was more than disappointed that President Clinton had done almost nothing to capitalize on the distrust of concentrated corporate wealth and power. Further, as Peter Edelman was to discover, Clinton would not fend off the relentless anti-government attacks of the GOP and, ultimately, caved into signing the 1996 Welfare Reform Bill. Galbraith was also concerned about Clinton's hesitation to restructure federal spending priorities, such as military programs like Star Wars (Parker, 2006, 631). In a complete reversal of the legacy of Robert Kennedy, in 1993 Clinton decided to largely abandon the public investment programs that he had outlined as a candidate. According to Galbraith's biographer: "Worse, the President seemed to embrace deficit reduction as a principle, not a tactic. 'I have a jobs program,' he proudly declared, 'and my jobs program is deficit reduction.' This was not a program Galbraith could support" (Parker 2005, 633). By extrapolation, it is not counterfactual to make the argument that if Galbraith could not support such an approach to governance at the federal level, then neither could Robert Kennedy have sanctioned it either. Engagement with and support of vibrant public investment programs was one of the primary avenues that Robert Kennedy endorsed and envisioned as necessary, so that it would be possible, at last, "to give voice to the poor."

Robert Kennedy envisioned a new role for government in the effort to create and help sustain vibrant public investment programs in alliance with both the private sector and the residents of local communities, working together in a democratic framework that would make civic participation and engagement a part of common practice. In such a creative embrace, RFK envisioned a kind of Jeffersonian flowering of government, citizens, and business. In such an arrangement, these three interdependent groups would not be placed at odds with one another, but rather would share in a creative dialogue with one another while actively working toward the common goal of realizing a sustainable and flourishing community that would be more democratic, more inclusive, and more just. Democracy itself, Kennedy believed, would be strengthened and more fully realized by giving voice to the poor. In fact, he believed that "to give voice to the poor" would have the potential to create a new historical reality: the incarnation of a revitalized communitarian vision for all Americans. The socioeconomic circumstances of the poor had to be changed if America's national community was to be transformed into a more egalitarian nation, as opposed to becoming a plutocracy of wealth for a privileged minority at the top of the economic pyramid. Kennedy knew that a rise in the median wage and greater income equality was essential if joblessness was to be consigned to the dustbin of history, if the poor were ever to escape their poverty, and if the establishment of an economic hierarchy at the expense of American democracy was to be avoided and averted.

Writing in 2011 about the loss of a more egalitarian national community since 1968 and the death of Kennedy's communitarian promise, one commentator took note of the fact that "we . . . need to look beyond proximate causes to deeper socioeconomic circumstances. The real median wage in the US has been stagnant for almost 25 years, and this despite the fact that per capita GDP has almost doubled. At the same time, income inequality is on the rise; the wealthiest 1 per cent of the population doubled its share of national income from 8 percent in the 1970s to almost 16 percent in the early 2000s. Between 1976 and 2006 roughly half of all real income gains were accrued in the richest 5 per cent of households." He continued: "According to World Bank economist Branko Milanovic, *had the wealth been more evenly distributed, the financial services industry might never have created the exotic financial instruments which proved so dangerous, and credit culture might never have emerged among the lower and middle classes*" (Dobos 2011, 15–16, italics added). This is an important insight.

The "credit culture" that emerged after RFK's death took the place of the kind of public-private investment paradigm that he had advocated between 1965 and 1968. If only it had become politically possible for Kennedy's paradigm of public-private investment to be followed, then there would not have been an incentive to foist a credit culture on the American people, insofar as better wages, jobs, and investments in communities would have obviated what became a forced reliance on credit. The reliance on credit by working-class families and the poor largely came into existence after wages stopped rising in the 1970s. The political shift from Robert Kennedy's paradigm took place when the right wing and conservative advocates of Ayn Rand's *Atlas Shrugged* philosophy connected to a laissez-faire economic doctrine and to neoliberal economic theory, which was adopted by both the Federal Reserve and US Treasury Department—as well as by policy makers in Washington who, like Alan Greenspan and Robert Rubin, uncritically and enthusiastically embraced "market fundamentalism" (Stiglitz 2003; Kozul-Wright and Rayment 2007). The neoliberal economic theory created a situation in which, according to Michael Hudson: "It seems absurd to call the present system's high taxes and public guarantees to foreign bond holders '*free enterprise*.' Under these conditions '*market fundamentalism*' becomes a euphemism for financial dominance over governments. It is merely another form of centralized planning, not the absence of planning. It is planning to impose dependency, not self-reliance" (Hudson 2005, xxxi, italics added).

Recent American history reveals that it has been the persistent habit of the right wing and those with conservative tendencies to scapegoat the government. This practice has largely defined the political climate of the first three years of the Obama presidency, as well the dominant nature of political discourse in America from 2008 through 2011 and, most likely, into the future. Yet as early as 1983, three leading American economists brought their research to bear on this conservative tendency and found that "there is simply no international comparative support for the idea that growth can be accelerated by *cutting* public spending for social security, income support, health, and education. There are other ways to escape from economic decline. But most monetarists prefer hardball to softball anyway, toughing it out in the current political climate rather than pursuing the complicated political compromises which would be necessary to move in other directions" (Bowles, Gordon, and Weisskopf 1983, 203). And so it came to pass that in August 2011, conservative Republicans and right wing extremists battled the administration of President Barack Obama over whether or not the nation's debt ceiling should be raised in the absence of cuts in social security, income support, health, and education. In other words, between 1983 and 2011, the fundamental economic lessons about social justice and economic sanity in America had not been learned. Political interests fighting for private gain and greed remained willing to throw out the welfare of the people with the bathwater of "debt and deficit" fears.

The events of August 2011 in Washington, DC, seemed to prove what Robert Kuttner had observed in 1984 about the continuing battle between egalitarian politics, on the one hand, and the general logic of the market system, on the other. Kuttner wrote: "*The difficulty of maintaining egalitarian policies against the steady thrust of the market system toward greater inequality is immense. Big money retains a potent hold on the limits of the possible. In a liberal democracy, conservative parties frequently govern; they usually can be counted upon to reintroduce policies that frustrate universalistic income redistribution, weaken labor movements, separate the dependent poor from the working poor, and erode the political constituency for equality. Egalitarianism never quite reaches escape velocity*" (Kuttner 1984, 267, italics added). Kuttner's assessment, it turns out, has been prophetic—as well as insightful.

Cognizant of the problems that Kuttner later identified, Robert Kennedy had already suggested an antidote in 1967. While speaking about the plight of the poor and overcoming the political barriers they face, Kennedy suggested to Marian Wright Edelman, head of the Children's Defense Fund: "I think what really has to happen is that you got to get an awful lot of them, you've got to get a whole lot of poor people who just come to Washington and say they're going to stay here until something happens and it gets really unpleasant and there are some arrests and it's just a very nasty business and Congress gets really embarrassed and they have to act" (Lemann 1991, 216). In the aftermath of the conversation, Marian Edelman passed Robert's suggestion on to Dr. King. This proposal resulted in King and Kennedy planning for undertaking the Poor People's Campaign in the middle of 1968. After King's assassination, in April 1968, it was left to King's lieutenants to carry out the plan. It was finally realized in a May 13, 1969, meeting at the White House between representatives of the Poor People's Campaign and President Richard Nixon, with several high-ranking members of Nixon's administration—including nearly half the cabinet—in attendance. Finally, there was an official audience with the executive branch to receive the pleas and complaints of the people. It was the legacy of the campaign of 1968.

Today, in the second decade of the twenty-first century, if we begin to push aside the vapid, incestuous, and disingenuous rhetoric of neoliberalism and the "Washington Consensus," then it becomes possible to discover that, in the current neoliberal capitalist order, just about everything from the formulation of United States government economic policy to IMF and World Bank policies are actually little more than contemporary variants of a "longstanding political and economic philosophy. The major difference between classical liberalism as a philosophy and contemporary neoliberalism as a set of policy measures is with implementation. Washington Consensus policymakers are committed to free market policies when they support the interests of big business, as, for example, with lowering regulations at the workplace. But these same policy makers become far less insistent on free market principles when invoking such principles might damage big business interests. Federal Reserve and IMF interventions to bail out wealthy asset holders during the frequent global financial crises in the 1990s are obvious violations of free market precepts" (Pollin 2003, 8). This policy approach also serves to explain why, in contrast to Roosevelt's New Deal, adopted at the height of the Great Depression, "the macroeconomic policy agenda of the Obama administration does not constitute a solution to crisis. In fact, quite the opposite: it directly contributes to the concentration and centralization of wealth, which in turn undermines the real economy" (Chossudovsky 2010, 3).

What is the effect of the neoliberal policy prescriptions on the democratic health of the United States? According to Michael Hudson, antidemocratic forces have now become politically, culturally, and financially synthesized into the structure of a modern American oligarchy, wherein "the emerging oligarchy is euphemized by the term '*managed democracy*,' which is antithetical to democracy in the traditional meaning of the term. It goes together well with 'post-industrial,' as if modern finance is promoting progress rather than retrogression" (Hudson 2005, xxxi, italics added). Yet there is retrogression the era of managed democracy and post-industrial economics and politics.

We discover that it represents a retrogression of the kind that has resulted in the creation of an entirely different America from the one that Robert Kennedy was attempting to build in the late 1960s.

Whereas Robert Kennedy continuously fought for policies and programs to genuinely eliminate poverty, we find in the decade of the 1990s a retreat from the RFK legacy by President Clinton and his neoliberal allies in the new American oligarchy. We discover that, contrary to Kennedy's inclusive and social-justice orientation to the governing of America, that "the poverty rate through Clinton's term was only slightly better than the dismal performance attained during the Reagan/Bush years. In short, rhetoric aside, the Clinton economy was never an alternative to neoliberalism, but rather a variation on the orthodox model that illuminates powerfully why a real alternative is so badly needed" (Pollin 2003, 174). Robert Kennedy already knew this in the 1960s and that is why he struggled so hard for a new politics that would serve as a viable alternative to a failed economic orthodoxy that was too tied to an ideological straitjacket of market fundamentalism, and too separated from the claims of democracy, citizen involvement, and the practical aspects of distributional justice.

On May 5, 1967, in an address at a Jefferson-Jackson Day Dinner in Detroit, Michigan, Robert Kennedy outlined the elements of his approach for starting to build and promote a new politics for the 1960s and ensuing decades. He mixed idealism with practical needs in a dangerous world. Both the domestic and international arenas were important to address in this regard. To seek a newer world required the invocation of a new politics that would be capable of sustaining a new developmental trajectory for both the United States and the rest of the globe. To effectuate a new trajectory of development for both the US other nations, it would be necessary to recentralize the dignity of the person and the human rights of each individual within the larger social, economic, and political framework. To this end, Kennedy identified the four key directions in which a new politics must move:

> First, we must above all find ways to liberate and enhance the importance of individual lives and actions; to protect ourselves against the great organizations—sprawling government bureaucracies, huge impersonal corporations, and universities as big as cities—which threaten to overwhelm and obliterate the importance and value of individual man ... Second, as we move to extend and deepen government protection of our people we must understand the new meaning of justice—ending the dependency which pervades our social

> programs, and which is the antithesis of democracy. Our greatest failure toward those who have been denied American justice is not simply that our poverty programs are pitifully weak; our greatest failure has been our refusal to recognize their rights as citizens . . . Third, we must begin to rebuild our sense of community, of human dialogue, of the thousand invisible strands of common experience and purpose, affection and respect that tie men to their fellows . . . Fourth, and most important, arching over all else, must be the quest for world peace; not the quiet of desolation nor the stability of tyranny, but a world of diversity and progress, in which armaments and violence give way to the forces of reason and compromise which are man's only hope for survival on earth. (Ross 1968, 357–358)

These were the humane and humanizing components of Robert Kennedy's thoughts, which he was in the midst of translating into political practice and policy when his life was terminated by an assassin's bullet.

After Robert Kennedy's assassination, these elements of the new politics that he advanced on behalf of labor, unions, the poor, the middle class, women, the excluded, and the disenfranchised all began to fade into history. In its place, there developed what Thomas Byrne Edsall identified as the "new politics of inequality." In the stream of history, the transformative era and new politics was singularly embodied in the person and politics of Robert F. Kennedy. After his assassination, everything was permanently changed. Into the abyss of leadership came the Wall Street bankers, the globalists from the Council on Foreign Relations, and their brothers-in-arms at the Trilateral Commission (Gibson 1994). These groups were all beholden to the global armaments industry, big oil, weapons manufacturers, and a policy of "war without end" (Klare 1972). Of these combined national and global powers, as well the ultimate ends to which they were directed, professor Stephen Gill has proposed that they be viewed through the historical lens of a changing global hegemony for the US in the 1970s and 1980s: "US hegemony has changed from an outward projection of US 'national' hegemony. What is emerging is a necessarily incomplete form of transnational, neoliberal dominance, one which is nevertheless anchored in US political and military centrality. *At the level of world order, then, the world is undergoing a shift from a relatively hegemonic to a post-hegemonic world order*" (Gill 1993, 246, italics added).

RFK wanted to turn away from violence, militarism, and materialism at the national and international levels. His quest for peace, both nationally and internationally, stressed dialogue, compromise, and reason.

That was how he helped to peacefully resolve the 1962 Cuban missile crisis, as recounted in his memoir of the event, *Thirteen Days*. He came to realize that the application of US military force in interventionism, as with Vietnam, was irrational and counterproductive. He came to realize that the pursuit of peace meant that nuclear war was suicidal, and that disarmament at every level made peace more attainable and also freed up needed funding for wars that mattered—such as the war on poverty. Robert Kennedy saw the trend toward a post-hegemonic world order evolving out of the ashes of the Vietnam War. He was already aware of this developing trend in global relations on March 16, 1968—the day he declared for the presidency.

To know and appreciate the implications associated with an evolving historical trend toward a post-hegemonic era serves to explain why Kennedy decided to conclude his announcement speech with an oblique reference to "our right to the moral leadership of this planet." RFK clearly understood what LBJ and the American primacy coalition did not understand, and never would, which is that genuine leadership is not hegemony. Robert Kennedy understood what humane and progressive leadership in a world of truly revolutionary change entailed. Leadership involved more than the threat of military force and/or military interventionism as the predominant policy for the United States. Rather, the historical record demonstrates Kennedy understood that "if important action is to be taken in the present international system, the United States must take that action. The United States must not just resort to vetoing the actions of others. It must take a positive lead. But taking the lead, and attempting to act like a hegemon, are two very different roles" (Doran 2009, 95).

President Lyndon Johnson and the US national security establishment did not comprehend the dynamics of the age of revolutionary change in which they were living, especially with regard to their commitment to waging war in Vietnam and throughout Southeast Asia. Robert Kennedy acknowledged this lack of comprehension by Johnson and the national security state much earlier than did many people who lived in this period. As the consensus for pursuing the war in Vietnam began to dissolve, Kennedy realized that the Johnson administration and the militaristic logic that drove its decision-making process was antithetical to the democratic foundations of the nation as well as both the moral and constitutional obligations of its leadership. "When we are told to forgo all dissent and division," Kennedy said in 1968, "we must ask—who is it that is truly dividing the country? It is not those who call for change, it is those who make present policy . . . who have removed themselves from the enduring and generous impulses that are the soul of this nation." Or, on another occasion: "I am dissatisfied with our society. I am dissatisfied with our country." His cadence resembled that of his brother, but his words had a harsher, angrier, more radical tone (Brinkley 1998, 230).

What we have witnessed since RFK sought to advance the growth of democratic institutions at home and abroad—whether through the Bedford-Stuyvesant renovation program to improve the life-chances of poor people in the ghetto, or through the Alliance for Progress, was designed as a social- and land-reform program for all of Latin America—the post-1968 era of world history demonstrates that "in the absence of global democratic institutions or other mechanism through which ordinary people can influence the formulation and application of supranational rules, we can expect regulatory capture with a spiral of increasing polarization that benefits a small minority at the top—and, unintentionally but not less inexorably, keeps down the bottom half of humankind" (Pogge 2011, 127). Whether unintentional or not, the authors of *Global Civil Society 2003* have written of this new breed of "regressive globalizers" that they *"see the world as a zero-sum game in which they seek to maximize the benefit of the few, which they represent, at the expense of the welfare of the many, about which they are indifferent at best"* (Kaldor, Anheier, and Glasius 2003, 5, italics added).

This shift was also reflected in the passage and signing by President Bill Clinton of the now-infamous Personal Responsibility and Work Opportunity Reconciliation Act of 1996. Instead of honoring the right of citizens to basic needs, as Robert Kennedy and Dr. King had envisioned, the Clinton "reform agenda" ended previously established provisions in law and practice for the most economically vulnerable recipients of federal assistance programs. Clinton's signature on the legislation marked the official close of the era of the New Deal, the Fair Deal, the New Frontier, and the Great Society. In their place, Clinton inaugurated the "Era of Economic Austerity" for the poor. On this matter, economist William Kern argued that this law runs counter to the protections of social and economic rights because it forced persons to submit themselves to the labor market, or robbed them of their right to life (Kern, 1998, 427). In short, President Bill Clinton drove the dagger through the heart of Roosevelt's "Second Bill of Rights," as well as key components and core values of Robert Kennedy's legacy simply with the fatal sweep of his pen. Clinton's 1996 retreat from the socioeconomic-justice legacy of Kennedy, King, and FDR demonstrates the fact that, beginning in the Reagan era, Wall Street has dominated and continues to dominate most areas of economic and social policy (Chossudovsky 2010, 54). According to a 2008 study of the Organization for Economic Cooperation and Development (OECD), levels of social inequality in the US are among the highest in the OECD countries, and that is because "the distribution of earnings widened by twenty percent since the mid-1980s—which is more than in most other OEDC countries" (Phillips 2010, 176).

The new politics of inequality is especially evident in the domestic politics of the United States, and it was reflected in the 1970s and early 1980s through the phenomenon of elite, powerful interests controlling the nation's taxing and spending policies, which became increasingly concentrated in the hands of the affluent. During the first three years of the Reagan presidency, budget cuts reduced spending for human resource programs by over $110 billion, with the largest cuts in those programs targeted for the poor (Gartner, Greer, and Riessman 1982; Block, Cloward, Ehrenreich, and Piven 1987; Perelman 2007; Edsall 1984; Gordon 1996; Bunch 2009; Williams 2003; Reed 1999; Blumberg 1980; Green 1985; Green 1981; Boggs 2000). Of all the various theories advanced to explain this historical occurrence, perhaps one of the best structural explanations for the retreat from Robert Kennedy's vision for American economic justice and shared prosperity—characterized by distributional fairness—was offered by Thomas Byrne Edsall, who noted: "As long as the balance of political power remains so heavily weighted toward those with economic power, national economic policy will remain distorted, regardless of which party is in control of the federal government" (Edsall 1984, 242).

Edsall's argument also happens to be well-illustrated by a series of events that transpired on May 2, 1997. On that date, President Bill Clinton spoke at the opening of a new memorial to FDR, during which he praised FDR as "the greatest president of this century." Yet only a few hours earlier, rather than honoring the legacy of FDR, Clinton ignored that legacy and agreed to a balanced-budget compromise with congressional Republicans. This agreement not only rested upon cuts in Medicare and Medicaid, but it also included significant tax cuts that largely accrued to the richest people in America. In 1996, Clinton advanced another agreement with the Republicans that resulted in the abolition of the federal guarantee of assistance to poor Americans under Aid to Families with Dependent Children—one of the central accomplishments of FDR's New Deal. It seemed that Edsall's prediction about the inevitable and inexorable distortion of national economic policy, by either major political party in office, had come to full realization. In fact, another commentator observed: "Together these agreements almost exactly inverted the programmatic legacy of Roosevelt's New Deal by cutting programs for the poor and working class and providing tax cuts for the wealthy. . . . This abandonment represented the culmination of the Democratic Party's 'New Liberalism.'" It also served to demonstrate that the traditional liberalism of the Democratic Party that had existed "from the late 1930s to the 1960s was no longer relevant or politically practical" (Klinkner 1999, 11–12). Clinton's New Liberalism shared nothing with the values, purposes, and policies that had surrounded Robert Kennedy's new politics of 1967 and 1968.

Perhaps the most blatant rejection of the FDR legacy came in 1999, in the waning months of his administration, when President Clinton engaged in reaching a major turning point in the process of financial deregulation. Under the Financial Services Modernization Act (FSMA), adopted in November 1999—barely a week before the historic Seattle Millennium Summit of the World Trade Organization (WTO)—US lawmakers set the stage for a sweeping deregulation of the US banking system. Clinton's secretary of the treasury, Lawrence Summers—ho was later appointed Chairman of the White House National Economic Council (NEC) by President Barack Obama—played a key role. The result of this legislation was that all regulatory restraints on Wall Street's powerful banking conglomerates were revoked with the stroke of a pen. Approved by President Clinton and ratified by the US Senate, FSMA meant that commercial banks could freely invest in each other's businesses as well as fully integrate their financial operations (Chossudovsky 2010, 35). What FSMA effectively accomplished was a repeal of the Glass-Stegall Act of 1933, a pillar of FDR's New Deal. It had been put into place following the 1929 Wall Street crash, which had come about in a climate of corruption, financial manipulation, and insider trading. Now the whole story was about to repeat itself during the presidency of George W. Bush with a Wall Street collapse in September 2008.

In short, America's economic catastrophe of 2008 could have been avoided. It was not inevitable. It was not the consequence of the so-called "natural evolution of capitalism." In fact, to argue that "had the wealth been more evenly distributed" is to make the argument that *if* Robert Kennedy's commitment to invest in the poor, wipe out the ghettos, raise wages and the minimum wage as well as spur job creation through public and private investment had been actively pursued as a matter of public policy, *then* a different financial, social and political environment in the US would have emerged. From this analysis, it then follows that **Robert Kennedy's social and economic policy prescriptions for advancing the interests and well-being of America's workers, the poor, the young, women and minorities would have likely averted the systemic practices which led to the financial crisis of 2008—(that has effectively bankrupted the United States)— is not a counter-factual argument."** Rather, the argument has now become what amounts to a demonstrable, objective, and evidentiary fact that has been borne out by history and experience—not to mention the economic data on growing disparities between classes and a worsening of economic indicators pointing to greater inequality (Wolff 2002).

Writing about the political dynamics at work in this process in 1986, historian Arthur Schlesinger, Jr., commented:

> *The rhythm of the political cycle predicts the replacement in due course of private interest by public purpose as the pervading national orientation. Many doubt that such problems as the decay of the infrastructure, the decline of heavy industry, the crisis of the cities, the growth of the underclass, a generation of young people reared in poverty, unprecedented trade deficits, the flight of jobs to the Third World, can be safely confided to a deregulated marketplace dominated by great corporations. If the unfettered market is structurally incapable of solving such problems, affirmative government becomes a functional necessity in the years ahead.* (Schlesinger 1986, 248–249, italics added)

Robert Kennedy understood this reality. Those who came after him in the Washington power structure either did not understand it, or simply failed to heed the warning signs. In either case, what is now undisputable is that attempts to depoliticize distributional issues by attempting to rely on markets could never work. In 1968, both Robert Kennedy and Dr. Martin Luther King knew that distributional issues were both moral and political issues that required democratic debate, citizen involvement, and a greater balance between the forces of private wealth and the public interest.

This understanding about distributional issues and social policy choices for America's national community was also reflected in *The Final Report of the National Commission on the Causes and Prevention of Violence* published in April 1970. The commission chairman was Dr. Milton S. Eisenhower, so the report is sometimes referred to as simply the Eisenhower Commission Report. The release date of the report happened to mark the second anniversary of the King assassination. The introduction to the report was provided by James Reston of *The New York Times;* in his opening sentence, Reston pointed out that "this report on violence in America was written for the President of the United States after the murders of Martin Luther King, Jr., and Robert Kennedy." In his reflections on the legacies of Kennedy and King, Reston's concluding sentences posed what he called "the main post-Vietnam question": "*Will the threat of public disorder be made the first order of business by the federal government? Will the resources of the nation be reallocated to 'establish justice, to insure domestic tranquility'?*" (*The Final Report of the National Commission on the Causes and Prevention of Violence* 1970, xiii, italics added).

In Appendix I of the report, entitled "Summary of Recommendation," members of the commission sought to provide a comprehensive answer to Reston's question. In their conclusion, the commission recommended that:

(1) *the time is upon us for a reordering of national priorities and for a greater investment of resources in the fulfillment of two basic purposes of our Constitution—to establish justice and to insure domestic tranquility.*
(2) *when our participation in the Vietnam War is concluded, we recommend increasing annual general welfare expenditures by about 20 billion dollars (stated in 1968 dollars), partly by reducing military expenditures and partly by use of increased tax revenues resulting from the growth of the Gross National Product.*
(3) *as the Gross National Product and tax revenues continue to rise, we would strive to keep military expenditures level (in constant dollars), while general welfare expenditures should continue to increase until essential social services are achieved.*
(4) *to aid in the reordering of national priorities, consideration should be given to establishing a counterpart of the Council of Economic Advisors to develop tools for measuring the comparative effectiveness of social programs, and to produce an "Annual Social Report" comparable to the present Annual Economic report.* (Ibid, 1970, 229, italics added)

This set of social policy recommendations were premised on the work of economist Kenneth Arrow's formulation of welfare economics. Arrow's formulation, in turn, was premised on the notion that markets cannot aggregate individual preferences to derive a social-cost function. From this, one can draw the implication that "a bold reading of Arrow's argument would suggest, then, that the satisfaction of social needs required a kind of decision making that went *beyond economics*, requiring choices that rested on *social* values of what is good and just for a community" (Brick 2007, 170). Both Robert Kennedy and Dr. King understood this concept very clearly. Yet in their respective efforts to address this reality, the great political difficulty that Kennedy and King faced was found in the dominant economic, social, and political reality of the late 1960s—the loss of confidence in the state and government (the defining feature of what Jurgen Habermas [1975] has called a "legitimation crisis") that was already clearly evident throughout US society. The various and interrelated elements of this social crisis were reflected in the speeches of both Robert Kennedy and Dr. King. Given the nature of this dilemma, the challenge being presented for resolution came in the form of one basic inquiry: *How could economic questions about the allocation of limited resources and distributional outcomes effectively be addressed by the state's policy makers?* The answer to this question was not simply an economic one—at its core, the answer to the question remained both a moral and a political one. Both Kennedy and King were the last American leaders of national prominence to make the case that "we are our brothers' keeper." Hence, the significance of the Eisenhower Commission Report is that it was the last will and testament of Kennedy and King for the country. The fact that the Nixon administration ignored its admonitions by ignoring its moral and political message set the country adrift for all of the ensuing decades. Therefore, the inevitable collapse of the US economy in 2008 provides us, in retrospect, with the true gravity of the loss that the world experienced in 1968 with assassinations of Kennedy and King.

Within the context of a functioning democratic society, the basic question still remains a political one that cannot be relegated to artificial economic sleight of hand, because it is not subject to solution by free market conservatives (Krippner 2011, 171). And so, given this dilemma: "*At a more fundamental level, even if economic outcomes could be depoliticized, how would individuals disadvantaged by market processes come to accept the outcomes generated by the market as legitimate?*" (Krippner 2011, 21, italics added). After all, "it was one thing for the market to govern in an era of abundance and quite another for the market to be the master in an era of permanent scarcity. In such an environment . . . markets could not resolve the divisive distributional issues that continually presented themselves. *These problems were inherently political; and without political resolution, leaving them to the market would only provide an opportunity for the underlying social tensions to fester and grow*" (Krippner 2011, 21, italics added).

Regardless of what political or economic theory was chosen to explain the crisis of the late 1960s and early 1970s, there was one immutable fact that could not be denied. It would be next to impossible to meet and respond adequately to "growing demands for social spending to ensure social harmony in a period in which economic prosperity was no longer as widely shared as it had been in the immediate postwar decades" (Krippner 2011, 18). Hence, from 1968 through the 1970s, this basic reality led to other related findings by political scientists who began to discuss the problems of the governability of advanced capitalist nations and, at the same time, having to confront the paradox of a situation where "the state was doing *more* but achieving *less* as a result" (Krippner 2011, 19, italics in original). In this atmosphere, after the assassinations of Kennedy and King, policy makers discovered how reliance on market mechanisms transformed the resource constraints of the 1970s into a new era of abundant capital. However, this brought its own problems, as the US economy was caught between an expansion of credit, on the one hand, and the imposition of a high-interest-rate regime, on the other. What the post-Kennedy and post-King era demonstrates is that policy makers turned to finance in an attempt to extricate themselves from problems they confronted in the guise of social crisis, fiscal crisis, and the legitimation crisis of the state (Krippner 2011, 22). But, as recent scholarship has now concluded, "if financialization offered a resolution to the crises of the late 1960s and 1970s, this resolution was necessarily a partial and temporary one." Therefore, given the Wall Street collapse of 2008 and the ensuing economic crises of the end of the Bush II presidency and the first term of the Obama presidency, it is clear that *"policymakers will once again face many of the difficult choices that they have manages to avoid for nearly three decades"* (Krippner 2011, 22, italics added).

Both Robert Kennedy and Dr. King had begun to point a way out of the economic darkness of the late 1960s and looming crisis of governance that came to define the 1970s. In the aftermath of the assassinations of Kennedy and King, and given the lack of genuine moral leadership within the United States at the close of 1968, the evolutionary trend toward the financialization of the global economy was under way. Further, with the ensuing spread of economic, social, and cultural values designed to be narrowly tailored so as to fit the requirements of a profit-oriented form of unregulated and unaccountable globalization, we discover that the 1970s (and the decades to follow) reflected levels of higher socioeconomic inequality. Such a result should not come as a surprise to anyone. Within the framework of a thoroughly globalized world economy, the richest and most powerful agents are best positioned to form alliances with one another, to lobby key political decision makers, and basically destroy the citizenship rights of ordinary citizens (Pogge 2011, 126). In such a world economy, every nation is affected and the global poor suffer the most from being excluded from even the most basic rights associated with citizenship. From this, it follows that as citizens are deprived of their rights as citizens, entire communities and nations ultimately suffer.

King accurately foresaw the prospect that such an outcome would be inevitable given existing trends in the America of 1967. He issued a moral warning about these trends: "In a real sense, all life is interrelated. The agony of the poor impoverishes the rich; the betterment of the poor enriches the rich. We are inevitably our brother's keeper because we are our brother's brother. Whatever affects one affects all indirectly" (King 1967, 181). Similarly, RFK warned on October 5, 1964:

> If we're going to permit what's going on in Harlem now, of those young children who grow up uneducated and untrained and dissatisfied with life and dissatisfied with their future and feeling that there is nothing in this system, then we're going to be in difficulty. Even if we look at this selfishly, we're going to be in difficulty . . . Sophocles said one time: "Well, what joy is there in day that follows day, some swift, some slow, with death the only goal?" Really, that is what many of our fellow citizens feel—whether they are in Appalachia or whether they're in Harlem or whether they're the white children who live in some of these other areas where they've no future . . . These, I think, are our responsibility. These are your responsibilities, just as they are mine (Guthman and Allen 1993, 129).

Both RFK and Dr. King were strongly and unequivocally committed to a stance against social injustice that made them—in King's words—"maladjusted." With respect to certain values and practices of the existing social order, and in particular the growth of militarism, King often stated in his sermons and speeches that he was proud of the fact that he continued to be maladjusted. For both Kennedy and King, the militarism that both guided and depleted American society was not working and was no longer feasible for the nation's future nor for the future of humanity itself. The word that Robert Kennedy employed for the concept of being maladjusted was *dissent*. The word was used throughout his October 22, 1966, speech at the University of California at Berkeley. Kennedy's dissent from the insanity of nuclear war was now a matter of record. In the most adverse and extreme circumstances, after the United States was brought to the brink of nuclear war over the presence of Soviet nuclear missiles in Cuba, he clearly understood that the geopolitical status quo was far from morally or politically acceptable. In fact, for RFK, the Cuban missile crisis had spelled out the reasons why this kind of status quo was entirely unacceptable and deserving of complete and utter condemnation. He would often remind his audiences that "we can do better." Throughout the course of his 1968 campaign, he would repeatedly communicate this thought when he closed his speeches with a quote from George Bernard Shaw: "Some men see things as they are and say, why? I dream things that never were and say, why not?"

9

Redefining Human Security in an Age of Insecurity

Both RFK and Dr. King believed that it was necessary and profoundly essential to refuse to adjust to a socioeconomic order in which people had become objects—things used in pursuit of riches by others and disposed of when no longer needed (Pepper 2003, 172). They were engaged in the process of developing a concept which, in succeeding decades, would come under the rubric of "human security." By definition, human security encompasses being committed to defending all of that which makes human life materially sustainable and qualitatively worthwhile. The scope of this vision of human security includes the following: preserving peace; protecting the environment; investing in health, education, and welfare of all peoples and classes in an inclusive manner; and advancing a humane global order that honors and protects the dignity of the person as the ultimate priority. In the tradition of Kennedy and King, professor Mark David Wood argues that the struggles for ecological integrity, human rights, and social justice should be explicitly linked to the goal of socializing production to satisfy human needs. Wood maintains that "capitalism is structurally incapable of lifting all boats. Competition among private property owners to increase their share of naturally existing and socially generated wealth inescapably results in socioeconomic inequalities . . . Only by constructing the US political economy on the basis of democratic control of productive property can the ideals of liberty, equality, and fraternity be fully realized" (Wood 2000, 7).

Wood's critique was prefigured in the 1977 classic book by Charles E. Lindblom entitled *Politics and Markets: The World's Political-Economic Systems*. Like Woods, we find in Lindblom's work that he is critical of the socioeconomic inequalities that are largely the product of the private sector assuming ownership of enterprise and stripping working people of their rights, access to decent wages, and the enjoyment of decent working conditions. Lindblom notes:

> Not by logic but by history, owners of capital have become the owners of the enterprise. Many of the characteristics of familiar private enterprise systems are not attributable to private enterprise and property as such but to this particular historical form of private enterprise and property in which owners of capital rather than workers own the enterprise. It is a form full of consequences for the distribution of wealth and authority, for job rights, for alienation, and for patterns of social conflict . . . The market-oriented systems of the world are all inheritors of this inequality. None have gone very far in experimenting with a private property market system from which the effects of marked inequality in wealth are eliminated. Yet market systems that do so can be imagined. They would be drastically different from any existing market system. (Lindblom 1977, 105)

In the stream of history, Robert Kennedy found himself caught in the matrix of a market economy that resulted in severe consequences for those outside its ambit of power, wealth, and authority. For the powerless, the poor, the voiceless, and the excluded of the ghettos, as well as the alienated youth of the 1960s, the market system had provided them with little more than an enforced inequality that made the ghetto a permanent prison. For the young, the ghetto was a capitalist culture that had permitted vast injustices to fester and become worse with time. The objects of their dissent ranged from the uncontrolled damage done by corporate polluters to the weapons culture and its corporate machinery that profited from investing in the Vietnam War.

From Wall Street to the Pentagon, from polluted rivers to coal plants, it had become clear to the vast majority of the young, the poor, the disenfranchised that the market system was not on their side. Realizing that this was the real state of affairs in American life, Robert Kennedy came to the University of California at Berkeley on October 22, 1966, and declared:

> The future does not belong to those who are content with today, apathetic toward common problems and their fellow man alike, timid and fearful in the face of new ideas and bold projects . . . It will belong to those who see that wisdom can only emerge from the clash of contending views, the passionate expression of deep and hostile beliefs. Plato said: "A life without criticism is not worth living." This is the seminal spirit of American democracy. It is this spirit which

> can be found among many of you. It is this which is the hope of our nation. For it is not enough to allow dissent. We must demand it. For there is much to dissent from. We dissent from the fact that millions are trapped in poverty while the nation grows rich. We dissent from the conditions and hatreds which deny a full life to our fellow citizens because of the color of their skin. We dissent from the monstrous absurdity of a world where nations stand poised to destroy one another, and men must kill their fellow man. We dissent from the sight of most of mankind living in poverty, stricken by disease, threatened by hunger and doomed to an early death after a life of unremitting labor. We dissent from the willful, heedless destruction of natural pleasure and beauty. We dissent from all those structures—of technology and of society itself—which strip from the individual the dignity and warmth of sharing in the common tasks of his community and his country. (Ross 1968, 219–220)

Robert Kennedy had recognized that the market society and system had created a social prison for millions of people. It was a prison that demanded a prison break in the realm of public policy and public consciousness. That is why Kennedy endorsed dissent as a needed and proper avenue for bringing about change in a democratic society—on the assumption that the society was still democratic enough to be changed through dissent based upon principled claims—in areas such as environmental protection, the recognition of civil and human rights, and calls for ending a militaristic culture of investment in war and a practice of foreign intervention in Third World nations. Following in the spirit of Robert Kennedy's own dissent and critique of America's market system, Charles Lindblom also expanded his critique of the market system in ostensibly democratic systems. In an article entitled, "The Market as Prison," he argued that the behavior of market actors can, by definition, be directed only through inducement. While the behavior of public officials is susceptible to direction through commands and voting, this is not the case with markets. Rather, unless markets can be enticed to do something, they simply will not do it. Hence, market actors, which wield important decision-making authority, can choose *not* to do things that a democratic polity might require—such as investing in the ghetto, hiring workers, curbing industrial pollution. In this way, the consequences of their choices can undermine the authority of the public system of decision-making as well as the welfare of society as a whole. What makes the situation even more dire and precarious is that the position of powerful market actors is radically different from the position of all other participants in the political economy as a whole.

For example, certain market actors may even possess the capacity to exercise veto power over the decisions of public policy. With this danger in mind, Lindblom concluded: "My main point . . . has been that market systems imprison policy. Those of us who live in those market oriented systems that are called *liberal democratic* exercise significantly less control over policy than we have thought. *And we are also less free than we may have thought. Such are the inevitable consequences of imprisonment*" (Lindblom 1984, 11, italics added).

It may also be said that the nature of this imprisonment has many direct ramifications for the culture of a society, its values, and its public priorities and preferences. By 2001, Lindblom recognized the nature of this economic imprisonment on American culture itself when he noted: "That the market system pushes participants toward materialism is usually a clumsy way to say either that it pushes them toward the pursuit of money or toward acquiring those performances and things that money can buy. This is an allegation that cannot be dismissed. It suggests an excessively commercial and therefore corrupt culture" (Lindblom 2001, 198). As America's culture was in the process of being transformed through its imprisonment by a market culture, so, too, American democracy was becoming less democratic, less responsive to the progressive hopes and aspirations of the majority of the citizenry, and less representative of policies conducive to the public interest while becoming more accommodating to the interests associated with the maximization of profits by large corporations. In his critique of the sources of America's "democratic deficit," Lindblom wrote: "It is the large enterprises that pose obstructions to political democracy. Through their spending and relations with government officials they exercise much more power than do citizens . . . [This is] a mammoth violation of the political equality deemed necessary for genuine rather than spurious democracy" (Lindblom 2001, 237). In many ways, Lindblom's assessment of the role of corporations in America was merely a reiteration of his earlier conclusion about their negative impact in America when he observed: "It has been a curious feature of democratic thought that it has not faced up to the private corporation as a peculiar organization in an ostensible democracy . . . [They] exercise unusual veto powers. They are on all counts disproportionately powerful. . . . The large private corporation fits oddly into democratic theory and vision. Indeed, it does not fit" (Lindblom 1977, 356).

In the late 1960s, both Robert Kennedy and Dr. King began to question the nature, structure, and distributional effects of the private enterprise market system as it was constituted in the United States. In so doing, they began to confront and threaten the very foundations of the American financial establishment. In their collective efforts and political alliance for advancing social-justice concerns, both Kennedy and King had come to be seen as powerful adversaries of the American establishment, as well as threats to its status-quo mentality. This perception of Robert Kennedy and Dr. King as threats to the war interests and system of racial subordination was shared throughout the power structure: from the US Chamber of Commerce to Hoover's FBI, from the businessmen contractors of defense industries who profited from Pentagon contracts to the CIA and the national-security bureaucracy of the United States government. They were perceived as threats to national security itself because they dared to question the fundamental organization of American society itself. In this crucial regard, in addition to the structural debate over the way in which private enterprise and the market system were operating in the US—to the disadvantage of workers, minorities, and women—there also was a concomitant debate over the larger purpose of the "permanent war economy" in the United States and the nature of its activity in the world. Robert Kennedy and Dr. King had persistently come to question the moral authority of the United States in its pursuit of what is often referred to as the "national interest."

The questions that Kennedy and King raised were not only questions about the structure of US governmental and business power, but also: what was the purpose of US governmental and business power? To understand the significance and scope of this question is to begin to understand the answer to how and why Robert Kennedy and Dr. King embodied a vision of power and purpose for the United States that was critically and fundamentally at odds with the understanding of those who were the power brokers of that era. As Richard Barnet explained in his book entitled, *Roots of War: The Men and Institutions Behind US Foreign Policy*, we discover that:

> ***The terrible problem for policy planners in mid-century America was that they did not and could not know what their long-term interests really were. To be sure, they used the code word "national interest" to sanctify policies they perceived to be in their own class interests, i.e., the ever-increasing capitalist system from which they, their friends and employers had amassed great wealth. But within a generation it had become clear that they lacked a sufficiently coherent understanding of the world and a sufficiently***

> ***flexible strategy to realize their parochial definition of the "national interest." The world was moving too fast.*** (Barnet 1972, 67, italics and bold added)

Given the fact that the policy planners not only lacked "a sufficiently coherent understanding of the world," but were also so inflexible that they could not escape the gravitational orbit of "their parochial definition of the 'national interest,'" it is clear why they would find Robert Kennedy's challenge to their power, privileges, and perceptions so threatening. The brother of an assassinated president was now running for president in 1968 on a peace platform that also sought a virtual end to US hegemony by declaring that there should be no more Vietnams. At the same time, Kennedy was also an advocate, along with Dr. King's powerful civil rights movement, of a drastic remaking of America's socioeconomic structures, business practices, and hierarchies of privilege, which had been constructed on a foundation of racism, exploitation, and genocide (both within the US, against American Indians, and around the world, as with Vietnam, Cambodia, and Guatemala).

What both King and Kennedy sought and advocated in 1967–1968 was the development of a new US political economy that would be more responsive to the broad claims of "coalition politics." What the civil rights movement and antiwar movement came to realize in this period was that democratic alliance-building was critical in the effort to advance social change and redirect US government policies. As Joshua Cohen and Joel Rogers have succinctly explained: "*The basis of democratic coalition-building is not the convergence of aims on any particular issue advantage or gain, but the convergence of aims on securing a political order within which those particular aims can be addressed with mutual respect. To recognize such convergence is not merely to accede to another strategy of advertisement for the left, but the possibility of a strategy of principle. It is to accede to the principle of democracy itself*" (Cohen and Rogers 1983, 175, italics added).

In his efforts to advance democratic alliance-building, it would be Robert Kennedy who offered the most explicit understanding of what democracy itself meant when transformed into a "strategy of principle." He believed that the principles of democracy could only be actualized through mutual respect and dialogue. He stated this idea rather clearly in an address on June 8, 1967, in Salt Lake City, Utah: "There can be no national progress or security, no better life for our children, if we respond to our critics with denunciations or epithets—for only through the dialogue of criticism and response can we discover and remedy our own mistakes. All of these are both symptom and cause of a general lack of respect which for a democratic society is the greatest danger of all. *This sense of apartness, of selfish unwillingness to share the concerns of our fellows, or even to listen to them, simply must be ended*" (Ross 1968, 345, italics added). Riots and violence were usually caused by a complete breakdown of dialogue between contending parties and groups. If the promise of American democracy was to be restored and its ideals finally realized after decades of denial and bitter strife, then it would be both necessary and incumbent upon every citizen to open his/her mind and heart to "the other"—or as Kennedy put it, "the stranger amongst us." For Robert Kennedy, the idea of "the stranger amongst us" included immigrants, people of color, and other excluded and disenfranchised groups who sought to join the national community as equal citizens. Only in this way could we become, in Robert Kennedy's perspective, "brothers and countrymen, once again."

Kennedy's approach of seeking to engage in dialogue—and thereby developing mutual respect between contending parties and interests—was at the center of his new politics. One example of this could be seen in the effort he made as he consistently sought to defend and advance the work of community development corporations (CDC). He expressed his support for the CDC-model, noting:

> It has been a long time since most leadership in this country has spoken to the poor and tried to understand the problems of their existence. We should not fear the conflicts that have arisen as new power groups contend with old, as political leaders are forced to meet the slum dwellers instead of ward-leaders. Every department of city government dealing with social welfare programs should feel challenged to justify their traditional response to the problems of the poor. They may not like it, but the price of their discontent will be stronger and safer communities for our children and ourselves. (Vanden Heuvel and Gwirtzman 1970, 90)

Kennedy's expression of what he believed was needed for an effective urban program for the benefit of the poor went beyond the confines of ambiguous phrases employed in the Poverty Act, such as the "maximum feasible participation of the poor." Robert Kennedy resented the fact that the practical expression of this phrase often allowed city halls throughout the nation to continue to assert control over poverty programs. The effect of such an approach left the residents feeling as though they were receiving little more than handouts from the white community. Alternatively, Kennedy demanded that there be "full and dominant participation by the residents of the community concerned," thereby making the community the central focus of decision-making and allowing the geographic neighborhood to become that area within the city that residents could truly consider their own. In Kennedy's words: "In the supposed interests of efficiency we have thus far provided municipal services only on a citywide basis; using the same kind of organizational structure, whether the city had 2,000 people or 2 million. This technique has proven unable to meet the special needs of the ghetto and should be replaced by a system which allows a recognizable community to organize and secure those services which meet its own unique needs" (Vanden Heuvel and Gwirtzman 1970, 91).

In making this argument, Kennedy was being quite practical with regard to the sensibilities and suffering of the residents, thereby revealing his compassion and empathy with their plight. At another level, he was attempting to bring into existence the concrete manifestation of his Jeffersonian democratic ideal, which saw citizenship as something that was exercised at the grassroots level. Yet what is also present and influential in the very nature of Kennedy's suggestion was a short-lived historical movement toward a European model of a social democratic welfare state, which "was observable in rudimentary form in the Great Society urban social policies of the 1960s. *Even then, the target of these policies was 'the poor' rather than either the working class or the whole citizenry as a matter of 'right.' In any case, the trend was halted by the stagflation crisis of the late 1970s*" (Smith 1988, 35, italics added). In the stream of history, these developments in Robert Kennedy's time grew out of "the antipoverty programs created by the Economic Opportunity Act of 1964 and other federal initiatives of that decade" and "represented an effort to undo the New Deal legacy by reconstituting racially biased programs or by compensating African Americans with new benefits" (Quadagno 2004, 181). These developments also entailed federal job training programs that targeted minority youths, along with federal housing programs that targeted urban ghettos.

In this undertaking, community action agencies worked to expand federal authority in urban racial politics by modifying the old political alignments and permitting the state to claim new powers. This was the environment in which Robert Kennedy was operating, while bringing his own programmatic idealism to bear on the problems. For Robert Kennedy, what mattered most was a restoration of basic human dignity and respect for those who had been the victims of a centuries-old pattern of racial discrimination, economic hardship (including slavery and its scars), and the burden of ingrained prejudice. Similarly, this legacy constituted the same challenge that Dr. King faced when he traveled to Memphis, Tennessee, to support a garbage workers' strike. King came to Memphis to underscore the need for all Americans to come to grips with socioeconomic injustice. Both Kennedy and King were attempting to bring about a new kind of consciousness in civil society that would ultimately result, it was hoped, in new kind of national community. They were both working for the creation of a new social condition of mutual respect between blacks and whites for those who suffered from economic injustice emanating out of institutionalized patterns of racial discrimination. In this struggle, King's visit to Memphis was designed to expose denial of the dignity that was due to African American sanitation workers, as both human beings and as American citizens deserving of equal treatment and equal protection. In fact, it was emblematic of the struggle and its underlying message that the striking garbage workers of Memphis all marched with a sign hung around their necks that read: "I am a man."

For the sake of this message and in furtherance of this cause, Dr. King, acting in harmony and in alliance with Robert Kennedy, had been planning another march on Washington, in the summer of 1968, so that the agenda of the "Poor People's Campaign" could finally be heard by the entire nation (Honey 2007, 173–190). The issue of distributive justice was a message that had to be addressed in all of its dimensions. It was not an issue that could be swept under the rug any longer. Dr. King wanted a revamping of the entire socioeconomic order of the United States. It was an idea that King had been planning with Robert Kennedy since 1967. According to Thurston Clarke, in the fall of 1967, Kennedy had "suggested to King through mutual friends that King lead an interracial coalition of poor people in a march on Washington. King embraced the idea and began planning the Poor People's Campaign. Soon after King's funeral, columns of impoverished Americans began marching on Washington" (Clarke 2008, 102).

Before King's assassination, his plans for the Poor People's Campaign, and for another march on Washington had been the subject of secret meetings within the national security establishment, and had come under very close scrutiny by Hoover's FBI, elements of the CIA, and other networks within the US intelligence community. Despite the restrictions of its 1946 charter regarding domestic spying, the CIA had an active operational interest in King. In fact, a review of CIA documents from this period clearly demonstrate that the CIA viewed the entire civil rights movement with a degree of trepidation that can best be described as paranoid (Melanson 1991, 128). Further, because both Dr. King and Robert Kennedy were opponents of the Vietnam War as well as active political leaders seeking to advance the cause of civil and human rights, both had become targets of official hostility within the governing circles of the US government and the ruling elite establishment (O' Reilly 1989; Pepper 2003; Friedly and Gallen 1993; Garrow 1983).

Like Malcolm X, both King and Kennedy were on a collision course with the FBI, CIA, and the US national security establishment (Carson and Gallen 1991; Marable 2011). Malcolm X, Martin Luther King, and Robert Kennedy were threatening the delicate balance of power within an American social structure that was grounded in racist practices and ideologies, distorted values that promoted the aggrandizement of wealth over the realization of civil and human rights, and an ideology of white supremacy that sought to maintain racial subordination. In addition to the material aspects of the struggle, there also was the issue of militarism and the collusion of state power with business interests in maintaining an unbalanced state that was anti-democratic in many fundamental respects.

Now the question becomes: *How did American democracy get to a point in the late 1960s where the leaders of social movements in a supposedly democratic society could be viewed as "enemies of the state" and become targets of assassination?* The provisional answer, it would seem, was provided a decade earlier, in 1956, when the sociologist C. Wright Mills first published his book entitled, *The Power Elite*. In his chapter entitled "The Theory of Balance," Mills explained:

> The idea that the power system is a balancing society also assumes that the units in balance are independent of one another, for if business and labor or business and government, for example, are not independent of one another, they cannot be seen as elements of a free and open balance. But as we have seen, the major vested interests often compete less with one another in their effort to promote their several interests than they coincide on many points of interest and, indeed, come together under the umbrella of government. The limits of economic and political power not only become larger and more centralized; they come to coincide in interest and to make explicit as well as tacit alliances. The American government today is not merely a framework within which contending pressures jockey for position and make politics. Although there is of course some of that, this

> government now has such interests vested within its own hierarchical structure and some of these are higher and more ascendant than others. There is no effective countervailing power against the coalition of the big businessmen—who, as political outsiders, now occupy the command posts—and the ascendant military men—who with such grave voices now speak so frequently in the higher councils. *Those having real power in the American state today are not merely brokers of power, resolvers of conflict, or compromisers of varied and clashing interest—they represent and indeed embody quite specific national interests and policies.* (Mills 1956, 266–267, italics added)

The vision of the national interest that was proposed by Robert Kennedy was in conflict with the vision that was embodied and entrenched within the minds of those who occupied positions in the American establishment of that era. Their alliances and secret deals had created a safe environment for them to plan "wars without end," and they were in no mood to listen to Robert Kennedy speaking about "No More Vietnams."

10

The Crisis of "Social Exclusion"

Looking at Kennedy's analysis of poverty and social exclusion on a global scale, we discover that his critique of the foundational elements of the problems holds true as well. From the perspective of 2011, we can see how a globalized economy operates in the absence of democratic institutions and how that impacts not just millions, but billions of people around the globe. In 2011, Pogge observed: "In the absence of democratic institutions or other mechanisms through which ordinary people can influence the formulation and application of supranational rules, we can expect regulatory capture with a spiral of increasing polarization that benefits a small minority at the top—and, unintentionally but no less inexorably, keeps down the bottom half of humankind" (Pogge 2011, 127). Even more explicitly, Latin American scholar professor James Cockroft has noted: "By reflecting and promoting the interests of monopoly capital, the US government implements a militarization of the world that threatens preventive military attacks upon sixty nations under the pretext of 'the war against terrorism.' This militarization serves to ensure and increase control over natural resources, the expansion of big financial and industrial capital, and the best possible conditions for US trade and investments" (Cockroft 2006, 262).

The scale and scope through which monopoly capital operates is global—hence, the use of the term "globalization." Globalization really, in essence, refers to the globalization of capital. Yet, to effectuate the rule of monopoly capital requires force. The force that the United States has historically exerted since the end of World War II in advancing the interests of monopoly capital has been nothing less than a remodeled version of colonialism and imperialism. By definition, this means, according to James Petras and Henry Veltmeyer, that "imperialism by its intrusive, disruptive, destructive and exploitative character inevitably generates permanent political, social and cultural forms of opposition. As a result, brief periods of consolidation are typically followed by prolonged periods of instability. The cycles of 'consolidation' and 'instability' reflect the sequence of imperial conquest: initial occupation and severe repression, followed by the fostering of imperial sponsored selection-elections, and the emergence of an apparently 'hegemonic' elite—followed by new waves of popular resistance in response to corruption, pillage and incompetence, leading to new revolts and perpetual warfare until the imperial regime withdraws or engages in genocide" (Petras and Veltmeyer 2007, 14).

The pattern outlined by Petras and Veltmeyer has been replicated in Latin America in its dealings with the United States throughout the twentieth century. It is a pattern that the European colonial powers employed during their stay in Indochina in the mid-twentieth century—until the United States took their place. It is a pattern that has characterized the history of the early twenty-first century in the cases of Iraq and Afghanistan, following the invasion of the two nations by the United States under George W. Bush and their continuing occupation under Barack Obama. What these two US presidents have failed to grasp are the inherent fallacies that invariably accompany the imperial project and its flawed design and execution, and the impossibility of its ultimate success. In their review of the historical record, both Petras and Veltmeyer have been quite skeptical about the long-term prospects for empire building, insofar as "empire-building is the result of deliberate, calculated acts and improvised interventions in circumstances and contingencies, which are out of the control of the imperialist elites" (Petras and Veltmeyer 2007, 18). The very omnipresence of imperialist institutions requires the spreading out of forces. According to Petras and Veltmeyer, we discover a new reality in the stream of history because "this suggests that omnipresence can lead to relative imperial impotence. In other words *omnipresence can be a weakness rather than a strength*" (Petras and Veltmeyer 2007, 11, italics added). Historian Paul Kennedy calls this phenomena "imperial overstretch."

Unlike either Bush or Obama, both John and Robert Kennedy came to comprehend the dynamics of revolutionary change throughout the Third World that characterized the 1960s. In both his Senate career and in the presidency, John Kennedy attempted to redefine US objectives and tactics in the lesser-developed countries along paths that he considered to be more realistic. Similarly, Robert Kennedy was greatly influenced by his brother's approach to the aspirations, needs, and challenges of the lesser-developed countries. Therefore he continued to champion his brother's views throughout both his term in the US Senate and in his campaign for the presidency. It had become Robert's contention that a profound revolution was sweeping the Third World. In responding to this revolution, Robert believed that the US could influence its direction and course only if America's leadership came to understand and respect the true nature of the upheaval.

In a college commencement address at Queens College, New York, on June 15, 1965, Robert Kennedy declared:

> Around the world—from the Straits of Magellan to the Straits of Malacca, from the Nile Delta to the Amazon basin, in Jaipur and Johannesburg—the dispossessed people of the world are demanding their place in the sun. For uncounted centuries they have lived with hardships, with hunger and disease and fear. For the last four centuries they have lived under the political, economic, and military domination of the West. We have shown them that a better life is possible. We have not done enough to make it a reality. . . . A revolution is now in progress. *It is a revolution for individual dignity, in societies where the individual has been submerged in a desperate mass.* It is a revolution for self-sufficiency, in societies which have been forced to rely on more fortunate nations for their manufactured goods and their education, cotton textiles and calculus texts. It is a revolution to bring hope to their children, in societies where 40 percent of all children die before reaching the age of five. This revolution is directed against *us*—against the one-third of the world that diets while others starve; against a nation that buys 8 million new cars a year while most of the world goes without shoes; against developed nations which spend over 100 billion dollars on armaments while the poor countries cannot obtain the 10 to 15 billion dollars of investment capital they need just to keep pace with their expanding populations. (Ross 1968, 423–424, italics added)

In the emerging world of the 1960s, Robert Kennedy saw the possibilities for a new kind of international community that would be more humane, inclusive, and just. This insight also had great significance in the way in which he was starting to re-imagine community, and the human experience of community in the United States itself. For Kennedy, both the world and the United States needed to change together so that the common problems of poverty, isolation, and alienation could be effectively overcome. At the center of Kennedy's vision was the need to restore emphasis on the dignity of the individual person.

Throughout Robert Kennedy's public career, "Kennedy's search for community was central to most—though not all—of the domestic issues he engaged . . . Kennedy would be drawn to the issue of poverty as a threat to all levels of community in the United States, and his policy proposals would reflect a consistent vision of the interrelationship between the individual, the local 'grassroots' community, and the national community" (Schmitt 2010, 6). It should also be noted that as an international statesman who dealt with these same basic problems with regard to Latin America, South Africa, and Southeast Asia, RFK also developed a strong sense of what an international approach to the problems of poverty involved and what kind of solutions these problems would necessitate if they were to be overcome.

RFK had already discovered the problem of "social exclusion," of the separation of the individual from the life of the community, as well as how individuals had become divorced from the decision-making structures and processes that were supposed to be the hallmark of American democracy. After his assassination in 1968, however, it would take until the 1990s for others to rediscover what he had already learned and about which he had spoken so eloquently in the late 1960s. Because of the evolving need to better comprehend the nature of these structural injustices, a new paradigm emerged in the 1990s in relation to the study of poverty in Europe: "This was the notion of social exclusion that was arguably a broader and more dynamic concept than traditional notions of poverty. It is notable that Amartya Sen . . . the international leader of poverty studies, has recently called for the adoption of '*social exclusion*' as a powerful new overarching concept for the study of human deprivation. Sen takes up the *social-exclusion paradigm* mainly because of its focus on the multi-dimensionality of deprivation and its emphasis on relational processes rather than the individual" (Munck 2005, 21, italics added). Both RFK and King already employed this concept in the 1960s as they addressed national and international inequalities and the effects of these realities upon individuals, classes, communities, nations, and international relations as whole (Dyson 2000; Schmitt 2010; Pepper 2003; Honey 2011; Jackson 2007).

In the year 2010, new studies were produced that provided firm evidence clearly demonstrating that we will not change our economic behavior unless we change the ways by which we measure our economic performance. Hence, it is extremely significant to finally and objectively be able to acknowledge that the very economic indicators by which we have traditionally measured both economic and social progress are now recognized by leading Nobel Prize winning economists as deeply flawed. President Nicolas Sarkozy of France had previously asked two

Nobel Prize-winning economists, Joseph Stiglitz and Amartya Sen, along with the distinguished French economist Jean-Paul Fitoussi, to establish a commission of experts to study whether gross domestic product (GDP)—the most widely used measure of economic activity—is really a reliable indicator of economic and social progress. In a word, their collective answer came back as a resounding no in their final report entitled, *Mis-Measuring Our Lives: Why GDP Doesn't Add Up* (Stiglitz, Sen, and Fitoussi 2010). The report's authors discovered that most people are worse off, despite the fact that the average GDP has been increasing. That is largely because the GDP is incapable of accurately measuring well-being. Hence, the authors of *Mis-Measuring Our Lives* conclude that: "To define what well-being means, a multi-dimensional definition has to be used . . . At least in principle, these dimensions should be considered simultaneous: (1) material living standards (income, consumption and wealth); (2) health; (3) education; (4) personal activities (including work); (5) political voice and governance; (6) social connections and relationships; (7) environment (present and future conditions); (8) insecurity, of an economic as well as a physical nature." In combination, the authors conclude, "all these dimensions shape people's well-being, and yet many of them are missed by conventional income measures" (Stiglitz, Sen, and Fitoussi 2010, 15).

On May 5, 1967, in an address at the Jefferson-Jackson Day Dinner in Detroit, Michigan, RFK specifically called into question the accuracy of the gross national product (GNP) and the Dow Jones Industrial Average as indicators for determining whether American society was sick or sound. Kennedy declared:

> And let us be clear at the outset that we will find neither national purpose nor personal satisfaction in a mere continuation of economic progress, in an endless of amassing of worldly goods. We cannot measure national spirit by the Dow-Jones average or national achievement by the gross national product. For the gross national product includes our pollution and advertising for cigarettes, and ambulances to clear our highways of carnage. It counts special locks for our doors and jails for the people who break them. The gross national product includes the destruction of the redwoods, and the death of Lake Superior. It grows with the production of napalm and missiles and nuclear warheads, and it even includes research on the improved dissemination of bubonic plague. The gross national product swells with equipment for the police to put down riots in our cities; and though it is not diminished by the damage these riots do, still it goes up as slums are

> rebuilt on their ashes. It includes Whitman's rifle and Speck's knife, and the broadcasting of television programs which glorify violence to sell goods to our children. (Ross 1968, 351)

In his final message to white South Africa at the University of Witwatersrand, Johannesburg, on June 8, 1966, on the subject of our collective slavery to corrupt systems and the selfishness induced by individualistically-oriented market systems, RFK observed: "Freedom is not money, that I could enlarge mine by taking yours. Our liberty can grow only when the liberties of all our fellow men are secure; and he who would enslave others ends only by chaining himself, for chains have two ends, and he who holds the chain is as securely bound as he whom it holds." He concluded his remarks by noting that "we all struggle to transcend the cruelties and the follies of mankind. That struggle will not be won by standing aloof and pointing a finger; it will be won by action, by men who commit their every resource of mind and body to the education and improvement and help of their fellow man" (Kennedy 1993, 255–256). In the early twenty-first century, it is striking to see just how much of Robert Kennedy's own assessment of the human crisis of development and deprivation, of inequality and large-scale injustice, can now be appreciated as a foreshadowing of the 2010 findings contained in *Mis-Measuring Our Lives*. To assert the validity of this comparison is not inappropriate and does not make this comparison into a counterfactual claim. Rather, it is an objective statement about Kennedy's insights and what we collectively lost when we lost him and his voice of conscience.

Far ahead of his time, Kennedy's insights reflect a deep sensitivity into the many dimensions of human purpose as well the multidimensional needs of a healthy national and international community. From his various speeches, personal musings, and public interviews, the record of the times convincingly demonstrates that RFK understood all too well that by uncritically and compulsively seeking to rely all too heavily on the externals of our existence—the material wealth that we aggrandize, the techniques we adopt that only seem to make life easier—we impoverish the internal dimensions of life that offer purpose, meaning, and a shared sense of common fate and destiny. Kennedy and King shared a critique of American society and culture. Their common bond and shared political purpose was to reclaim America and the world from the abuses of an unconstrained capitalism in search of endless profits, and the iron cage of the market mentality so that the bonds of true human community and common purpose could be given new meaning. However, the civic order, the corporate and financial elites of Wall Street, and the power brokers in Washington of his time failed to recognize what Thoreau had criticized as "improved means to an unimproved end." In response, Kennedy indicated that he believed the GNP, Dow Jones average, and technological advances had brought a false sense of security to his fellow citizens in an age of deep insecurity.

Reflecting on these themes, Daniel Rogers, professor of history at Princeton University, wrote: "In these contexts the era's great debate about the poor was more than a debate about policy. *It was a debate between visions of society*. In the more partial, pluralistic communities of the late twentieth century, who was inside and who was outside the imagined spheres of obligations and responsibilities? Who belonged? Whose needs required public response? Whose claims counted? In a world of deepening inequalities, who stood inside the social contract and who stood outside it altogether?" (Rogers 2011, 200, italics added). These were the questions that resonated through the 1960s and forward into the 1970s, 1980s, and 1990s.

Dr. King had consistently warned that "western civilization is particularly vulnerable at this moment, for our material abundance has brought us neither peace of mind nor serenity of spirit" (King 1967, 172). In expanding upon King's perspective, one commentator noted: "Long before globalization was in mode he knew that a global system, dreamed of by corporate imperialists, would harmonize standards across the globe down to the lowest common element. Social responsibility would be regarded as inefficient in a global free market and demands for a living wage would be a targeted source of inefficiency and purged wherever possible" (Pepper, 2003, 172). In the year 2011, Michigan's Republican governor made just such an argument as he set out to destroy the collective bargaining rights of labor. On the global stage, such a practice has been commonplace since the 1970s for the World Bank and the International Monetary Fund (IMF), through the employment of "structural adjustment programs" designed along the prescriptive lines of the neoliberal economic model.

11

"Tribune of the Underclass" and "Global Statesman"

Within the United States of the 1960s, Robert Kennedy's embrace of social justice concerns was evident as he dealt with protests ranging from lunch-counter boycotts throughout the South and freedom rides in Selma, Alabama, to gatherings in the agricultural fields of Delano, California with Caesar Chavez and the United Farm Workers (UFW). Aware of the dangers of social exclusion and alienation from the large society, Kennedy launched community development projects dedicated to slum and ghetto redevelopment, as showcased in Bedford-Stuyvesant, New York. Robert Kennedy's journey in the stream of history had made him into what historian Arthur Schlesinger called "the tribune of the underclass" (Schlesinger 1978, 778–80).

Looking abroad, the statesmanship of Robert Kennedy was clearly apparent in his travels. In South Africa, Kennedy was a vibrant advocate for the end of racial apartheid. He traveled throughout Latin America to urge that the social reform goals of the Alliance for Progress be extended, that democratic governments and reforms replace the exploitative dictatorships and oligarchies of a feudal past, and that the benefits of modernity be shared by all, from access to health and education to employment and jobs for those able to work. Robert's transformative vision for freeing South Africa from the bondage of apartheid, and his vision for freeing the peasants of Latin America from the tyranny of dictators and landowners through land reform and a reformulated definition of their rights and power as citizens, served to make him not only a tribune of the underclass, but also a truly global statesman.

In keeping with the central theme of this book, I am working to reframe and to reinterpret the historical record so that a truer image of Robert Kennedy can finally emerge that allows him to be finally understood as a global statesman. Clearly, this does not mean that he was a statesman in the political mold of a Henry Kissinger, whose record in office as both Nixon's Secretary of State and National Security Advisor was premised on the ideological foundation of *realpolitik* and the further expansion and consolidation of US hegemony, regardless of the human consequences for Third World peoples. Also, the model of conventional establishment statesmanship that Kissinger embodied does not constitute the approach to statesmanship that RFK exhibited; for example, Robert Kennedy would not endorse or engage in planning by the US to overthrow a democratically elected head of state, as Kissinger did with Salvador Allende in Chile. Both Kissinger and Nixon endorsed the CIA plan to work with a military junta led by Augusto Pinochet to remove Allende from power. To Robert Kennedy, such a plan was anathema to the kind of foreign policy that the US should pursue, because it violated the principle of the democratic consent of the people and would work to undermine the fabric of the entire inter-American system. How do we know this for sure? Because Kennedy condemned such a policy in a press statement issued on June 28, 1966, regarding the consequences stemming from the military overthrow of President Illia of Argentina. Kennedy's office issued this statement:

> Senator Robert F. Kennedy (D-N.Y.) said today that the overthrow of the elected government of Argentina by a military junta is a grave setback to inter-American solidarity and to the Alliance for Progress. '*On my recent visit to Argentina,*' Senator Kennedy said, '*I was very impressed with the dedication shown by President Illia and his government and the progress he has made under serious pressure from both the military and the followers of Juan Peron*.' Senator Kennedy indicated his strong belief that '*whenever a democratically elected is overthrown by the military, severe damage is done to the entire fabric of the inter-American system. If real progress is to come in Latin America, it must be with the democratic consent of the people.* (Ross 1968, 443, italics added)

Based on his record, it can be argued that Robert Kennedy would have admired Allende's efforts at land reform, meeting the needs of the poor, and even Allende's tenacious and audacious nationalization of the copper and oil industries of Chile so that the economic benefit of Chile's resources would be enjoyed by the Chilean people and not exported elsewhere. In short, Kennedy would not have subscribed to the neoliberal model of which Kissinger was both an advocate and an active power broker in seeking to bring about its implementation.

Before neoliberalism became a formal ideological model under President Reagan in the 1980s, its main tenets were already present inchoate within the philosophical framework of David and Nelson Rockefeller and their business and banking allies in the 1960s. There is no congruence between the Rockefeller/Nixon/Kissinger approach to US government policy toward Latin America and the approach invoked by John and Robert Kennedy. The efforts of John and Robert Kennedy represent a commitment to resist a set of economic beliefs that subordinates all social and development considerations to the demands of private capital and the world market. In particular, Robert opposed such an approach because he viewed it as anti-developmental, lacking in attentiveness to the inherent democratic and social justice aspirations of the majority of people throughout the Third World, and antithetical to realizing the legal and moral mandates that reside at the core of claims to human rights and human dignity. There is a great deal of evidence in the historical record that supports such a depiction of Robert Kennedy and his policy positions on Latin America, the proper role of US business interests in Latin America, and RFK's strong advocacy of the rights of the people of Latin America to act in their own best interest. A key case in point is when Kennedy made public his disagreements with Nelson Rockefeller and the role of Standard Oil in Latin America's affairs in 1965.

In the case of Peru, in the summer of 1965 Robert Kennedy challenged Peruvians to act for themselves:

> In the conversation I had with the students at the Peruvian-American Cultural Institute, I heard many complaints and criticisms, but not once was I told about what they thought or what they supposed should be done in this or that problem. I think that the action is up to you people. President Kennedy had to act against some large firms; Argentina has cancelled its oil contracts; years ago Mexico nationalized its oil, and what happened? It is up to you not to get overwhelmed and to act according to your interests and according to what you consider is more convenient. And nothing can happen, as nothing happened before. (Colby and Dennett 1995, 539)

Robert Kennedy's comments upset both LBJ and the Rockefeller brothers, David and Nelson. In fact, it was reported that: "The Johnson White House was not amused. The stories have him in effect saying: '*Go ahead and nationalize. Others (Argentina, Brazil, and Mexico) have done this. In the end, things work out*'" (Colby and Dennett 1995, 539–540, italics added).

In 1965, Robert Kennedy continued to make an argument that President Kennedy had already made in 1963, thereby incurring the wrath of David Rockefeller. David went beyond the classical liberal argument of the market as the basis for individual liberty—a theme sounded by Nixon, Ford, Reagan, Bush I and II, and Clinton, as well as by right wing elements of the Tea Party, from 2009 onward. Instead, David Rockefeller suggested that US policy should not merely prefer private enterprise, but should oppose public enterprise and its creation out of private corporations—irrespective of the public's grievances or the true nature of the corporation's crimes. Rockefeller's argument was a precursor to what would come to be known in the coming decades of the 1980s and 1990s as "neoliberalism." It is an economic model that privileges private corporate power, disparages democracy, and seeks to get the government out of its traditional role of protecting the civil and human rights of people by embarking upon a reduction of social and health services, outlawing labor unions, reducing wages, and privatizing governmental tasks and public entities. In all cases where it has been applied, it has ended with severe austerity measures being put into place. In 1963 and 1965, what David Rockefeller especially wanted from the executive branch was a general US policy that discouraged all nationalizations. He "wanted to set up rules that not only extended to corporations abroad an extraterritorial imperial right to assert the US Constitution's guarantee of fair compensation to persons when property is seized, but also included 'indemnification,' a much broader legal term that encompassed legal exemption from liabilities or penalties incurred by one's actions" (Colby and Dennett 1995, 665–666).

This ongoing battle between John and Robert Kennedy, on the one hand, and David and Nelson Rockefeller, on the other, was part of a larger struggle over the nature of US hegemony, the policies that the United States would pursue throughout the Third World, and a final resolution of the issue of what kind of emphasis should be given to social reform versus the business community's preoccupation with economic growth as an end in itself. During President Kennedy's tenure in office, he did not rely on US businessmen for advice on inter-American affairs and they decried their lack of influence (Rabe 1999, 180). However, only two months after the assassination of President Kennedy in Dallas, the entire calculus of power and influence changed. The Rockefellers and their business allies immediately moved to make sure that their influence would be felt in the higher circles of the Johnson administration. The bitter battles with John and Robert Kennedy over social reform in

Latin America were going to be decisively dealt with in no uncertain terms. Therefore, according to historian Stephen Rabe, a significant shift in US policy would start to become evident as early as January 1964, when it was announced that "bankers, traders, and investors [had] formed the Business Advisory Group on Latin America, which subsequently joined the larger Council for Latin America. David Rockefeller of Chase Manhattan Bank headed both business groups, which included representatives from major corporations like Standard Oil of New Jersey and International Telephone and Telegraph" (Rabe 1999, 180).

For the Rockefeller brothers and their business associates, John and Robert Kennedy's leaning and emphasis toward basic social reforms and political liberalism had sent counterinsurgency as social reform, and the task of nation-building—understood as a commitment to promoting land reform, education, as well as the provision of decent health care and jobs with a living wage—down the wrong developmental path. Because of the Kennedy commitment to promoting genuine and comprehensive social reform, the Rockefellers strongly believed that the Kennedy brothers were responsible for leaving an enduring legacy of democratic baggage that would be extremely difficult for subsequent US administrations to throw off (Colby and Dennett 1995, 667). As it turned out, they need not have worried. Both President Johnson and Vice-President Hubert Humphrey met regularly with business lobbies, such as the Business Advisory Group and the Council for Latin America. And so it was that the businessmen from Rockefeller-sponsored groups throughout the US financial establishment appreciated hearing Johnson talk about "property rights" (Rabe 1999, 180–181). In fact, as early as February 1966, "the vice president informed Johnson that Rockefeller and his colleagues '*believe that a substantial change in policy has occurred within the US government within the last two years in regard to the question of private enterprise in Latin America.*' The Kennedy people had made economic growth secondary to social reform. But now with those priorities reversed, the business community was now '*most happy with US policy*'" (Rabe 1999, 181, italics added).

Given the perspective of the Rockefellers as emblematic of the capitalist classes of which they were a part—and alliances that they led—it can be concluded that:

> The Western capitalist prescription for development is a model which always leaves intact the dynamic of exploitation and the machinery of repression—regardless of what concessions or reforms may be instituted. It is a model which sees human labor as one more resource to

> be exploited (as cheaply as possible). It is a model which ties people to a treadmill of conspicuous consumption, warping the promise of human potential. It is a model which is built upon competition and advocates cooperation only in the self-interest of the most powerful. It is a model of development which buys stability for business at the price of shattered and stunted lives; offering people a t-shirt, a pair of sneakers, plastic dishes, maybe a radio or a watch, in place of freedom. (Sklar 1980, 52)

Because of the inherent incompatibility of this corporate/capitalist model with its alternative—an agenda that centralized concerns with human rights, humane progress, and genuine development within Third World nations—Robert Kennedy was on a collision course with Rockefeller banking and business interests. By 1965, it had become clear to all major parties that the political and economic philosophy that Robert Kennedy was committed to realizing would become a roadblock to the interests of many financial elites. In particular, Robert's political and economic approach to the problems of the Third World were a matured and updated version of John Kennedy's—whose views Rockefeller-ites had hated, and had opposed at every turn. Hence, Robert Kennedy constituted an enduring problem for the Rockefeller oil, banking, and corporate interests—not to mention their financial allies.

In contrast to the Rockefellers and their corporatist ideology, Robert Kennedy was, in both substance and in practice, a global statesman beyond a narrowly defined national interest. His compassion for the millions of suffering and oppressed people around the globe was intimately connected with his personal belief in and commitment to the power of progressive social movements, democratic aspirations, and the advancement of civil and human rights. In this unique sense, Robert Kennedy blended his roles as both a tribune of the underclass and a global statesman. It would be in this combination of political roles that Kennedy would, in Tennyson's phrase from his poem *Ulysses*, be at work "to seek a new world." In the meantime, the Rockefellers would be at work trying to preserve the old world, and sought to do so through the tired cynicism of *realpolitik* (Colby and Dennett 1995, 397, 667).

The Alliance for Progress had been launched by JFK with the signing of the Charter of Punta del Este in early 1961. As the foundation of the Alliance for Progress, the Charter is "a remarkable, almost revolutionary document." The Charter is noteworthy because, for the first time in recent history, "it spoke with frankness of the place of social and institutional reforms in the process of development" (Feder 1970, 206).

This was a history that Robert Kennedy helped to form and shape. It was also a legacy that he would inherit after his brother's assassination. In light of the foregoing discussion, it should also be obvious from the historical record that President Kennedy's initiatives, as outlined throughout the Charter, were significantly at odds with the worldview and priorities of businessmen who were also leading bankers. It was a battle that would continue long after President Kennedy's assassination. Robert Kennedy would take up the cause where his brother left off, continuing to combat and oppose the Rockefeller worldview. It would be a battle that would come to define Robert Kennedy's Senate years as he continued to try to revive the social reform elements of the Alliance for Progress.

The reason for Robert's reluctance to surrender the battle to the Rockefellers and to the Johnson administration was because of his personal fidelity to the cause of human rights and his personal preoccupation with human suffering. Robert Kennedy committed himself to do all that he could to alleviate human suffering wherever possible, whether in Latin America, on American Indian reservations, in apartheid South Africa, or in the ghettos of America's inner cities. There are many examples that could be cited, some of which come out of the period of Robert Kennedy's 1968 presidential campaign. Two journalists of this era, Jules Witcover and Jack Newfield, had the unique opportunity to view Robert Kennedy up close and in action. Their views on Kennedy's connection to the world of suffering and his identification with the victims of social injustice, the poor, minorities, and the excluded speak volumes about the personal and public faces of Kennedy. According to Jules Witcover:

Robert Kennedy was obliged to become a public figure but he remained in most ways a private man; he gave his hands and his voice and his life to the public; his warmth, his soft, almost playful good humor, he kept mostly for his family and those others closest to him. One of the most hopeful developments as he campaigned, however, was that the private man was blending into the public man; in time, had he been given the time, the bulk of the nation might have come to know him as his intimates did. His special constituency—the have nots—seemed already to have accepted him thus (Witcover 1969, 331).

Another example of Kennedy's identification with and personal commitment to those who suffered was recorded by Jack Newfield. According to Newfield, in the midst of the presidential campaign, on Saturday, March 30, 1968, "despite laryngitis and a cold, Kennedy went to Flagstaff, Arizona, to preside at a hearing of his Senate subcommittee on Indian Education. The night before, when several members of his local campaign organization complained of his wasting time on the hearings when he could be out meeting voters, Kennedy snarled, *'You sons of bitches! You don't really care about suffering!'"* (Newfield 1969, 274, italics added). This is a clear example demonstrating that Kennedy did not endorse the practice of "internal colonialism"—which American Indians suffered on reservations—any more than he approved of colonialism practiced by the European powers since the nineteenth century, or the American version of neocolonialism as practiced by the US under Lyndon Johnson throughout Southeast Asia, during the course of the war in Vietnam.

Robert Kennedy's domestic political opponents were often on the receiving end of his righteous indignation when it came to the plight of America's poor and dispossessed. When authors Gerard Colby and Charlotte Dennett commented on Robert Kennedy's sensitivities and moral indignation in their history of this era, they observed:

> If Lyndon Johnson was troubled by having such a sensitive rival, so, too, was one of his strongest supporters on Vietnam, Governor Nelson Rockefeller. Nelson also had felt Bobby Kennedy's sting. Migrant laborers, whether Indians, African American, or Mexican Americans, were one of Kennedy's special concerns. The orchards of Rockefeller's New York were no more spared Kennedy's senatorial investigations than were the vineyards of Governor Ronald Reagan's California. *Rockefeller did not appreciate Kennedy's calling for a state investigation of health conditions at migrant camps. Reagan had even less use for Kennedy's urging labor leaders to unionize migrant farm workers.* Kennedy supported Caesar Chavez's striking grape pickers and sponsored legislation to grant migrant farm workers collective bargaining rights. This struck at the foundation of the cheap-labor code of agribusiness. (Colby and Dennett 1995, 577–578, italics added)

Robert Kennedy's capacity to upset the convenient regime of elite businessmen, bankers, and politicians within the US—as was the case with Reagan and Rockefeller—was a quality of his that was duplicated in his approach to foreign affairs. Like John Kennedy, Robert was an apostle of social justice and social change. This characterized Robert Kennedy's twin roles as tribune of the underclass and global statesman.

Of John F. Kennedy's foreign policy approach, policies, and his general attitude toward social change throughout the Global South (the "Third World"), one economic historian has made the case that "his foreign aid program was supposed to further economic development and free Third World nations from the backwardness and inferiority which were central to colonial and neo-colonial arrangements. *He favored nation-to-nation agreements and was willing to bypass the private banks and the 'free market.' He showed no interest in aggressively demanding that recipients adhere to the other conditions favored by the international banking community*" (Gibson 1994, 62, italics added). In 1963, David Rockefeller called upon President Kennedy to shift foreign economic aid away from government-to-government aid. The primary reason that Rockefeller was so adamant about this particular issue was that "such aid allowed governments in underdeveloped countries to fund publicly owned enterprises that competed with privately owned (often American controlled) companies. Local government aid, in turn, encouraged political independence from Washington and greater national sovereignty—including nationalization of American holdings. David wanted Kennedy to proclaim a shift in foreign-aid policy toward private entrepreneurs, both American and allied local investors, on the grounds that private enterprise per se was the basis of political freedom" (Colby and Dennett 1995, 665).

Given the progressive nature of the Kennedy policies, it should be evident why the various private power constituencies—predominantly represented by US businessmen, bankers, and the IMF—remained stubbornly resistant, recalcitrant, and unimpressed. John and Robert Kennedy had actively sought to bring about a peaceful revolution on behalf of the oppressed, excluded, and disenfranchised within the United States and internationally. In these efforts, both men gave practical expression to FDR's approach to Latin America, as boldly enunciated and practiced under his Good Neighbor Policy. During the entire three-year span of the New Frontier, it was clear that the Kennedy brothers had sought to launch a policy toward all of Latin America that reflected a major ideological and policy shift—a change that would reflect a purposeful discarding of old economic dogmas, theories, and categories.

In 1961, this new Kennedy-inspired approach and philosophy would come to mean that "development was not any more a purely economic matter—of more capital investments, of slightly improved price and credit policies, of more efficient marketing channels or better farm management—but a function of fundamental changes in basic institutions. Economic growth had to be preceded, not only accompanied, by social reforms as the new basis for an economic growth take-off" (Feder 1970, 206). The political agenda of JFK and RFK would appear to be nothing short of radical in the eyes of domestic financial elites from Wall Street to the US Chamber of Commerce. Other elements of this elite-backed financial web of opposition and hostility to the Kennedy brothers would come to include the International Monetary Fund (IMF), the World Bank, and Rockefeller and J. P. Morgan banking interests—all of which seemed to view the Kennedys' approach to a peaceful revolution in Latin America as nothing less than treason. At the very least, it was treason with regard to this elite's particular interpretation of the capitalist edict and the financial norms that they had created to make the system work for them in pursuit of their own best interests. According to one leading scholar on the subject: "The Charter dogma clashed almost at once with US business which looked at land reform of any shape or kind as a threat to US interests and investments abroad as subversive" (Feder 1970, 208).

From the establishment's vantage point, their opposition to the Alliance for Progress was essential to their survival as well as the survival of the system they served. All of this was threatened by JFK and RFK. Evidence of the establishment's fear is abundant in the history of the early 1960s. A review of establishment publications reveals that:

> Early in 1962 the editors of *Fortune* expressed their concern that the Alliance for Progress and other Kennedy administration programs were being heavily influenced by the doctrine of the Economic Commission for Latin America, a group established in 1947 under United Nations auspices. *Fortune* charged that this doctrine favored *dirigisme*, that is, a type of economic nationalism which included economic planning to achieve rapid growth. . . . *Fortune* wanted Latin nations to pursue a conservative economic policy focused not on internal development and improving the standard of living, but on fulfilling the traditional role within colonial and neo-colonial relations of exporting wealth and allowing foreign domination of their economies. This was precisely the policy that Kennedy had repeatedly rejected. (Gibson 1994, 59)

This was the central point of contention. The Kennedys wanted an end to colonial and neocolonial practices, while the Rockefellers and their allies wanted nothing less than a continuation of these very same policies that had served them and their profit-making ventures in the Third World so well for so long. Hence, the question to be resolved was: *Would the United States continue to participate in a continuation of colonial and neo-colonial relationships with the Third World or not?* Even after both John and Robert Kennedy were assassinated, this debate resurfaced in the Nixon administration.

In the early 1970s, the US Senate authorized the Church Committee to investigate CIA abuses. The Church Committee released its findings in a report entitled, *Alleged Assassination Plots Involving Foreign Leaders*. At the time, the report represented the most comprehensive documentation of the dark side of US foreign policy operations ever published. A large part of the focus was on the Nixon/Kissinger/CIA/ITT corporate connections to the overthrow of Chilean democracy. The removal of Chile's democratically elected socialist president, Salvador Allende, was viewed as necessary by affected business interests in Chile, including International Telephone and Telegraph (ITT), not to mention the economists at the University of Chicago led by Milton Friedman, who were euphemistically dubbed the "Chicago boys" because of their excitement over the possibility of making Chile a financial laboratory to experiment with their neoliberal economic model of privatization, deregulation, and labor-union busting, thus spurring their Rockefeller-like version of economic growth.

Both the CIA and the foreign policy team within the Nixon administration came together to agree on a strategy that would undermine the democratic socialist government of Allende and replace it with a US-sanctioned and developed economic model of neoliberal governance (Dallek 2007, 227–242). Though the experiment of Allende's government with democratic-socialism might benefit the poor, labor, and the excluded classes of Chile, it was, in the final analysis, fundamentally "not good for US business interests." Therefore, the Nixon administration decided to comply with domestic US business interests and their agenda by setting into motion a series of covert operations and overt financial moves designed to, in both Nixon's and Kissinger's words, "make the Chilean economy scream" (Colby and Dennett 1995, 664).

Following this strategy, the US government became complicit in destabilizing Allende's tenuous base of political support. The roots of this decision lay with Nelson Rockefeller and his former advisor, Henry Kissinger. The history of the era reveals that "Nelson, as a member of the Nixon Foreign Intelligence Advisory Board, was aware of the anti-Allende policy in the Nixon White House. The National Security Council's Special Group (called the 40 committee during the Nixon administration) was chaired by Kissinger . . . '*I don't see why we need to stand by and watch a country go Communist due to the irresponsibility of its own people,*' Kissinger told a June 1970 meeting of the Special Group" (Colby and Dennett 1995, 664, italics added).

If Robert Kennedy had only lived to become president, then neither Nixon nor Kissinger would ever have made it to the White House, or been empowered to issue these kinds of statements. Had Robert Kennedy attained the presidency, it seems evident from this historical record that his respect for democratic elections, as well as his fidelity to the cause of human rights, would have been instrumental in the task of rerouting and redefining the traditional responses of US national security structure, as well as official US foreign policy, from one of interventionism to global cooperation with peoples and movements seeking social justice. Such a move would have eventually resulted in the formal recognition of the value and preeminence of human rights, as exemplified in Kennedy's speech to the Canadian Press in Toronto, Canada, on April 14, 1964:

> **We must recognize that the young in many areas of the world today are in the midst of a revolution against the status quo. They are not going to accept platitudes and generalities. Their anger has been turned on the systems which have allowed poverty, illiteracy and oppression to flourish for centuries. And we must recognize one simple fact: they will prevail. They will achieve their idealistic goals one way or the other. If they have to pull governments tumbling down over their heads, they will do it. But they are going to win their share of a better and cleaner world.** (Ross 1968, 425, bold added)

Robert Kennedy's words still ring out as prophetic and prescient in the first decades of the twenty-first century, as the "Arab Spring" or "Arab Awakening" in early 2011 served to demonstrate. Throughout North Africa and the Middle East, dictators and autocrats would soon come tumbling down in Egypt, Libya, and Tunisia. Similarly, Robert Kennedy's words still ring out as prophetic and prescient in the aftermath of the revolutions that took place in the Eastern Europe of the late 1980s and early 1990s, as East Germany, Poland, and the Baltic nations—Estonia, Latvia, and Lithuania—declared their independence from the Soviet Union. And similarly, Robert Kennedy's words still ring out as prophetic and prescient in the aftermath of the Bush II administration, as Latin American nations liberated themselves from the International Monetary Fund (IMF) and, at the same time, left-leaning social movements placed progressive leaders into elected office from Venezuela to Bolivia, from Brazil to Ecuador, from Peru to Argentina (Ali, 2006; Petras and Veltmeyer 2009; Petras 2003; Petras and Veltmeyer 2005; Petras and Veltmeyer 2007; Robinson 2008; Hart 2002).

These progressive developments within Latin America stand in sharp contrast to imperial policies of the administration of George W. Bush. In the aftermath of the September 11, 2001, attack on New York's World Trade Center, the foreign policy apparatus in Washington adopted what James Petras and Henry Veltmeyer have called "retro-colonialism." In this model, the attempt to promote the same old hegemonic strategies of the American Empire involved a combination of repressive and regressive policies, among which it is possible to identify "retro-colonialism and its corollary of military-based empire building, subsidizing economic policy and occupation of geo-strategic territories," and which all reflect "the framework for understanding the key features of the period after September 11, 2001" (Petras and Veltmeyer 2003, 61). Yet the policies of retrenchment, retro-colonialism, and geostrategic plans for maintaining US hegemony have continued to meet with fierce resistance from a majority of social movements across the Global South. Instead of capitulating to the threat of US military forces, we find an increasing number of what I have called "counter-hegemonic alliances" throughout the multicentric regions of the Global South, from Latin America to Africa, from the Middle East to Asia (Paupp 2007; Paupp 2009).

Furthermore, a leftist alternative to the "Washington Consensus" of the late 1980s and early 1990s has emerged through the anti-globalization efforts and dialogues initiated through the World Social Forum (Starr 2005). Under the banner of a bold and ambitious slogan declaring that "Another World Is Possible," the World Social Forum has gathered under its umbrella a renewed set of calls for fair trade, boycotts, and a return to local markets in the face of corporate offensives launched by multinational capital. In so doing, the people of Latin America are engaged in the task of reinventing and remaking democracy for themselves (Starr 2005). The World Social Forum has effectively contributed to the global struggle of many social movements, from many different regions and nations, via the task of formulating strategies and policies capable of resisting any further intrusion of neoliberal experiments at the expense of the majority of the people. In short, since its inception in Porto Alegre in 2001, the World Social Forum has provided a platform that facilities cooperation between diverse social movements (de Sousa Santos 2005).

In significant measure, these trends and efforts represent the spirit of Robert Kennedy and his legacy of revolutionary change that he advocated. While Robert Kennedy emerged out of a corporate/capitalist system, it would be inaccurate to simplistically claim that he was a product of the capitalist system. Rather, Kennedy had always, throughout his entire public career, actively opposed capitalism's worst abuses and the way in which it was employed by the leading US establishment elites, corporate interests, and an ideology of profit before people. His approach was evident in the way he dealt with the prosecution of Jimmy Hoffa, who had allowed organized crime to infiltrate the Teamsters Union, and in his battles with David and Nelson Rockefeller over the treatment of migrant workers, the Vietnam War, and US policy in Latin America. Therefore, in this critical respect, without committing the error of being counterfactual, I am arguing that Kennedy would share in endorsing the modern critique of the current version of global capitalism that has been offered by Boaventura de Sousa Santos. Santos, a member of the World Social Forum and a leading professor of sociology at the University of Coimbra, Portugal, who has noted:

> *Although neo-liberal globalization—the current version of global capitalism—is by far the dominant form of globalization, it is not the only one. Parallel to it and, to a great extent, as a reaction to it, another globalization is emerging.* It consists of transnational networks and alliances among social movements, social struggles, and non-governmental organizations. From the four corners of the globe, all these initiatives have mobilized to fight against the social exclusion, destruction of the environment and biodiversity, unemployment, human rights violations, pandemics, and inter-ethnic hatreds, directly or indirectly caused by neo-liberal globalization. (de Sousa Santos 2005, xvii, italics added)

These global trends of the late twentieth and early twenty-first century serve to reveal the importance and ongoing significance of Robert Kennedy's progressive views on social reform and revolution. These trends also stand as a glaring indictment of the policies pursued by Nixon and Kissinger in continuing the war in Vietnam, as well as in their complicity in attempting to reverse the trends toward social change in Chile during the early 1970s. In the aftermath of Allende's overthrow by a US-backed Chilean military junta on September 11, 1973, led by General Augusto Pinochet, the entire Chilean nation was placed under martial law. The ensuing government-sanctioned assassinations of the junta's domestic political opponents, human rights abuses, unconstitutional governmental practices, and draconian police-state tactics employed by the junta would shake the conscience of the world. Those progressive forces and voices around the world who had placed faith in the Alliance for Progress and social reform emphasis in the policies of John and Robert Kennedy were horrified to discover and to witness the mounting evidence of US complicity in what can only be described as crimes against humanity after the 1973 coup. Peter Kornbluh, director of the National Security Archive's Chile Documentation Project, noted that "Pinochet's atrocities, with Washington's ongoing assistance, mobilized church and solidarity groups who transformed human rights into a movement, and a potent political issue on Capitol Hill. The '*Chile Syndrome*'—supplementing the Vietnam Syndrome of national reticence to US military intervention in distant lands—reflected growing public demand that US foreign policy return to the moral precepts of American society" (Kornbluh 2003, 222–223, italics added). It was as if Robert Kennedy's 1968 call for no more Vietnams had come back to life in the early 1970s.

Predictably, Henry Kissinger would complain in his memoirs that "the issue [of Chile] arose in America at the worst possible time." In Kissinger's imperial view, "in the aftermath of Vietnam and during Watergate, the idea that we had to earn the right to conduct foreign policy by moral purity—that we could prevail through righteousness rather than power—had an inevitable attraction" (Kornbluh 2003, 223). Yet, as Kornbluh notes, "in spite of Kissinger's objections—indeed, because of them—Chile became the battleground for the first major fight between the executive branch and Congress over human rights and US foreign policy. Between 1974 and 1976, Congress passed a wave of precedent-setting human rights legislation in an effort to directly or indirectly block the Ford administration's support for Pinochet—laws that institutionalized human rights as a component of US bilateral relations with other nations" (Kornbluh 2003, 223).

This record of legislative achievement in the field of human rights can, in many ways, be directly related to the legacy and human-rights commitments of Robert Kennedy. Evidence for this assertion can be found in all of the efforts of Robert's brother, Senator Edward Kennedy (aka Teddy), to curtail both economic and military assistance to Chile. Commenting on this precise point, Kornbluh reviewed Edward Kennedy's record, noting: "Senator Kennedy must be credited with being the most outspoken congressional critic of Pinochet and US assistance to his regime. Soon after the coup, Kennedy condemned the '*continued silence of the government of the United States which has not issued a single public expression of remorse over the military coup which toppled a democratically elected government, or over the deaths, beatings, brutality, and repression which have occurred* in that land' (Kornbluh 2003, 224, italics added). Following this initial statement, the record also demonstrates a sustained effort by the Senator:

> Kennedy convened the first Senate hearings on Chile only seventeen days after the coup took place. On October 2, 1973, he offered a *"sense of Congress"* resolution urging the president to *"deny economic or military assistance, other than humanitarian aid, until he finds that the government of Chile is protecting the human rights of all individuals, Chilean and foreign."* In December 1974, Kennedy successfully obtained a $25 million cap on economic aid to Chile in the foreign assistance appropriations bill, which the Ford administration simply ignored; at the same time, Kennedy also sponsored the first limits on US military aid and training to the Chilean junta. In July 1976, Congress passed the far more comprehensive Kennedy amendment, banning all military assistance, credits, and cash sales of weapons to Chile—marking the first time Congress has terminated military aid to another government because of human rights abuses. (Kornbluh 2003, 223–224, italics added)

In reviewing the Kennedy legacy in the stream of history, there are many notable milestones in its evolution and progress. Starting with John F. Kennedy's inauguration in January 1961, the president made numerous references to Latin America and the need for social progress. Only three months later, the Alliance for Progress was officially launched by the Kennedy administration. After the president's death, Robert Kennedy took it upon himself to explain the purpose of the Alliance and the Charter, making it clear that the Charter contained policies, intentions, and hopes for expanding human rights and socioeconomic justice for all peoples throughout the Americas. In the aftermath of Robert's assassination, Senator Edward Kennedy took up the cause, reflected in his human-rights legislative work after the 1973 coup in Chile. This is the enduring significance of the Kennedy legacy. What is reflected in the work of all three of the Kennedy brothers is a fearless commitment to social change that transcended the zeitgeist of the businessmen of corporate America, who cared little or nothing about human rights. In the case of Robert Kennedy, in particular, we see ever-present in his thoughts and speeches a spirit of openness to other economic and political experiments in a world of diversity.

In many ways, there was much that Robert would have appreciated about Chile's experiment with democratic socialism, given his non-intervention philosophy as expressed in his "no more Vietnams" speech. Hence, it is highly unlikely that Kennedy would have pursued the path taken by Nixon and Kissinger.

In assessing the historical validity of this claim, consider historian Peter Winn's comments on the Allende legacy:

> Although Allende's road to socialism was controversial and generated severe economic dislocations, social tensions, and political polarization, his term in office in many ways represented the apex of democracy in Chile. Under Allende, illiterates and eighteen-year-olds received the right to vote and the entire population was mobilized by the Popular Unity and its opponents. Grassroots participatory democracy was promoted in residential neighborhoods, and economic democracy—although imperfect—was created in Chile's larger workplaces through worker co-management and in rural cooperatives that replaced the great landed estates of the past. Although the press and other mass media were partisan and polemical, all political views were represented. Allende's Chile was striking for its political pluralism and both representative and direct democracy. The contrast between Allende's and Pinochet's Chile could not be greater. (Winn 2004, 19; *See also:* Huneeus 2007; Roht-Arriaza 2005; Ensalaco 2000)

Interestingly enough, the same things could be said about the profound and fundamental differences between the America of John and Robert Kennedy as opposed to the America of Nixon, Ford, Reagan, and Bush I and II. For both John and Robert Kennedy, it can be said that their political orientation and worldview was derived from many different sources. Among these sources, the Kennedys found inspiration in the New Deal years. The political and moral leadership of Franklin Roosevelt was a philosophical and practical starting point for what would eventually become the "New Frontier," as well as the inspiration for Robert Kennedy's 1968 quest for the presidency. Hence, in this regard, the sources for their thinking were multifaceted, but all of these sources and tributaries converged within a particular moment in the stream of history.

12

The Legacy of FDR and his "Second Bill of Rights"

On January 11, 1944, President Franklin D. Roosevelt proposed a "Second Bill of Rights." In it, he declared that every American is entitled to:

1. The right to a useful and remunerative job in the industries or shops or farms or mines of the nation;
2. The right to earn enough to provide adequate food and clothing and recreation;
3. The right of every farmer to raise and sell his products at a return which will give him and his family a decent living;
4. The right of every businessman, large and small, to trade in an atmosphere of freedom from unfair competition and domination by monopolies at home or abroad;
5. The right of every family to a decent home;
6. The right to adequate medical care and the opportunity to achieve and enjoy good health;
7. The right to adequate protection from the economic fears of old age, sickness, accident, and unemployment;
8. The right to a good education. (Sunstein 2004)

In combination, these provisions were not to be seen as mere privileges, but as rights to which every person is entitled as a citizen. These provisions also presented an altered conception of governance and the role of the state towards its citizens. The entire concept of the state underwent dramatic transformations in the New Deal era, largely reflecting the philosophy and new priorities being injected into the culture, party system, and policy practices and preferences of Franklin Roosevelt. Professor William Leuchtenburg, in commenting on this transformative era and its enduring legacy, notes: "The Great Depression and the New Deal brought about a significant realignment of the sort that occurs only rarely in party history in America. The Depression wrenched many lifelong Republican voters from their moorings . . . No less important was the shift in the character of the Democratic party from the conservative organization of John W. Davis and John Raskob to the country's main political agency for reform . . . The New Deal transformed the nature of American politics by drastically altering the agenda" (Leuchtenburg 1995, 274–275). The concept of a democratic state and the nature of democratic governance would undergo a radical transformation in the FDR years of a Great Depression, a New Deal and a world war. In this one basic respect, Roosevelt had "altered the fundamental concept and its obligations to the governed," in the words of historian Isaiah Berlin, by initiating "a tradition of positive action" (Borgwardt 2008, 35).

This new and transformative perspective had arisen out of a new historical consciousness that was born of the Second World War. With victory assured, Roosevelt was preoccupied with one ultimate question: *What would be the nature of the peace?* Just as the war had been a shared international endeavor, with the United States acting as just one participant among many, now, with peace on the horizon, the question had become what kind of world order could emerge after victory. From Roosevelt's vantage point, the answer was to be found in making a connection between the war that had just been won against fascism, on the one hand, with building a new national and global effort to combat poverty, economic distress, and uncertainty on the other. Therefore, in his innovative and bold speech of January 11, 1944, Roosevelt concluded that "the one supreme objective for the future," the objective for all nations, was captured "in one word: Security." In commenting on this linkage, law professor Cass Sunstein, quoting Roosevelt, has noted:

> Roosevelt argued that the term "*means not only physical security which provides safety from attacks by aggressors*," but includes "*economic security, social security, moral security.*" All of the allies were concerned with not merely the defeat of fascism but also improved education, better opportunities, and improved living standards. Roosevelt insisted that "*essential to peace is a decent standard of living for all individual men and women and children in all nations. Freedom from fear is eternally linked with freedom from want.*" In connecting the two freedoms, he argued first and foremost that "*America could be free from fear only if the citizens of 'all nations' were free from want.*" (Sunstein, 2004, 11, italics added)

In other words, once the war was won, it was going to be essential to move ahead with the implementation of these rights. Hence, he believed it was inevitable that there was "a close connection between this implementation and the coming international order" (Sunstein, 2004, 13). Roosevelt's articulation of this vision had begun almost a full four years earlier, but now it had matured into "the foundation of a Global New Deal," which implied a reciprocal relationship between state and citizen. In this Global New Deal, the state would be obliged, in the words of historian Robert Westbrook, "to provide and protect a minimal level of subsistence for the individuals who comprise it" (Borgwardt 2008, 34).

In Roosevelt's famous "Four Freedoms" address of 1941, he focused on the evolution of and transformation of the content of the phrase *"freedom from fear and want."* Roosevelt had mentioned an earlier version of the idea of a list of freedoms in a press conference on June 5, 1940, as a response to a question about how he might "write the next peace" (Roosevelt 1972, 498). Roosevelt's "Four Freedoms" speech file also contained a December 1940 clipping from the *New York Post*, quoting the joint proposals offered by Protestant and Catholic leaders in Britain and advocating:

1. That extreme inequalities of wealth be abolished,
2. Full education for all children, regardless of class or race,
3. Protection for the family,
4. Restoration of a sense of divine vocation to daily work, and
5. Use of all the resources of the earth for the benefit of the whole human race. (Borgwardt 2008, 36)

Of these trends in the early 1940s, historian Elizabeth Borgwardt has observed: "These debates in Britain were part of a transatlantic surge of interest in the relationship of domestic social welfare provisions—individual security—to wider war and peace aims—international security" (Borgwardt 2008, 36). In the transatlantic dialogue of the period, between 1941–1942, the so-called "Beveridge Report" was produced in Britain. The report addressed itself to a consideration of the economic contours of the postwar world with its primary purpose being "designed to abolish physical want." It was instrumental in helping Roosevelt to rethink the relationship between individual security and international security. According to Borgwardt, it is evident from the American press coverage of the time that:

> [The Beveridge Report was seen as] a British "blueprint for postwar New Deal," which would stand as "the first attempt to translate the four freedoms into fact" by giving life to "at least one of the rights

> specified in the Atlantic Charter—the right to live without hunger or destitution." This use denotes a definite shift in the way Americans were deploying the phrase "freedom from want" from FDR's earlier articulation two years earlier, regarding the "fear of not being able to have normal economic and social relations with other nations." Linking individual security to international security was becoming a fresh way of framing US national interests. (Borgwardt 2008, 36–37)

These shifts in thinking about politics, international relations, and human rights were destined to emerge again in the early 1960s in many of the speeches given by both John Kennedy and Robert Kennedy. There were a number of reasons for this to happen. Among them was the fact that untrammeled individualism as a social norm was not viewed as a sustainable social ethic by either FDR or the Kennedy brothers. Further, emerging out of the 1940s was the work of four so-called "conscience liberals" who made major contributions to the United Nation's Universal Declaration of Human Rights in 1948: China's Peng-chung Chang, Lebanon's Charles Malik, Panama's Ricardo Alfaro, and France's Jacque Maritain. What made them so influential in their own time, and in the thinking of the Kennedy brothers, was the fact that "all four theorized 'security' in ways that included an important role for community, duty, and social bonds" (Borgwardt 2008, 37). This intellectual linkage was evident in the signature line of JFK's inaugural address: "Ask not what your country can do for you, ask what you can do for your country." Similarly, the theme resonated in all of RFK's speeches about the need to restore the bonds of community, of brotherhood despite racial differences, and of human purpose in a communitarian bond.

Underlying all of these rights was a strong and indelible notion that the fulfillment of human rights is the bedrock of social justice. From this premise, the 1948 Universal Declaration of Human Rights sparked an ongoing debate over the obligation of governments to ensure the welfare of individuals by protecting not only their civil and political rights, but their social and economic rights as well. This was a driving force in remaking political philosophy and social policies in the 1940s. It was a force that would resurface and reverberate through the Kennedy years and well beyond—on into the twenty-first century. This is the great insight and theme that connects the legacy of FDR with the legacy of Robert Kennedy. Building on the idea that social and economic rights could never really be divorced from the recognition of civil and political rights was central to Robert's political program and philosophy. In this effort, Robert came into conflict with right wing and conservative movements when he made moral and political claims with respect to the inherent rights of the poor and dispossessed in a healthy democracy. The record shows that Robert came into political conflict with these groups because of the ideological orientation of right wing and conservative movements that habitually saw the articulation of the rights to health, work, housing, education, and employment as conflicting with the efficient workings of a market economy.

Despite these assaults on socioeconomic rights, the fact remains that since the 1930s, if not before, America's top leaders had persistently supported and promoted a human-rights agenda that included social and economic rights. Tragically, despite this long history of support for socioeconomic rights, we discover in twentieth century American history that the final direction of the struggle was largely shaped by those social forces that placed profits before people (Farnsworth 2004; Fuchs 2007; Selznick 1992; Brinkley 1995; O'Connor 1984). Robert Kennedy was the last major national political figure to oppose this direction. Rather, Robert consistently sought to bring about a vision of the American economy that was inclusive, justice-oriented, and less focused on the market as the final arbiter of public policy. For example, Kennedy's initiative for Bedford-Stuyvesant was centered upon the creation of actual socioeconomic justice for the poor, jobs, employment and decent housing as the central priorities for the nation. Hence, Robert Kennedy wanted to make markets accountable to all of the people—not make people accountable to the markets. This is precisely what Robert Kennedy undertook to do. He worked to develop an alternative vision of how government itself, working with average citizens and private enterprise, could forge new bonds of civic cooperation that could enable the American people to rediscover a communitarian bond with one another, reform their civil society, and make government and business more accountable to the democratic aspirations of the people as a whole—principles now common to the social democracies throughout the European Union.

RFK dedicated much of his senate career and presidential campaign to setting forth proposals, new approaches, and policies to remake a failing welfare state, to deal more effectively with the enduring problems posed by poverty, and to create a more inclusive democratic union by overcoming the problems posed by seemingly implacable divides—whether they be class, racial, and/or socioeconomic divides. As always, it was clear that Kennedy remained preoccupied with the suffering of the most vulnerable within American society: the children, the excluded, and the dispossessed. In this undertaking, Kennedy confronted great obstacles. For example, in the summer of 1967, Congress did move to revise the Aid to Dependent Children Program (ADC), but hardly along the lines that Kennedy had suggested. The Congressional version proposed that all mothers receiving assistance be compelled to accept jobs and leave preschool-age children in public nurseries, and that states be given incentives to take custody of illegitimate children. Testifying before the Senate Finance Committee against these proposals, on August 29, 1967, Robert Kennedy declared:

> *The objective of enabling welfare recipients to obtain productive employment is of course laudable; indeed, as I have indicated, I believe it is the only hope we have for avoiding deep division in our society which the creation of a permanent class of welfare poor would bring. But attempting to bring about employment by compulsion is not the way to do this.* There are many mothers who should not work. Some, particularly in progressive states and cities, will be excused from working. But in other states with less enlightened welfare programs, many will either be driven off the welfare rolls or will be discouraged from applying, and *they will still be poor*—a little more invisible, for the time being, than they are now, but no less poor, no less miserable . . . the provision giving states an incentive to provide custodial care for illegitimate children is also punitive. Once an illegitimate child is born—although we may have wished to discourage that from happening—his best hope is to grow up in some kind of family structure. (Ross 1968, 160, italics added)

Kennedy was angered to discover that laws and policies were designed to blame the victim for their own victimization:

> Study after study shows that the worst thing that could be done is to consign him to an institution. So we punish illegitimacy by punishing the illegitimate child . . . In the meantime, also we must not continue to place a premium on broken homes as the condition for obtaining public assistance. And we must not end up by venting our own frustration in a measure punishing the poor because they are there and we have not been able to do anything about them . . . *It is not as though people choose to be poor, to need welfare assistance . . .* We cannot afford to bury our heads in the sand. Our nation has been ripped apart this summer by violence and civil disorder that have taken dozens of lives and caused billions of dollars of property damage. *We face in our cities the gravest domestic crisis to confront this nation since the Civil War. We are not going to solve that crisis by forcing welfare recipients to accept training for jobs when we have absolutely no idea whether jobs will be available to them after their*

> *training. We are not going to solve that crisis by punishing the poor and hoping that they will bear that punishment silently, invisibly, graciously, without bitterness or hostility for their "benefactors."* (Ross 1968, 169–170, italics added)

Commenting upon this tortured history, from domestic politics to international relations, Noam Chomsky has observed:

> Throughout the reconstruction of the industrial societies, the prime concern was to establish a state capitalist order under the traditional elites, within the global framework of US power, which would guarantee the ability to exploit the various regions that were to fulfill their functions as markets and sources of raw materials. If these goals could be achieved, then the system would be stable and resistant to feared social change, which would naturally be disruptive once the system is operating in a relatively orderly fashion. In the wealthy industrial centers, large segments of the population would be accommodated, and would be led to abandon any more radical vision under a rational cost-benefit analysis. (Chomsky 1991, 348)

This pattern of co-optation was clearly evident more than a decade before the appearance of the Universal Declaration of Human Rights. The earliest drafts of the 1935 Social Security Act (SSA)—which laid the foundation for the US welfare state—expressly included provisions for comprehensive health, social insurance, and work programs. However, "a highly truncated version emerged following the long and contentious battle between advocates of social and economic rights and powerful business groups whose interests were threatened by the prospect of fulfilling human rights" (Abramovitz 2011, 47) By the time of FDR's death, the powerful business groups were well on their way toward a retrenchment of their power and influence.

Reflecting upon the revenge of corporate, banking, and financial interests, as well as the capitulation of the liberals in the Democratic party, historian Alan Brinkley has noted:

> *By 1945, American liberals, as the result of countless small adaptations to a broad range of experience, had reached an accommodation with modern capitalism that served, in effect, to settle many of the most divisive conflicts of the first decades of the century.* They had done so by convincing themselves that the achievements of the New Deal had already eliminated the most dangerous features of the corporate capitalist system; by committing themselves to the belief that economic growth was the surest route to social progress and that consumption, more than production, was the surest route to economic growth; and

> by defining a role for the state that would, they believed, permit it to compensate for capitalism's inevitable flaws and omissions without interfering very much with its internal workings. *They had, in effect, detached liberalism from its earlier emphasis on reform—its preoccupation with issues of class, its tendency to equate freedom and democracy with economic autonomy, its hostility to concentrated economic power.* They had redefined citizenship to de-emphasize the role of men and women as producers and to elevate their roles as consumers. (Brinkley 1995, 269, italics added)

All of these accommodations were viewed by Robert Kennedy with contempt. That helps to explain, in large measure, why RFK had no patience with most liberals and consistently rejected most of these liberal assumptions in his speeches. RFK believed that liberals' accommodation of the abuses of a capitalistic-corporate culture had sacrificed community and the bonds of trust that cement people, and had eviscerated the value of work, employment, and jobs by not providing millions of Americans with a living wage. This was especially true for minorities, women, and poor whites.

By the time of John F. Kennedy's inauguration in 1961, the New Deal order was beginning to crack under the strains of racism and Jim Crow laws that had emerged after the first Reconstruction. These problems had not been adequately addressed under the New Deal, and in some ways had been made worse through bureaucratic racism and ineptitude (Gerstle 2001; Massey and Denton 1993; Lieberman 1998; Katz 1993; Satter 2009; Fairclough 2001; Rich 1993). In addition to and concurrent with these domestic upheavals, the new administration of the Kennedy brothers had to deal with both the growing moral force of a domestic civil rights movement and the disintegration of the remnants of Europe's nineteenth century imperial international order. Both colonialism and imperialism were falling apart under the strain of anti-imperialist and nationalist social movements as the nations of the Third World demanded decolonization, independence from the imperial powers of Europe, and the formal acknowledgment and enjoyment of their legal rights under the international law principles of sovereignty, self-determination, and formal independence.

It was into this national and global setting that the Kennedy brothers came to power. They arrived with an agenda to address the civil rights claims of African Americans and to redress the wrongs of the past with a domestic program that would become the nation's Second Reconstruction. In this respect, the administration of JFK would begin to take on the complexities of domestic and foreign policy under the rubric of the Cold War and in conjunction with emerging claims of civil and human rights from the Third World. It became evident to the Kennedy brothers that a domestic civil-rights revolution had to be undertaken in conjunction with a revolution in US foreign policy. Put simply, events at home and abroad had conspired in such a way that they started to converge under the banners of revolution, rights, and human dignity. It was a time to rethink, reformulate, and readdress the ways in which governmental and social policies could augment and support the collective drive for principled change.

In responding to this challenge with intelligence and moral conscience, both JFK and RFK would have to call upon "the better angels" of human nature. Yet the Kennedy brothers were building on the legacy of FDR in making their claims, setting forth new policies, and seeking to advance—at home and abroad—the cause of human rights. In this regard:

> ***The human rights ideas embedded in the Four Freedoms and the Atlantic Charter—as well as in the 1942 Declaration of the United Nations, the document which further internationalized the Charter—had reshaped the concept of the national interest by injecting an explicitly moral calculus. While the international initiatives infused with moralistic ideas were hardly a new development, now mobilized and mainstream constituencies were arguably paying attention and reacting in a way they had not before. These vocal constituencies were quick to shout about "the betrayal of the Atlantic Charter" when confronted with the cold realities of US policies that ignored British colonialism, strengthened status quo ideologies such as national sovereignty, or facilitated racial segregation and repression.*** (Borgwardt 2008, 43–44, italics and bold added)

For the Kennedy brothers, building on FDR's legacy and expanding its moral claims in the decade of the 1960s would require courage and the ability to employ their consummate skills as politicians and leaders in the midst of Cold War hysteria. In this task, both John and Robert Kennedy confronted a domestic and global challenge that would have to be morally, legally, economically, and politically addressed in such a way that, in the context of a US foreign policy, the United States could somehow find a path that would incorporate Third World claims, aspirations, and demands into its calculus (Fredrickson 1997). As far as the Kennedy brothers were concerned, what was now required for taking the next progressive step toward realizing a true and genuinely democratic political order was a new concept of the "national interest"—a more inclusive national interest that would serve to solidify FDR's legacy and political order, wherein progressive liberals, in alliance with mass movements (notably labor), would work with the national/federal government in order to effectuate a more inclusive and just society for all. This was the democratic order that emerged out of the 1930 and 1940s.

The FDR legacy, as the Kennedys understood it, had brought together both democratic and modernizing themes within the framework of a new brand of progressive liberalism that advocated governmental action to achieve economic stability, protect social security, and expand political representation. Far from being nonideological, the democratic order—as defined by FDR—saw the dynamics of political transformation in terms of sharp conflicts with forces to its right and left. However, by the early 1960s, if their agenda was to be realized, effective, and transformative, the Kennedy brothers knew that new networks of domestic power that had emerged since the end of World War II would have to be dealt with. Hence, armed with this understanding of the political context in which they lived, we find that John and Robert Kennedy began to undertake efforts that could begin the process of dismantling the corporate, banking, military, and financial grip that the US government and national security structure had allowed the nation to abide in without democratic accountability or transparency since the late 1940s. In this sense, as far as the Kennedy brothers were concerned, FDR's political legacy was about to be advanced and matured in the stream of history as it traversed the decade of the 1960s.

Tragically, this promised advance was short-lived. The assassination of John F. Kennedy abruptly brought this progressive direction to an end. Commenting upon this point, Professor David Plotke noted:

> In 1962 and 1963 reform efforts were presented as an extension of prior democratic commitments, and the administration had sufficient resources to begin . . . New official attention to poverty underlined the administration's links with the New Deal legacy of state-based reform . . . The title of Michael Harrington's book, *The Other America: Poverty in the United States,* signals the distance traveled from the 1930s, when poverty engulfed entire social groups and threatened much of the country. The grim course of events enhanced reform prospects in the short term, as Kennedy's assassination was interpreted as not only the brutal end of an individual's life but as a violation of a democratic national commitment to a new course of reform. Thus, remembering and honoring Kennedy meant pursuing his reform

> efforts, even supporting measures more ambitious than those his administration had supported. (Plotke 1996, 352–353)

After his brother's assassination, Robert Kennedy was on his own. He would become the nation's most influential and pivotal voice for proposing more ambitious measures than those of John Kennedy's New Frontier or Johnson's Great Society. It is an often neglected historical fact that "It was Johnson who declared war on poverty, but he did so looking over his shoulder at Kennedy, and Kennedy, not Johnson, was the political sponsor of the war's main strategies" (Lemann, 1988, 39). In this undertaking, Robert believed that a progressive political order still had a chance to be renewed, and this was the message of his senate years and his presidential campaign. The promise of such a renewal was ended when his life was ended by an assassin in 1968. Hence, the high-noon of progressive political reform that began in the 1930s and 1940s had reached its apex in the 1960s. Robert Kennedy was attempting to guide it into a new reform phase as the old Roosevelt coalition began to crumble and dissipate (Branch 2006). Kennedy was the last American politician of sufficient stature and influence to even try to build a new progressive governing coalition.

By 1969, the rise of Richard Nixon marked the ascendancy of a new conservative alliance that would eviscerate and eventually shred the coalition that Robert had been attempting to build. In its place, neoconservatives hijacked social reform and turned it into a crusade to dismantle both the welfare state and the social safety nets that went with it. The social contract of the New Deal and New Frontier would be replaced by the 1980s with a corporate-friendly, anti-welfare state ideology under the auspices of emerging neoconservatives. Ronald Reagan would join forces with Britain's Margaret Thatcher to turn the ideology of laissez-faire capitalism into the mantra of privatization, deregulation, and tax cuts for the super-wealthy classes and the corporate interests of their respective nations. By the 1990s, Bill Clinton would join forces with Britain's Tony Blair to announce that a corporate-friendly neoliberalism had arrived on the political and economic scene that would surrender the "commanding heights" of governance from the hands of the state, and leave most major governing decisions about the direction of the economy to the largely unfettered and unregulated marketplace. As Daniel Yergin and Joseph Stanislaw astutely noted in their book, *The Commanding Heights: The Battle Between Government and the Marketplace That Is Remaking the Modern World*, the situation for almost a century has been one that has never reached a final or consummate resolution. They note: "*Where the frontier between state and market is to be drawn has never been a matter that could be settled, once and for all, at some grand peace conference. Instead, it has been the subject, over the course of this century, of massive intellectual and political battles as well as constant skirmishes. In its entirety, the struggle constitutes one of the great defining battles of the twentieth century. Today the clash is so far-reaching and so encompassing that it is remaking our world—and preparing the canvas for the twenty-first century*" (Yergin and Stanislaw 1999, 11, italics added).

Now, at the close of the first decade of the twenty-first century, there is little immediate hope that the legacy of Robert Kennedy can be revived. This is not to say that Robert Kennedy's legacy does not have application and relevance in the current circumstances. On the contrary, it does. However, the caveat is that unless public anger over the financial crimes of Wall Street and citizen frustration with the lobbyist-driven corruption of Washington result in widespread calls for an end to the unconstitutional practices of the military-industrial complex and those responsible can finally be criminally prosecuted, politically regulated, and made accountable, there is little hope. In short, the task before the American people is to realize and act on the fact that the hidden forces and interests that have corrupted the entire American political and financial systems must now be placed under stringent democratic controls so as to make the wealthy, privileged, and private interests of the nation accountable to the larger public interest.

Writing on this evolving problem in the late 1990s, Professor Edwin Amenta astutely noted:

> Although it is possible, it seems unlikely that reform-oriented regimes like those of the middle 1930s will ever appear again in the absence of a significant break in the connection between money and politics in America. That connection is far more powerful than it was during the 1960s or the 1930s. Until then, the future of social policy is likely to remain on hold. A national commitment to health and a program to providing work for all those who need it in the manner of the WPA will have to wait. In the meantime, we will endure with the divided system of social policy that was the legacy of the New Deal. (Amenta 1998, 269)

From the perspective of historian Alan Brinkley, the New Deal experiments have proved to be unsustainable:

> The new liberalism proved inadequate to the tasks it set for itself. The efforts to create economic growth and full employment through consumer-oriented fiscal policies floundered after 1973 in the face of global competition, environmental degradation, and deindustrialization. The welfare state failed to solve the problems of deteriorating inner city communities and rising violence; ultimately it could not even withstand assaults from those who believed it had helped create those problems. The white liberal commitment to the struggle for racial justice wavered as the relatively straightforward legal and moral issues of the early 1960s gave way to more complicated and controversial economic ones . . . In the face of these and other frustrations, postwar liberalism ultimately seemed to exhaust itself—to become paralyzed by its inability to find satisfactory answers to the problems it had so eagerly embraced. (Brinkley 1995, 270)

In an even more dismal tone, Carl Boggs in his book, *The End of Politics: Corporate Power and the Decline of the Public Sphere*, asserted:

> My core argument is that by the 1990s American society had become more depoliticized, more lacking in the spirit of civic engagement and public obligation, than at any time in recent history, with the vast majority of the population increasingly alienated from a political system that is commonly viewed as corrupt, authoritarian, and simply irrelevant to the most important challenges of our time . . . In such a historical context the deterioration of the public sphere has potentially devastating consequences for citizen empowerment and social change, not to mention the more general health of the political domain itself—hence the "crisis within a crisis." Sadly, despite the much easier access to educational facilities and technological outlets, most people seem to have lost hope for remedies to social problems within the existing public realm . . . *This epochal triumph of antipolitics is not merely a matter of failed leaders, parties, or movements, nor simply of flawed structural arrangements, but also mirrors a deeper historical process—one tied to increased corporate colonization of society and economic globalization—that shaped virtually every facet of daily life and political culture. De-politicization is the more or less inevitable mass response to a system that is designed to marginalize dissent, privatize social relations, and reduce the scope of democratic participation.* (Boggs 2000, vii–viii, italics added)

In an earlier age of robber barons, before their great trusts were brought under control, Theodore Roosevelt had remarked: "*In no other country . . . was such power held by the men who had gained these fortunes . . . The power of the mighty industrial overlords of the country had increased with giant strides . . . the government [was] practically impotent . . . Of all forms of tyranny the least attractive and the most vulgar is the tyranny of mere wealth, the tyranny of a plutocracy*" (Josephson 1962, 448, italics added). In retrospect, these were essentially the same forces against which both FDR and the Kennedy brothers were forced to contend. Indeed, at the close of the first decade of the twenty-first century, these are essentially the same forces against which we—the majority of the people on the planet—must now contend.

What will still continue to remain at stake in this ongoing contest between the Kennedy legacy and the plutocracy are the core principles of American democracy itself, along with the moral, ethical, and legal mandates of our international law regime regarding both civil and human rights. The battles in this arena continue to rage from the 1960s on into the early twenty-first century. To more fully appreciate this connection in the stream of history, it is helpful to return to the words of Robert Kennedy. Speaking in circumstances that were not unlike those we face in 2011, Robert Kennedy delivered a provocative and quite controversial speech on March 24, 1968, at the Greek Theatre, Los Angeles, California, in which he reminded his audience:

> Surrounded as we are by crisis in Vietnam, civil strife in our great cities, and a division among our young people, which often erupt in dramatic forms, it is easy to overlook the most profound crisis of all: *The unprecedented and perilous drift of American society away from some of its most treasured principles* . . . This is not simply the result of bad policies and lack of skill. It flows from the fact that for almost the first time the national leadership is calling upon ***the darker impulses of the American spirit***—not, perhaps, deliberately, but through its action and the example it sets—an example where integrity, truth, honor, and all the rest seem like words to fill out speeches rather than guiding beliefs. Thus we are turned inward. People wish to protect what they have. There is a failing of generosity and compassion. There is an unwillingness to sacrifice and take risks. All this is contrary to the deepest and most dominant impulses of the American character—all that which has characterized two centuries of history. (Guthman and Allen 1993, 335–338, italics added)

Kennedy's speech was immediately dubbed "the darker impulses speech" by the press. The speech reflected Kennedy's recognition that his campaign had helped to liberate a spirit in the country that reflected the empowerment of people who were no longer convinced of the invulnerability of LBJ, nor of the inevitability of conflicts at home and abroad (Carter 2009).

In many respects, Kennedy's 1968 speech can be read in 2011 as a commentary upon a nation that has lost faith in an Obama administration that, like the Bush administration before it, has been too loyal to Wall Street and too dedicated to continuing war expenditures in Iraq and Afghanistan, and in a two-party system that is too connected to corporate and banking interests at the expense of the majority of the people, as summed up by the rallying cry of "I am one of the 99 percent." In fact, one could argue that the rallying cry of October 2011 by the national Occupy Wall Street movement had, in effect, been foreordained by events that transpired in the early part of September 2011. As in Kennedy's own time in 1968, the America of the first decade of the twenty-first century has been on a rather unprecedented course, moving on a trajectory that was taking it farther from its democratic principles and practices. In this key respect, the trajectory seemed to reach its climax in August 2011.

In early September 2011, the United States Congress had finally resolved its long debate over a "debt deal," which allowed the federal government to raise the nation's debt ceiling. In reaching this deal, corporate interests and the Tea Party movement had both appealed to Americans' darker impulses when they advocated cutting social programs to balance the budget and lower the nation's deficit (without raising taxes on the wealthiest 1 percent). Writing about this battle and its larger meaning in *The Nation*, Ilyse Hogue critically observed:

> Most of the endless rehashing of the debt deal has correctly focused on the fact that corporate interests and Tea Party politics have prevailed again, at the expense of the middle class, children in poverty, students and the elderly. But too little attention has been paid to the blow this drawn-out debate has dealt to the foundational principles of our democracy . . . The debt deal's final resolution of what essentially amounted to a hostage crisis by that minority represents a complete unmooring of official decision-making from the will of the American people. The past few weeks could be the final straw that leads to a collapse of confidence not just in this government but in the American project of self-governance. At a time of so much great need in our country, sending the message that citizen involvement is futile is dangerous not just to the substance of one debate but to the core principles that allow us to call ourselves a democracy. Are we really prepared to risk that? (Hogue August 29/September 2011, 6–8)

In the same issue of *The Nation*, on the same subject, Dean Baker commented: "Unfortunately, the people who control the national agenda care little about the devastation they have wreaked with their greed and incompetence. Their philosophy of government is that a dollar that goes to the middle class and the poor is a dollar that should be going to the wealthy. This means that as long as Social Security, Medicare and Medicaid are still providing income and security to ordinary Americans, they will be pushing to pare these entitlements back. And they are prepared to use everything in their power to accomplish their goals" (Baker August 29/September 2011, 9).

Despite these powerful corporate and right-wing interests, the people of the United States and the people of the world have been pushing back. This pushback is evidenced in the front-page cover article of *The New York Times* dated Wednesday, September 28, 2011: "Protests Rise Around Globe as Faith in the Vote Wanes: Many Are Driven by Contempt of Political Class." The first paragraphs of the article reads:

> Hundreds of thousands of disillusioned Indians cheer a rural activist on a hunger strike. Israel reels before the largest street demonstrations in its history. Enraged young people in Spain and Greece take over public squares across their countries. Their complaints range from corruption to lack of affordable housing and joblessness, common grievances the world over. But from South Asia to the heartland of Europe and now even to Wall Street, these protestors share something else: wariness, even contempt, toward traditional politicians and the democratic political process they preside over. They are taking to the streets, in part, because they have little faith in the ballot box. (Kulish, *NYT*, September 28, 2011, A-1)

Only twelve years earlier, professor Carl Boggs predicted such an outcome. Boggs had come to this conclusion after examining the underlying historical causes of a long-standing impasse between the government and the corporate sector, on the one hand, and civil society on the other. He ascribed this impasse to the "increased corporate penetration of modern American life (what I call 'colonization'), a phenomenon that has been speeded up and intensified by such forces as economic globalization and the information revolution. In many ways, the predatory system of privilege and power is devouring its own (increasingly precarious) foundations. *The grandiose ambition of American elites to extend their domination throughout the world, while ostensibly a sign of great national economic, political, and military strength, has turned into a deadly bargain for the population as a whole, auguring long-term political weakness rather than the heightened power that now seems to be the most visible outcome*" (Boggs 2000, 9, italics added).

Professor Boggs' assessment has been reinforced with the passage of time and unfolding events. The grandiose ambition of American elites has become a global phenomenon and, in its wake, massive global suffering and global protests have ensued. By September 2011, global protests emerged that are not unlike the global protests of 1968. Between August and September 2011, protests in Britain exploded into a rampage as many young Londoners smashed store windows and set fires in London and beyond. In Spain, which has been hit hard by the developed world's highest official rates of unemployment, at 21 percent, many have lost all faith that politicians of either party could find a viable solution. Meanwhile, hundreds of thousands of people turned out in New Delhi to vent their outrage at the condition of Indian politics. One banner read: "If your blood is not boiling now, then your blood is not blood." The two major parties in Germany, the Christian Democrats and the Social Democrats, have seen tremendous declines in membership as the Greens have made gains, while Chancellor Angela Merkel has watched her authority plummet over unpopular bailouts. In short, around the globe, there is a feeling that the various political systems have failed their citizens and, as a result, the people have lost a sense of responsibility for one another (Kulish, *NYT*, September 28, 2011, A-8).

These were the tragic outcomes that Robert Kennedy was trying to avoid as he campaigned for the presidency in 1968. He had presented his communitarian vision as the beginning of a way out of the impasse. For Robert Kennedy, the empowerment of the average citizen was central to his vision. It was a vision that extended beyond the United States and permeated his view of what a just world order would look like. As a person-centered national leader and as a global statesman, Robert Kennedy had proposed and campaigned on a message for human betterment and the recognition, protection, and defense of human dignity that was grounded and rooted within a commitment to civil and human rights, jobs, employment, and projects for building a genuine community—both nationally and internationally. It was this fidelity to a humane and progressive social vision that placed him at odds with the Wall Street bankers and financiers, who sought an untrammeled monopoly over the lives of not only American citizens, but the entire global community—from Latin America to Africa, Asia, Europe, the Middle East, and Russia. Kennedy's own fervent defense of nationalist aspirations and the human-rights agenda attached to those aspirations were thematically and practically combined in such a way that his message created a fundamental divide within and between the ruling class elites. It would not be resolved by Kennedy's assassination. True, his life and progressive message was largely terminated by his death in the context of 1968, but it was a message that would be revived over the course of the coming decades and become a global call to action at the dawn of the twenty-first century.

13

From a "Second Bill of Rights" to a "Second Reconstruction" and a "Global New Deal"

Just sixteen years after Roosevelt's speech, the 1960 Democratic Convention in Los Angeles witnessed its presidential nominee—John F. Kennedy—articulate an economic strategy that went far beyond where Roosevelt had left it. JFK set forth an economic strategy that was in the stream of the history of the 1960s and could be compared to Roosevelt's, but Kennedy's went far beyond Roosevelt's statement of goals by producing an actual program to achieve those goals. That was because, according to sociology professor Donald Gibson, "much of Kennedy's program was aimed at achieving these goals" and therefore "his program was focused to a much greater degree on generating the economic progress that would be necessary" so that "it included an aggressive set of policies to produce that result" (Gibson 1994, 32).

Due to the judicial activism of the Warren Court and the social pressures placed on both the executive branch and the Congress, the Kennedy years would witness the unfolding of not only a political revolution, but also a Constitutional revolution in the body politic. After all, as one legal scholar has observed: "If the past cannot fully control the future, the Constitution cannot establish its legitimacy by setting down a fixed set of rules that we can agree on in advance and that are fair to all. Its legitimacy must come, perhaps paradoxically, from its openness to the future, and from the fact that people in the past, in the present, and in the future can and will disagree about its meaning" (Balkin 2011, 9). Therefore, "what makes an imperfect constitutional system democratically legitimate is that people have the ability to persuade their fellow citizens about the right way to interpret the Constitution and to continue the constitutional project. What makes this legitimacy democratic is that constitutional redemption is not the product of isolated individuals but the work of the entire public. Taken together, citizens have the resources to move the Constitution closer to their ideal of what their Constitution means and should mean" (Balkin 2011, 9–10).

This perspective is also shared by law professor Cass Sunstein, who has asked: "Why does the American Constitution lack Roosevelt's second bill? Why hasn't it become a part of our constitutional understandings?" Sunstein asserts: "I will contend that much of the answer lies in nothing abstract or grand, but in a particular and hardly inevitable event: the election of President Richard M. Nixon in 1968. If Nixon had not been elected, significant parts of the second bill would probably be a part of our constitutional understanding today. In the 1960s, the nation was rapidly moving toward accepting a second bill, not through constitutional amendment but through the Supreme Court's interpretation of the existing Constitution" (Sunstein 2004, 4–5).

One could further argue that but for the assassination of Robert Kennedy, it would appear from the record that his election as president in 1968 would have made progress toward a second bill inevitable. The legacy of John Kennedy's New Frontier was updating and building upon the FDR legacy. Robert was on record and in practice as thoroughly committed to building a new progressive coalition on domestic issues from ending poverty to advancing civil rights, as well as working to end the war in Vietnam. Hence, there are objective historical reasons for asserting that Kennedy was committed to not only the legislative passage of a second bill of rights, but also to ending both the war in Vietnam and the ingrained foreign policy that allowed the national security apparatus to engage in other United States military interventions in the Third World. To begin with, in the electoral arena, Nixon's narrow victory over Hubert Humphrey was largely the product of his having made a promise that he had formulated a "secret plan" to end the war in Vietnam. When coupled with Humphrey's reluctance to divorce his candidacy and platform from Johnson's war policies, it seems, in retrospect that Nixon's victory was assured. On the other hand, RFK was a well-known peace candidate and a "dove" on Vietnam who would have had little difficulty with the Nixon style and lack of candor. Some might view this statement as being counterfactual, but that is clearly not a position that I would take. Rather, I continue to contend that, in the stream of history, it is an argument that is defensible based on the historical record and the trends that were cresting in the late 1960s (Klinkner and Smith 1999). Further, it is also an argument that reflects an appreciation of the huge ideological differences between RFK and Nixon on almost every issue in contention in 1968. Finally, my conclusion on this matter is supported by the fact that it was Nixon who appointed a very right-wing conservative judge to be Chief Justice of the US Supreme Court: William Rehnquist. Nixon chose Rehnquist with the intention of reversing many of the social justice gains that had characterized the Kennedy years.

A review of the history of the Kennedy years demonstrates that in "the process of elaborating on and adding to Roosevelt's *Economic Bill of Rights*, the 1960 party platform included many of the initiatives later taken by Kennedy" (Gibson 1994, 32, italics added). Once in office, JFK adopted many proposals and policies that were consistent with FDR's Second Bill of Rights, but he also took various aspects of Keynesian economic theory and tried to provide a revamped Keynesian theory with a "much greater focus on expanding and improving the productive base of the economy and included many actions not derived from Keynes" (Gibson 1994, 33). While it is true that the Kennedy program inaugurated in 1961 was one that remained intensely committed to the national interests of the United States, it is also true that this national commitment did not show any disdain for other nations or denigrate the importance of their advancement, progress, and improvement. Significantly, according to professor Donald Gibson, the thrust of Kennedy's foreign policy did not "view the progress of the United States as in any way at odds with the progress of other nations, nor did he seek such progress for the purpose of world domination." In fact, Kennedy's governing philosophy and policies in foreign affairs demonstrated that "his goals for other nations and other peoples were completely consistent with his goals for the United States, even if his capacity to affect global trends was more limited" (Gibson 1994, 34). This same worldview, outlook, and governing perspective also characterized the views of Robert Kennedy. Taken together, the Roosevelt and Kennedy legacy is one that can be viewed as one that sought to embark upon putting into place a "Global New Deal." As such, it was antithetical to imposing a Pax Americana or US hegemony on the world. To the chagrin of Wall Street, the Rockefellers and their allies, the Pentagon, and the CIA, the Kennedy agenda represented a sharp break with traditional US foreign policy.

For example, we find that this Kennedy-inspired worldview was very much in evidence on March 13, 1961, when, in a bold and innovative redirection of foreign affairs, President John F. Kennedy announced the inauguration of the "Alliance for Progress." At its core, the Alliance for Progress was a progressive, social reform-oriented program designed for advancing cooperative development with Latin America. In the spirit of John Kennedy's inaugural address, the purpose of the Alliance constituted a "special pledge" to "our sister republics south of our border" in which the United States, he said, would at last convert "good words" into "good deeds." According to historian Robert Dallek, when JFK announced the Alliance and "talked about 'creating an American civilization where spiritual and cultural values are strengthened by an ever-broadening base of material advance,' he was not referring to merely the United States. Indeed, by '*American civilization*,' he was joining the cultures of north and south into a single civilization, diverse in language and custom, but united by ideals and values" (Dallek 2006, 93, italics added). This more broadly conceived and universalistic perspective reflected what shared membership in the international community of nations should be, and what it should look like. It was also an initiative that represented what the Kennedy brothers believed would help to redefine real democracy—not only in the United States, but also around the globe.

For the Kennedy brothers, outworn slogans and dogmas were not sustainable or politically realistic in the new era of the 1960s. The economic conventions of the past had to be replaced so that Wall Street, bankers, and multinational corporate interests would not continually have the last word over the direction and emphasis of US foreign policy—especially in Latin America. Empty slogans and ideological rhetoric could not be relied on as a substitute for genuine reform and change in a revolutionary age of global change. Therefore, John and Robert Kennedy believed that whether these slogans and old dogmas emanated from the ranks of racists, white nationalists, and segregationists, or from the boardrooms of wealthy Wall Street bankers, financiers, and men of commerce—committed to the corporate bottom-line irrespective of the human costs—it did not matter. From the perspective of JFK and RFK, the stream of history was moving beyond the sole control of narrowly defined class interests that resided within traditional national and global hierarchies. In this new decade of the 1960s, the Kennedy brothers believed that for the United States and the world to thrive in the near future, as well as in the decades ahead, progress would depend in large measure on inclusive and humane norms. In their view, these norms and principles would be critical for how people understood and undertook their social obligations within the context of both the national and international community.

In the 1960s, the entire economic and political governing structure had come under collective scrutiny. Civil right leaders like W. E. Du Bois and Martin Luther King understood this fundamental historical fact:

> The black predicament in the United States was a matter both of legal discrimination and systematic economic dependence and impoverishment. This meant that freedom for blacks involved more than ending formal segregation; it required basic changes that provided the entire polity with economic self-rule through meaningful work and guaranteed income. Thus, both civil rights leaders understood these goals to be ultimately universal ones, available to all and therefore necessitating fundamental reforms that were not race specific. At the same time, King and Du Bois also saw the black condition in the United States as part of the larger global narrative of imperial authority. Independence for the colonized world and liberty for African Americans were parallel objectives, to be pursued jointly, as both remained united by the historic fact of European empire. (Rana 2010, 343)

In many crucial respects, the Kennedy brothers shared this perspective with Du Bois and King. In particular, RFK took all this to heart even more so in the years following his brother's assassination. More attuned to the world of pain and suffering, Robert was able to identify with the victims, the vulnerable, and the excluded. Embodied within JFK's inauguration of the Alliance for Progress were the philosophical seeds, worldview, and foundation that RFK would come to build upon. Social reforms and economic reforms had to go together insofar as "progress consists in spreading the benefits which society can distribute to the largest possible number of beneficiaries, and in eliminating the institutional barriers which given social systems set up to prevent their diffusion" (Feder 1970, 206). This is what made the Charter of the Alliance for Progress unique and new, because the Charter had consciously and purposefully incorporated this perspective as the basic dogma of an international policy agreement.

It was a perspective that was completely endorsed and expanded upon by Robert Kennedy during his years as a senator from New York. In his 1967 book, *To Seek a Newer World*, RFK asserted:

There is no such thing as "pure" economic development in Latin America. Development depends on change—on a new balance of wealth and power between men. Economic development requires hard political decisions; it depends on political leadership, political development, political change . . . *Advocates of emphasis on economic development have argued that social reform is inefficient and economically disruptive—the classic example is the contention that land reform depresses agricultural production—and that, like other luxuries, it must await the achievement of economic success. But that view, in my judgment, ignores the fundamental connection between development and reform: that revolutionary social and political change is the necessary base for economic development* (Kennedy 1967, 80, italics added).

In this statement, Kennedy clearly differentiated himself from those conservative economists who saw development primarily in terms of a mathematical model that privileged economic profit-making over and above human needs. In later years, the approach that Kennedy rejected would be actively embraced by Milton Friedman and the Chicago School; by Ronald Reagan and his "magic of the marketplace" mantra; by Bill Clinton's "New Democrats," who embraced the North American Free Trade Agreement (NAFTA) as the wave of the future; and by George W. Bush in his attempts to put the neoliberal model on steroids by linking the mantra of economic growth alongside "democracy promotion" in the Middle East. The historical record is clear with regard to Kennedy giving primacy and priority to social reform as the necessary prerequisite to economic development as a social project. Hence, Kennedy's version of how the Alliance for Progress should be undertaken reflected his strongly held view: "The Charter gave highest priority to agrarian reforms. It *encouraged* the 'effective transformation of unjust structures and systems of land tenure and use' through peaceful and legal means to avoid that it be achieved by revolution, as in Cuba and many other countries throughout the world" (Feder 1970, 206, italics in original).

Unlike those who came after him in the stream of history, such as the Chicago boys like Milton Freedman or the neoliberal economists of the Reagan/Bush/Clinton years, RFK, in the tradition of JFK, refused to try to reduce the realization of human freedom to a strict economic calculus, such as in the so-called "Washington Consensus." Rather, RFK astutely maintained that "we cannot buy or plan or manage this vision into existence. We must believe it and create and hold fast to those beliefs and dreams, however strongly the urgencies of the moment tempt us from that path. For economic development, social reform, education, land reform, and all the rest are, like the shadows of Plato's cave, only the material cast of the great realities of human freedom. No matter how brilliantly we build, how generously we pour forth our treasure, how wisely we use our power, if we neglect the reality behind the act, then we will surely fail." Therefore, Robert Kennedy's adherence to the primacy of democratic principles over and above econometric models empowered him to differentiate between two kinds of leadership: "Leadership in freedom cannot rest on wealth and power. It depends on fidelity and persistence in those shaping beliefs—democracy, freedom, justice—which men follow from the compulsions of their hearts and not from the enslavement of their bodies" (Kennedy 1967, 125–126). Kennedy's perspective on this matter had both domestic and international implications.

On the domestic side, Robert understood the importance of a strong democratic theory and principles in shaping a community of persons who would share common values, beliefs, and goals; this was central to his vision and political program. Kennedy consciously linked the ideas of freedom, justice, and democracy together—it was not an accident. These three components of a truly strong democratic theory lift people beyond the kind of deterministic thinking that characterizes so much economic theory and modeling. As professor Benjamin Barber would later make note of in his book, *Strong Democracy: Participatory Politics for New Age*, it is essential to both understand and appreciate the fact that *"far from positing community a priori, strong democratic theory understands the creation of community as one of the chief tasks of political activity in the participatory mode. Far from positing historical identity as the conditions of politics, it posits politics as the conditioner of given historical identities—as the means by which men are emancipated from determinative historical forces"* (Barber 1984, 133, italics added).

It is clear that RFK consistently spoke about freedom as the foundation of democratic participation and action. On August 7, 1962, in a speech at the Seattle World's Fair, he stated:

> We know that freedom has many dimensions. It is the right of the man who tills the land to own the land; the right of workers to join together to seek better conditions of labor; the right of businessmen to use ingenuity and foresight to produce and distribute without arbitrary interference in a truly competitive economy. It is the right of government to protect the weak; it is the right of the weak to find in their courts fair treatment before the law. *It is the right of all our citizens to engage without fear or constraint in the discussion and debate of the great issues which confront us all.* We understand this

> regardless of the extent to which we may differ in our political views. We know that argument in the open is one of the sources of our national strength. (Ross 1968, 4, italics added)

The ideas contained in his 1962 speech were the themes that would come up repeatedly throughout the entire span of Kennedy's public career and service. We find the message repeated in his constant thematic uniting of the ideas of democracy, justice, and freedom as interdependent components of a healthy and participatory democratic order of governance. Kennedy's enduring capacity to unite these components of strong democratic theory stood in stark contrast to those who would invoke the tunnel vision of the "magic of the market"—along with the fictions of the free market, such as the putative freedom and equality of bargaining agents. Kennedy clearly understood what Professor Barber would come to criticize about the ideological centralization of focus on the alleged magic of the market: "it cannot generate public thinking or public ends of any kind; because it is innocent about the real world of power . . . because it uses . . . the illusions of the free market and of the invisible hand and the simplistic utilitarianism (Mandeville, Smith, and Bentham) by which the pursuit of private interests is miraculously made to yield the public good" (Barber 1984, 144). For Robert Kennedy, the alternative to taking this narrow neoliberal and/or neoconservative approach was to articulate the importance of (1) respect for the human rights, dignity, and worth of people—by acknowledging the central importance of their freedom and autonomy—which, in turn, would lead to (2) a form of citizenship that could (3) build a community of persons who shared a common consciousness. Kennedy often expressed this notion in his phrase about "citizens bound together in common purpose." Similarly, building upon a long democratic tradition of what constitutes citizenship, Professor Barber wrote: "*Citizenship and community are two aspects of a single political reality: men can only overcome their insufficiency and legitimize their dependency by forging a common consciousness. The road to autonomy leads through, not around, commonality*" (Barber 1984, 216–217, italics added).

To bring this discussion full circle, having addressed the twin components of freedom and democracy, we need to unite these ideas with Kennedy's conception of justice. Kennedy often spoke of justice in terms of fairness. The idea of justice as fairness was central to his political and moral worldview. After all, it was the unfairness of the welfare system that created more problems for the poor. It was also the enduring unfairness of economic life without land reform that created situations of injustice for the landless peasants, farmers, and laborers of Latin America, Asia, and Africa. Kennedy often used justice as fairness as the means through which he could speak of the more humane norms that ought to guide the political judgments of citizens who were members of a democratic society. In Kennedy's view, there nothing more unfair than the negative effects of unemployment and underemployment, which he believed lay at the heart of the poverty problem. It is this enduring problem that retains the duel capacity to not only deprive people of their dignity, but also to destroy the possibility of a democratic community. This is largely because the persistence of poverty and unemployment creates a social reality that separates people from one another. On July 12, 1967, speaking on the floor of the US Senate, Kennedy stated: ***"The crisis in unemployment . . . is significant far beyond its economic effects—devastating as those are. For it is both measure and cause of the extent to which the poor man lives apart—the extent to which he is alienated from the general community. More than segregation in housing and schools, more than differences in attitudes or life style, it is unemployment which marks the urban poor off and part from the rest of America. Unemployment is having nothing to do—which means having nothing to do with the rest of us"*** (Ross 1968, 141–142, italics and bold added).

Only four years after Robert Kennedy's assassination, professor John Rawls wrote his classic book entitled, *A Theory of Justice.* Rawls explains what justice requires, what a just society should look like, and how justice fits into the overall good of members of a just society. In many respects, it is clear that Rawls' theory of justice is more of a moral theory of justice than a pure democratic theory. Yet, despite its emphasis upon justice as a moral theory, it is a major contribution to democratic thought because it prioritizes the importance of a democratic political regime which, Rawls argues, is a requirement for justice. Like Robert Kennedy, we find that Rawls appreciates the role a democratic regime plays for more than just limited instrumental reasons. Rather, what Rawls envisions is what Kennedy envisioned—that is, how a conception of justice as fairness can provide guiding principles that can help to provide a democratic regime with forms of guidance that it can use in guiding the political judgments of all citizens within in the society as they work to exercise their responsibilities as citizens (Cohen 2003, 87).

All of these interrelated issues ultimately center upon making a choice. Robert Kennedy believed that the most basic truth and central reality about effective democratic governance is that citizenship and participation in a democracy require choices-- moral and political choices. This is what effectively separates the democratic path outlined by Kennedy, Barber and Rawls, from the more purely economic path of governance outlined by the Rockefellers and their financial allies, as well as those who prescribed the various neoliberal and neoconservative worldviews and economic models that came after 1968. It is only with Robert Kennedy's death and the deliberate closing of the door on his message that we find an historical disjunction between his advocacy about the need to make a political choice for a strong democracy that exhibits the components of justice, freedom, and democratic accountability versus those who saw "economic growth"—in isolation from political discourse and debate—as a convenient placebo for having to make hard choices.

The ideology of economic growth—in isolation from concerns with economic justice, from the requirements of a participatory democracy, and cut off from the transparency that accompanies genuine political accountability—also marks the historical turn from Robert Kennedy's message and legacy to the ascendancy of the conservative, right-wing corporate drift that America and the world embarked upon after 1968. In this critical respect, I would argue that it was the adoption of an ideology of economic growth as an end in itself that made a democratic deficit possible by removing any real discussion or struggle over issues of distribution, justice as fairness, or participatory demands from those seeking to make a strong democracy work on behalf of the excluded, marginalized, and dispossessed. In the words of professor Alan Wolfe: "Unlike political choice, economic growth offered a smooth and potentially harmonious future—instead of divisive, possibly ugly, and certainly disruptive struggles over re-distributional issues" (Wolfe 1981, 10).

Similarly, Russell Hardin has also taken note of the differences between the dominant discourse and worldview during Robert Kennedy's time and the decades after his death. Hardin exposes the ideological and philosophical gulfs of Kennedy's time and the great economic debates of that era, noting: "The economic conflict had both a domestic and an international form: greater equality versus untrammeled liberty, communism versus the free market. The institutional form of the domestic issue was central planning, versus laissez faire" (Hardin 2000, 43). However, in the aftermath of Robert Kennedy's assassination, we find that a tectonic shift took place that has altered the stream of history. According to Hardin:

> Now . . . we seem to be in an era in which the economic division is no longer crucial because we have reached near-consensus on how to handle the main economic problems: we generally handle them by letting them handle themselves. With the passing of the division over economics, there is no similarly cogent, simple dimension on which to organize political contests. We may have to deal with economic crises in the future, and we may disagree over how to do that, but we seem to have accepted . . . a basic reliance on the market and have increasingly given up on central planning to organize our economies. The former left-right antagonism has been reduced to a very short spread from those who prefer more generous welfare programs to those who prefer somewhat less generous welfare programs, and the difference between the two positions represents a very small fraction of national income. Radical reorganization of the economy to achieve some degree of equality or fairness is now virtually off the agenda. (Hardin 2000, 43)

In Kennedy's time, by contrast, his central message placed the goals of equality and fairness at the center of the political and economic agenda. It is this insight into the historical record of Robert Kennedy's legacy that leads us to a new appreciation of his message and meaning within the stream of history. In large measure, the recognition of Kennedy's message as a radical challenge to the privileges, hierarchical structure of the status quo, and growing wealth gap within the United States leads us into a new perspective on how to assess where we were in 1968 and where we have traveled since that time. It is a radical proposition insofar as it challenges us to reconsider the various national and international implications of democratic principles as governing principles in our collective political life and in our national and international community.

In this critical regard, we can view both the consciousness and statesmanship of Robert Kennedy in terms of what Professor Ronald Dworkin has called the "integrated liberal." Kennedy was a whole person in the sense that he did not separate his private morality from his public views, policies, and positions. Because Kennedy was able to unite his inner life with his public persona, we discover the possibility that a moral man who is in public life can also embody a public morality that reflects his inner priorities, his personal preferences, and his self-knowledge about his place within the larger political community. According to Dworkin: "The integrated liberal will not separate his private and public lives . . . He will count his own life as diminished—a less good life than he might have had—if he lives in an unjust community, no matter how hard he has tried to make it just. That fusion of political morality and critical self-interest seems to me to be the true nerve of civic republicanism, the important way in which individual citizens should merge their interests and personality into political community" (Dworkin 2000, 233). By this definition, Robert Kennedy was an integrated liberal because he viewed his own self-interest as connected to the collective national well-being and welfare of all people. Kennedy could not comfort himself with the antiseptic of a free-market economic model as his alpha and omega points because, in the words of Dworkin, "an integrated citizen accepts that the value of his own life depends on the success of his community in treating everyone with equal concern" (Dworkin 2000, 233). Treating all citizens with equal concern defines the legacy of Robert Kennedy. This same view also defined Kennedy's view of the international order and what should be the nature of US foreign policy. Kennedy's political consciousness led him to embrace a particular brand of statesmanship. In other words, Robert Kennedy's style of statesmanship demonstrated the fact that he saw himself as both an American citizen and a global citizen.

On international issues, while Robert Kennedy sought a more justice-oriented domestic order, he also strenuously advocated a new kind of approach to US foreign policy that would reflect his policy preference of no more Vietnams. This position was a defining moment in Kennedy's 1968 presidential campaign, for it signaled that he intended to radically redirect US foreign policy. In keeping with his progressive ideas and policies about social reform and civil and human rights from Latin America to South Africa, it was clear that Kennedy had rejected US interventionism and CIA-backed terrorism as reflective of his goals or consistent with America's stated ideals. However, by the time of the 1977 inauguration of President Jimmy Carter, it became clear that the rejection of Robert Kennedy's no-more-Vietnams position was a matter of policy: "*Carter's macro-economic policy became indistinguishable from the recommendations of the Republican party. He resolved the contradiction between growth and social justice by giving up on the latter. Promising starts toward avoiding the imperial temptation were dropped when they proved to be politically troublesome. . . . Policies toward the world's majority—the poor—were nonexistent*" (Wolfe 1981, 228–229, italics added). Carter had given in to political pressures that wanted neither domestic nor international justice concerns to restrain the profit-making potential of banks, corporations, or military contracting. Further, foreign markets and foreign nations were viewed by both Wall Street and the Pentagon as a necessary means to keep their version of economic growth expanding without engaging in a the struggles of a democratic political process that had the capacity to reduce their strength, influence, and wealth within the American hierarchy of class privilege.

Having retained the capacity to intervene in the Third World with more Vietnams, which they believed could lead to greater economic growth through imperial expansion abroad, the elites in the US Establishment clearly did not want to accept or adopt Robert Kennedy's formula. It would make their goal of easy economic growth more problematic and, at the same time, it would open up to greater democratic debate the potential for a radical redistribution of wealth in the US itself, thereby threatening their place in the economic hierarchy—a place largely achieved through maintaining a domestic economic order predicated on wealth inequality, the maintenance of racial divisions within the US labor market, a minimum wage locked into a no-growth status and, in place of rising wages, an emerging commercial credit market that would make bankers and financiers richer. Remarking on this trend, Professor Wolfe candidly observed:

> Rapid economic growth, it was felt, could expand the pie sufficiently so that it would not have to be cut in a different way. And expansion overseas could create an imperial dividend, a periodic bounty from empire that would augment the sugar in the pie in the first place. Between them, economic growth and the imperial dividend created a whole new approach to government, one that would not so much exercise political power to make choices as it would manage expansion and empire to avoid choice. Growth, in other words, was transpolitical. While liberals blame conservatives for America's impasse and conservatives say that the fault lies with liberals, the truth is that growth allowed policies that substituted economic performance for political ideology. (Wolfe 1981, 10)

By 1981 it had already become evident that "to return to a discredited liberalism would be no more a solution than to flirt with a faddish conservatism, for the economic conditions that support both no longer exist. The United States no longer has a liberal tradition, nor does it possess a conservative one" (Wolfe 1981, 261). Regardless of party, America would drift inexorably rightward from the Carter presidency through the Reagan years, from the Bush years to the Clinton years, and again back to a Bush. By the time of Obama in 2008, the die had been cast. The politics of economic growth theories and the alleged magic of the market had eclipsed the legacy of Robert Kennedy. But this was not the end of the story—nor of the enduring relevance of Kennedy's legacy. The failure of the neoliberal market model—as well as of neoconservative models—in the late 1990s and the early twenty-first century has produced for America and the rest of the world the politics of austerity.

According to Ian Bremmer in *The End of the Free Market,* a review of recent history reveals:

> By 2000, global foreign direct investment topped $1.4 trillion, a level not exceeded since. Multinational corporations and a host of smaller companies went global to both drive down production costs and target new customers: the hundreds of millions of people within emerging market states moving from poverty toward a middle-class lifestyle. Neither an economic slowdown in the early 1990s nor the damage wrought by the 9/11 attacks a decade later could challenge the dominance of the liberal economic model. Private wealth and private investment, and private enterprise appeared to have carried the day. But as the sun sets on the first decade of the twenty-first century, that story has already become ancient history. The power of the state is back. (Bremmer 2010, 19–20)

Yet, while the power of the state might be coming back into vogue, that does not guarantee that it will be advancing the needs of the poor or addressing the problems wrought by massive inequalities and a general lack of fairness in American society. On this point, Professor Stanley Hoffmann has noted: "The powerful and wealthy defenders of private interest have largely succeeded in making the political representatives of the people their dependents, and thus they have limited the obligations (taxes) and sacrifices these representatives could have imposed on the public, and particularly on its more prosperous members. The forces of self-interest, moreover, have often had help from the Supreme Court. Tocqueville's prediction about the dangers of democratic individualism was, alas, not wrong; however, the victim has not been freedom but what John Rawls called fairness in society" (Hoffmann 2011, 6).

By late 2011, Christopher Hedges noted with chagrin:

> Liberals lack the vision and fortitude to challenge dominant free market ideologies. They have no ideological alternatives even as the Democratic Party openly betrays every principle the liberal class claims to espouse, from universal health care to an end to our permanent war economy to a demand for quality and affordable

> public education to a return of civil liberties to a demand for jobs and welfare of the working class. The corporate state forced the liberal class to join in the nation's death march that began with the presidency of Ronald Reagan. Liberals such as Bill Clinton, for corporate money, accelerated the dismantling of our manufacturing base, the gutting of our regulatory agencies, the destruction of our social service programs and the empowerment of speculators who have trashed our economy. The liberal class, stripped of power, could only retreat into its atrophied institutions, where it busied itself with the boutique activism of political correctness and embraced positions it had previously condemned. (Hedges 2011)

The signs of this directionality were already evident in Kennedy's day, which is why he advocated a social-justice approach at home and abroad. Kennedy understood that only an inclusive social-justice agenda that delivered fairness for all classes could overcome the dangers associated with growing wealth inequalities and the imbalance of political influence that accompanied them. Further, only a no-more-Vietnams foreign policy could revive the economic health of the United States, spur investments in people and projects, and create a viable and cooperative international environment in which the rest of the world would not hate and resent the United States. Kennedy understood that economic growth could not be predicated upon imperialism and neocolonialism, or what was to become neoliberal and neoconservative doctrine. Markets should not be superior to political debate and discourse. Robert Kennedy understood that hard political choices were necessary if structural violence and injustices were to be overcome at home and abroad. This was not to be the case from late 1968 through 2008. Furthermore, between 2008 and 2012, global trends have actually worsened as the world has moved toward austerity measures (Posner 2010; Martinez 2009).

After more than three decades of listening to the official mantra from Wall Street and Washington that free markets are the best and most efficient way to govern the economy of not only nation-states but the entire globe, more scholarly evidence has accumulated to conclusively demonstrate that this belief is little more than a myth. In fact, since 2008, it has now become patently obvious that the ideology of "free markets" has fundamentally distorted American politics in profound ways—not the least of which has been the sundering of moral discourse from economic and political debates about the wisdom of this model and its guiding assumptions. One clear and notable consequence of the free-market myth is that it has made both the free market and the prison system seem natural and necessary, thereby leading to a system of mass incarceration in the prison-industrial complex. In large measure, this has been accomplished under the auspices of the neoliberal economic model, because the influence and reach of this model has affected other institutional and cultural dimensions that mediate the neoliberal ideology. As a result, the application of this model has affected the criminal justice and prison systems of all neoliberal countries, generating rising levels of income inequality and wealth disparities, influencing ethnic diversity and migration patterns, and impacting the composition of labor markets, as well as other political and institutional factors (Harcourt 2011, 226).

With the legacy of Milton Friedman's Chicago school of economics now firmly entrenched throughout America's legal system, economy, and culture, it has now become obvious, in the words of Professor Bernard Harcourt, that "it is time, well past time, to sever our contemporary assessment of economic organization from the rhetoric of the free market, natural order, and market efficiency. It is time to pull them apart: to purge economic and social analysis of the myth of natural order and the misleading language of liberty. It is time to dispense entirely with terms like 'natural order,' 'spontaneous equilibrium,' 'free markets,' 'liberate de commerce'—terms that do no more than obfuscate the real work that needs to be done. At the end of the day, the notion of 'free market' is a fiction" (Harcourt 2011, 242). The false promises of the Reagan era died in the Bush II years, as George W. Bush advanced the agenda of a corporate republic, bringing the methods and mentality of big business to public life. According to economist James K. Galbraith, the first decade of the twenty-first century revealed the presence of a new kind of state—the "predator state." The predator state emerged in a coalition of lobbies, doing the bidding of clients in the oil, mining, military, pharmaceutical, agribusiness, insurance, and media industries. The world watched as a predator state evolved in the United States—intent not on reducing government, but rather on diverting public cash into private hands (Galbraith 2008). The rise of the predator state has exposed the reality that the real economy is not a free-market economy. Rather, it is a complex combination of public and private institutions. The real problems and challenges—inequality, climate change, the infrastructure deficit, the sub-prime crisis, and the future of the dollar—are problems that cannot be solved by further incantations about the market. They will be solved only with planning, with standards and other policies that transcend and even transform markets (Galbraith 2008). This is the route on which the legacy of Robert Kennedy offers enlightenment to a new generation, as Americans and the rest of the world seek to reclaim the human future for humane policies, human rights, and the centrality of the dignity and worth of the individual person.

As Professor Alan Wolfe had predicted in 1981, the United States finds itself trapped in a seemingly hopeless situation:

> In an age of austerity, economics seems more relevant than politics, as people are told to sacrifice their security, their neighborhoods, their regions, and their ideals for the sake of an increased rate of return. The irony is that, under conditions of austerity, politics *must* be made to triumph over economics, for only through a revitalization of the collective energy of all people can an effort be made to find a way out of the impasse. America, as its citizens prove every day, does have the capacity to make itself whole again, but it can only do so by taking advantage of the social ideals of all, not the economic appetites of a few. (Wolfe 1981, 261, italics in the original)

As Robert Kennedy predicted in the 1960s, we find in the early twenty-first century more studies, more data, and more accumulated evidence to prove that "laws are a mechanism by which power can be democratically redistributed, changes in institutions can be created to ensure greater fairness, and a social floor guaranteeing minimum humane conditions can be established" (Heymann and Earle 2010, xii). On October 17, 1964, in a speech before the International Association of Machinists, Buffalo, New York State Council, Robert Kennedy said: "I think it's time different parts of this country stopped competing for business by depressing the standards of their workers. I think it's time industry stopped fleeing this state to go to states where the daily wage is $1.50. And to stop this flight, I believe we need a minimum [hourly] wage of $1.50 for New York and for the entire nation" (Ross, 1968, 149). Kennedy realized in 1964 what studies in the twenty-first century have confirmed again and again: "The most common way for working men, women, and their families worldwide to exit poverty is through work. Education is a ladder out of poverty, because it gives access to better jobs. Jobs define people's income as well as the conditions under which they work and live, which in turn affect their own health, the health of their families, and future opportunities for their children" (Heymann 2010, xiii). In the decades between 1945 and 1970, America was home to booming technological progress amidst a stable relationship between rich and poor. In those years, America was a true middle-class society.

It was only when the government decided to abandon the goal of full employment, to fight inflation by throwing people out of work, and to use high-interest rates like a bludgeon, that inequality began to threaten the American dream (Galbraith 1998). These policies reflected a complete rejection of Robert Kennedy's call for jobs, education, decent pay, and social justice for all.

Contrary to the dominant discourse of neoliberal economic dogma, it has become abundantly clear now, at the dawn of the twenty-first century, that we need to redefine the notion of community. This is a necessary enterprise not only on a national scale, but on a global scale. For, as Robert Kennedy argued throughout the 1960s, decent working conditions are attainable, needed, and constitute a human right at home and around the globe. Corporations should not be allowed to trample on the lives of billions of people, disrespectful of those people's human rights and unaccountable to anyone for the violations of those rights. Rather, as Kennedy argued in the 1960s, it is the job of government in every nation around the globe to ensure that a national and a global culture is constructed that will forge a common consensus that is empowered and capable of sustaining a long-term investment in people—as opposed to the traditional practice of advancing profit-driven considerations that destroy communities, destroy lives, and destroy hope for a better future.

By once again taking up Robert Kennedy's call to seek a newer world, it is incumbent upon our current generation to recognize that "while the mechanisms for ensuring the global enforcement of a foundation of decent working conditions require planning, cooperation, and courage, they are no more complex and demanding than other global challenges the world has undertaken. The principal arguments against change in this area have been that decent working conditions are unaffordable and that the world could never reach consensus on the needed changes." However, despite these claims: "There is no evidence that countries cannot compete while having strong labor standards or that they cannot create and keep jobs while ensuring that those jobs are good jobs. The belief that individuals should have decent working conditions and that work should support the health and welfare of individuals and their families is held across the full range of economies, political systems, and geographies" (Heymann and Earle 2010, 160). This is the first time since the dramatic post-1970s ideological swing to the right that challenges to market fundamentalism could be made with any real hope of success. Recent history demonstrates:

> The pressure on policy makers to adopt free-market policy prescriptions has been enormous. But the empirical evidence remains. The data simply do not support the OECD-IMF orthodoxy . . . Stepping outside the confines of a simple demand-supply framework, it is possible to imagine that much more is at work in countries with poor employment performance than inflexible labor markets. There is a less elegant but more convincing story to be told about the declining economic well-being of the less skilled in developing countries, a story in which low-skilled workers have borne the brunt of weak aggregate demand, massive economic and demographic shifts, and, of course, labor market deregulation. (Howell 2005, 339)

These are all elements and components of free-market capitalism—especially the variety of free-market capitalism that Edward Luttwak has termed "turbo-capitalism" (Luttwak 1999). Luttwak has defined turbo-capitalism as the phenomenon of private enterprise liberated from government regulation, unchecked by effective trade unions, unfettered by concerns for employees or investment restrictions, and unhindered by taxation. As early as 1999, while acknowledging the great efficiency of turbo-capitalism, he also described the already evident signs of the major upheavals that it could cause, as well as the inequities, broad dissatisfaction, and widespread anxiety that it was capable of producing.

By 2008, Kevin Phillips was lamenting the price that America was about to pay due to reckless finance, failed politics, and the overall global crisis of American capitalism (Phillips 2008). He was joined in this lament by Lance Taylor, Arnhold Professor of International Cooperation and Development. Director, Center for Economic Policy Analysis at the New School for Social Research. In Taylor's assessment of the new global situation, one thing was starkly clear: the world had witnessed the final collapse of free-market macroeconomics. Keynes had been correct after all, and we were now in the process of witnessing what Taylor called "Maynard's Revenge" (Taylor 2010). What was left largely unaddressed in all of this was the socioeconomic critique of the late Seymour Melman, who noted in 2001: "The US military economy is a partnership of government and business. It is managed by a central administrative office, based in the Pentagon, which is the largest single managerial entity of the whole economy and the core of America's permanent war economy" (Melman 2001, 98). Further, Melman revealed that "the decision power of Pentagon management has reached that of the state. After all, the fiscal 2000 budget plan of the Department of Defense—about $265 billion—exceeded the economic product of entire nations. The state management has become a para-state, a state within a state" (Melman 2001, 109). Tragically, the American warfare state has continued to eclipse the American welfare state—and with it the larger cause of social justice at home and abroad. In the name of fighting terrorism, the foreign policy of the US has, since 2001, expanded its capacity and investments to wage war while depleting its economic base. It has largely been a prescription for social, moral, economic, and political disaster. It has been an expansive expenditure since the end of World War II, primarily dedicated to the protection of multinational corporate interests overseas and the maintenance of US hegemony and domination over global affairs (Paupp 2007; Paupp 2009; Paupp 2012; Paupp 2014). In short, the pursuit of US hegemony has been a wealth-depleting investment that has primarily buttressed the American version of Europe's nineteenth- and twentieth-century projects of imperialism and colonialism. The main difference is that the US has used a balance of coercion and consensus to run its informal empire instead of maintaining a physical presence in all of its spheres of influence.

By 1961, JFK had already renounced and denounced the imperial and colonial policies of Great Britain and France. Therefore, he did not want the United States, under his leadership, to embark upon hegemony or the pursuit of US primacy. President Kennedy demonstrated his moral leadership for all humanity when he spoke as an advocate for a Nuclear Test Ban Treaty between the United States, the Soviet Union, and Great Britain. Following the 1962 Cuban missile crisis, both he and Robert were truly transformed men. JFK was determined, in the aftermath of that crisis, to invoke the full powers of the presidency on behalf of world peace, nuclear disarmament, and bringing an end to the Cold War.

Only a few months before his assassination, JFK declared in his "peace speech" at American University on June 10, 1963, that it was time to move beyond military solutions to global problems and to move away from the threat of military force—especially when it came to nuclear weapons. JFK asked his audience to consider this question: "What kind of peace do I mean? What kind of peace do we seek? Not a Pax Americana enforced on the world by American weapons of war. Not the peace of the grave or the security of the slave. I am talking about genuine peace, the kind of peace that makes life on earth worth living." It was the pursuit of peace, not American hegemony or the capacity for military intervention in other nations, that defined President

Kennedy's approach to foreign policy. This same sentiment was reiterated by Robert Kennedy on March 16, 1968, in the final sentences of his presidential candidacy announcement, in which he concluded: "these are not ordinary times and this is not an ordinary election. At stake is not simply the leadership of our party and even our country. It is our right to the moral leadership of this planet." It should be understood that when RFK refers to "our right to the moral leadership of this planet," he was not equating moral leadership with the capacity of the US military to impose political domination on other nations, or with the geopolitical practice of imposing great-power hegemony over other nations. Rather, he was referring to a truly moral leadership regarding global issues that would be capable of generating a consensus among all nations. In other words, it was not a unilateral US foreign policy, but rather a policy that was designed to evolve with the needs and demands of an expanding and diverse international community of nations. In a world of diversity, composed of diverse political systems, cultures, and traditions, it would be counterproductive to seek to impose an American "solution" to every single problem. Therefore, a consensus born of reason, free choice, and free will—not coercion—was what RFK meant when he spoke of moral leadership.

It was a theme to which he returned time and time again in his speeches at home and abroad. On March 18, 1966, in Oxford, Mississippi, at the University of Mississippi Law School Forum, he spoke of moral leadership in the following terms:

> In every continent—from Jaipur to Johannesburg, from Point Barrow to Cape Horn—men claim their right to share in the bounty which modern knowledge can bring, and they claim also the justice which they have heard proclaimed in that document which list the inalienable rights of man. I have seen scrawled on the sidewalks of Indonesia, and on the walls of Africa of in Latin America, not *Workers of the World Unite*, but *All Men Are Created Equal*, and *Give Me Liberty or Give Me Death*. They draw their hope for change and for a better life from the example of the United States. They look to us for hope and help. And the real question before you, before all young Americans, is whether we will help to bring about that future, or whether we will not help and stand by. (Guthman and Allen 1993, 137, italics added)

On June 6, 1966, speaking in South Africa at the University of Cape Town, Kennedy spoke of the same kind of moral challenge in international terms when he declared:

> We must recognize the full human equality of all of our people—before God, before the law, and in the councils of government. We must do this not because it is economically advantageous, although it is; not because the laws of God command it, although they do; not because people in other lands wish it so. We must do it for the single and fundamental reason that it is the right thing to do. We recognize that there are problems and obstacles before the fulfillment of these ideals in the United States, as we recognize that other nations, in Latin America and Asia and Africa, have their own political, economic, and social problems, their unique barriers to the elimination of injustices. (Guthman and Allen 1993, 240)

This statement is one of many he made that reflects his personal version and vision of what constituted America's "right to the moral leadership of this planet."

Both JFK and RFK were born into the tumultuous years of the Great Depression. Both served in the military during the Second World War and were mature young men at the time of the founding of the United Nations. They watched as the Third World's collective demands to be free of European colonialism and imperialism gained renewed momentum, even as the demands for greater civil rights within the United States were ascendant. In this respect, both JFK and RFK were caught up in the social pressures and movements of their time, which extended beyond the borders of the United States to South Africa, Latin America, and Asia (Massie 1997; Gerstle 2001; Borstelmann 2001; Nelson 2001; Dudziak 2000). All of the major themes and challenges accompanying the destruction of Jim Crow segregation in the American South and, in Robert Kennedy's speeches about the problem of racial apartheid in South Africa, would serve to make the issues of human rights and dignity more than just platitudes in the political speeches and statesmanship of JFK and RFK. In this key respect, their careers would be largely defined and eventually measured by the prominent role they embraced as activists in the cause of seeking social justice and as apostles of change for millions of people in America and around the world who had been victims of white supremacy, imperialism, and segregation.

14

An "Alliance for Progress" with the Third World

As advocates for new rules, new institutions, and new policies in both government and in the private sector, the Kennedy brothers were engaged in attacking the foundations of a variety of establishments within the United States and internationally. This would bring them both into sharp conflict with some of the most dominant and hostile elements of the Anglo-American establishment that had economically and politically benefited from these systems of exploitation. Businessmen, bankers, and imperialists all benefited from a continuing adherence to these systems of exclusion and subordination insofar as the maintenance of these very systems reinforced their privileged places in a hierarchy of socioeconomic, cultural, and geopolitical dominance. The hegemony and primacy of their power was laid upon these foundations; the imperial powers of Great Britain and France had spent most of the nineteenth and early twentieth centuries establishing colonial empires in Africa, Asia, India, and the Middle East. Along with American banking and various commercial interests, these European powers were able to extract vast reserves of wealth from Third World nations through the exploitation of natural resources, even as they established markets that were beneficial to their commercial interests. International bankers, businessmen, and the elements of an ever-expanding and emerging global military-industrial complex were the primary beneficiaries of these arrangements (Leffler 1992). It was against this network of forces that JFK and RFK aligned themselves in their struggle to establish a New Frontier that was more humane, inclusive and democratic.

The Kennedy brothers realized that the aftermath of World War II had unleashed revolutionary tides and social movements calling for radical change in the economic and political relationships of nations and peoples. The end of World War II had served to reignite the Third

World's collective aspirations for the legal recognition of sovereignty—which included other goals as well, such as freedom from the threat of superpower intervention, freedom from superpower alignment, and freedom from the legacy of colonial and imperial policies. In the post-1945 world that John and Robert Kennedy inherited, Third World nations continued, with an accelerated urgency, to make their claims for autonomy, self-determination, and independence from this globally imposed Anglo-European system of dependence and oppression (Lee 1995; Holland 1994; Statler and Johns 2006).

To employ Frantz Fanon's term, the nations of the Third World had been struggling since the end of World War I to escape their status in the international hierarchy as the "wretched of the earth" (Fanon 1968). In the spirit of the early 1960s, Fanon emphatically declared:

> *The young nations of the Third World are wrong in trying to make up to the capitalist countries. We are strong in our own right, and in the justice of our point of view. We ought on the contrary to emphasize and explain to the capitalist countries that the fundamental problem of our time is not the struggle between the socialist regime and them. The Cold War must be ended, for it leads nowhere. The plans for nuclearizing the world must stop, and large-scale investments and technical aid must be given to underdeveloped regions. The fate of the world depends on the answer that is given to this question.* (Fanon 1968, 105, italics added)

In the stream of history, a review of events demonstrates that the international origins of anti-colonial nationalism had been simmering since the so-called "Wilsonian moment" of 1919 (Manela 2007). It was a transitional period in which "the anti-colonial movements of 1919—commonly viewed only in the contexts of their national histories—profoundly transcended national enclosures in their genesis, conduct and aims. They were shaped by transnational networks of nationalist activists who imagined themselves as part of a global wave, operated explicitly on an international stage, and aspired to goals that were specifically international; namely, the recognition of the peoples and territories they claimed to represent as self-determining, sovereign nation-states within a new international society whose structure and dynamics would reflect Wilsonian precepts" (Manela 2007, 13). The human force of these movements and the profound spirit of liberation from colonial domination that drove them were destined to shape much of the history of the twentieth century. It was primarily for this reason that "the experience of the Wilsonian moment cemented ideological and political commitments to anti-colonial agendas, and the movements launched then did not disappear with its demise. The colonial authorities moved to stem the anti-colonial wave, and the popular momentum of the spring of 1919, driven by international events, could not last indefinitely. In its wake, however, political programs and organizations committed to self-determination became more powerful and more pervasive than before" (Manela 2007, 221).

As the world entered the Cold War era, these pressures would intensity. For, in the stream of history:

> Although Third World nationalism had begun to flower in most cases between the World Wars, it was only during the Cold War context that it grew to irresistible maturity . . . The concurrent hardening of the bipolar conflict and softening of the European empires meant that the anti-colonial struggle, and the embryonic nations to emerge from it, could be plotted along two definitional axes. The first was ipso facto oppositional: resistance to white supremacy and imperial rule, expressed as nationalism. The second, expressed as neutralism and eventually embraced by a significant number of newly emancipated nations, reflected the desire for independence not only from European landlords but from the Cold War dichotomy as well." (Parker 2006, 153–154)

By the decade of the 1950s, the Bandung Conference would further articulate the nature, depth, and scope of Third World demands and expectations (Tan and Acharya 2008). In the post-1945 world, the nations of the Third World took the victorious Allied nations to task for their hypocrisy in continuing to hold on to their empires, and began to try to make them accountable to the promises contained in the Charter of the United Nations. Only in this way would the entrenched interests and classes behind empire, colonialism, and imperialism begin to be forced to live up to the principles that they ostensibly fought to obtain in their global war against totalitarianism and fascism. The United Nations Charter itself would enshrine these ideals within the framework of a new liberal order, thereby making it harder for the forces of white supremacy and international capitalist rule to remain immune from the human-rights and civil-rights claims of millions of people at both the nation-state level and internationally.

For Robert Kennedy throughout the 1960s, the various national and global struggles of the poor in the slums and in the cities were increasingly conjoined with the perceived need to establish a more viable, justice-oriented, and inclusive national and international community.

This dual focus provided Kennedy with the moral and political space to make an argument for advancing human dignity that transcended the borders of the United States. RFK came to understand that the problem of social exclusion constituted a global challenge—one that every nation would eventually have to confront, address, and ultimately resolve. Because of Kennedy's unique capacity to understand the global connections that exist between different peoples and cultures, he was able to address the commonality of these struggles in such a way that he inspired the idealism and activism of a generation of young people. When addressing the problems of race and the city within the United States, he was also aware that his assessment applied with equal force to the cities and racial divides of the entire globe. In his 1967 book, *To Seek a Newer World*, RFK noted: "The crisis in employment is the most critical of our failures. It is both measure and cause of the extent to which the poor man is alienated from the general community. More than segregation in housing and schools, more than differences in attitude or life style, it is unemployment that sets the urban poor apart. *Unemployment is having nothing to do—which means having nothing to do with the rest of us*" (Kennedy 1967, 34–35, italics added).

Robert Kennedy's sensitivity to these common problems extended to Latin America. While others merely quoted statistics about the problems of degradation, poverty, unemployment, illiteracy, disease, and malnutrition, Kennedy observed it, felt it, and incorporated the experience into his being. From his personal experience and travels abroad, he noted: "To travel in Latin America, to see the terrible reality of human misery, is to feel these statistics with stunning force . . . Everywhere, in and around every major city, are the slums; incredible masses of tin or tar-paper or mud huts, one room to each, with what seemed like dozens of children coming out of every doorway. They are *barriadas* in Lima, *callampas* in Santiago, *villas miserias* in Buenos Aires, *favelas* in Rio de Janeiro and *ranchitos* in Caracas. They are all the same: vast numbers of peasants who have come to the cities in search of a better life, but find no work, no schools, no housing, no sanitary facilities, no doctors, and too little hope—their life bearable only because the countryside is so much worse" (Kennedy 1967, 72).

In 1970, a Twentieth Century Fund Study on the Alliance for Progress offered its reflections on the dynamic interplay between land reform and peasants who had been excluded from political participation throughout Latin America. The authors of the study supported the views of RFK on the scope and nature of the challenge when they noted: "An orderly agrarian reform requires that a society commit itself to heavy investment in its peasants. The peasants of most Latin American countries are numerous, deprived, and excluded from participation in politics. Therefore, an effective public program to give them land, capital, education, technical services, equal access to the market, and a voice in political affairs *amounts to a social revolution.* It is also enormously expensive. The Alliance for Progress gave this great and costly social change high priority in its program for inter-American cooperation" (Levinson and de Onis 1970, 228, italics added).

In addition to these challenges, other commentators on the dangers facing the Alliance for Progress have noted the great "counter-reform efforts" that were launched by US investors and businessmen with real estate, commercial or industrial interests in Latin America. These elites were committed to fighting the Kennedy program to the bitter end to preserve their privileges and access to wealth, despite the human and civil rights costs to the majority of the people affected by these arrangements. Recognizing this sociopolitical reality and the socioeconomic powers driving it, one commentator suggested that: "Only this can explain why so many resources were put behind the great Counter-reform of the 1960s, why so little was and is heard about American support for land reform in Latin America, and why it was decided to resolve the reform issues by military means. It would take a considerable reform in US national policies to allow land reforms in Latin America and at the same time force US business to accept the consequences. The truth seems to be that land reform in Latin America threatens the whole infra- and supra-structure of American economic hegemony in the hemisphere" (Feder 1970, 223).

This was the social, economic, and political world that JFK and RFK inherited. Caught within the stream of history, the Kennedy brothers were courageous enough to acknowledge the sea-change in international affairs and wise enough to embody a form of statesmanship that also contained a genuine, substantive, and coherent response to these claims. For example, Robert Kennedy was critical of those governments in Latin America that placed the needs of their people and social reform on the back burner of history while, at the same time, continuing to spend huge amounts of capital on arms and weapons:

> The budgets of many Latin American governments contain nearly as much for arms as they do for capital budget investment on the roads, dams, and schools that are essential to development. . . . We should lead the way toward cutting down arms sales to Latin America.

> Our military representatives in each of these countries should clearly understand this to be our policy. Frequently, in the past, it would appear that they have not, or if they do, they have ignored it—promoting the purchase of military equipment and the importance of the military establishment itself. Of the needlessly advanced weapons in Latin America, most were purchased—not donated by the United States; it is arms purchases, not grants, that use up valuable foreign exchange. As we are the major supplier of military arms, we should make the major effort to cut down arms sales to Latin America and other countries around the world. (Kennedy 1967, 120–122)

In addition to critiquing conventional arms sales by the United States to Latin America, RFK was also conscious of the emerging reality that "the spread of nuclear weapons cannot increase the security of any Latin American nation." Thus he argued, "we should therefore strive for a nuclear-free zone even if Cuba elects not to join to it, even if Cuba remains outside the treaty and outside the inter-American system" (Kennedy 1967, 122). As it turns out, Kennedy was quite prescient and truly ahead of his time in arguing for a nuclear-weapon free zone (NWFZ). Many Latin American nations subsequently joined to create one. From arms sales and the spread of nuclear weapons to the related problems of poverty, inequality, and lack of social reform, RFK was a leading figure who was involved in the midst of all of these struggles. Evidence of Kennedy's statesmanship in this arena is exemplified in remarks that he made to Venezuelan labor leaders in 1965. Kennedy painted a picture of a united Latin America playing an independent and influential role in the future of global affairs: "Latin America can and should take independent initiatives in the councils of the world, not only in matters of special interest to this continent, or to developing countries, but on worldwide concerns from disarmament to the peaceful settlement of disputes of Asia and Africa. Latin America can, for example, take the lead in assuring fair treatment in world trade for the developing nations." He then specifically made the point that "as nations one step removed from the confrontations of the great power, Latin American actions and proposals add substantially to hopes for settlement of conflicts" (Ross 1968, 434).

One cannot help but think that Kennedy was referring to the events associated with the 1962 Cuban missile crisis when the Organization of American States (OAS) joined together in combination with one another to condemn the introduction of Soviet nuclear missiles into Cuba. At the same time, looking forward prospectively in the stream of history, one cannot help but be struck by Kennedy's sensitivity to the Third World's desire to avoid confrontations between the USSR and the US. Kennedy's remarks anticipated the rebirth of the Non-Aligned Movement (NAM) of the 1970s, whose member nations sought not only to opt out of the battles of the Cold War, but also to establish a new and independent path for development across the Global South. NAM was inaugurated in 1955 at the Bandung Conference (Tan and Acharya, 2008). In the aftermath of World War II, it can be said that "the Third World was not a place. It was a project. During the seemingly interminable battles against colonialism, the peoples of Africa, Asia, and Latin America dreamed of a new world, they longed for dignity above all else, but also the basic necessities of life (land, peace, and freedom). They assembled their grievances and aspirations into various kinds of organizations, where their leadership then formulated a platform of demands" (Prashad 2007, xv).

In the early 1960s, both JFK and RFK entered into a place within the stream of history that demanded a response from the United States in terms of a foreign policy that would be able to both accommodate those aspirations and, at the same time, deal with the perceived threats that emerged out of waging a Cold War with the USSR. In this critical sense, it can be said of the Kennedy years that "every policy is a product of its era, of the ideas, events, and perceptions that shape the time before it is enacted. The Kennedy-era policy of engagement emerged from the debates of the 1950s, not only within the government but also outside of it" (Rakove 2013, 1). By the spring of 1968, RFK's speeches on the subject harked back to his brother's policy of engagement with the nations of the Third World and the NAM movement. In mid-April 1968, RFK decried the diminished moral authority of the United States in the world. Kennedy alluded to the Declaration of Independence, noting that "by the unilateral exercise of our overwhelming power, we isolated ourselves. To many of our traditional allies and neutral friends, we behaved as a superpower, ignoring our own historical commitment to 'a decent respect for the opinions of mankind.'" (Kennedy, cited in John Herbert, "Kennedy, Calling U.S. Power-Obsessed, Appeals for a New Policy," *NYT*, April 18, 1968, 34). The "decent respect [for] the opinions of mankind," a phrase coined by Thomas Jefferson and often cited by RFK, was in large part a casualty of the 1960s.

In the 1970s, NAM was supplemented by calls for a New International Economic Order (NIEO), which harked back to the aspirational agenda that was formulated during the 1955 Bandung Conference (Prashad 2012). As had always been the case during and after JFK's thousand days in the White House, Robert Kennedy's primary preoccupation with the agenda and challenges of Latin America centered around the relationship between security on the one hand, and conflict resolution combined with economic development on the other. In this respect, RFK was furthering and enhancing JFK's quest for peace around the globe (Sachs 2013). Kennedy made it clear to the Venezuelan labor leaders that "the first concrete step that can be taken toward world leadership in this area is the formation of a nuclear-free zone in Latin America. That alone could show the way for dozens of nations on two other continents and it could lead the way toward conventional arms reductions as well" (Ross 1968, 434).

What Kennedy proposed would eventually be referred to as the construction of a "security community" for the promotion of a sustainable peace. Among the attributes of such a security community was the practice of "confidence-building," which allowed nations to enter into bilateral forms of cooperation. This process of confidence-building is precisely indicative of what transpired between Argentina and Brazil from 1985 to 1988. Following their countries' transitions to civilian democratic rule, democratically elected officials in both Brazil and Argentina were empowered to transform their nuclear policies from an expression of regional rivalry into a means to advance regional tension reduction, political solidarity, and economic integration (Paupp 2000, 62–64). This process also had the added benefit of strengthening their fledgling democracies. Hence, the processes of democratization led to the overt use of foreign policy as a means of protecting newly established democracies. Democratic consolidation and civilian control over the armed forces was thereby secured by pursuing this strategy. Hence, it can be concluded—in non-counterfactual terms—that Kennedy's prescription for regional peace in Latin America through the establishment of nuclear-free-weapon-zones (NFWZ) possessed the dual benefits of reducing the threat of conflict between nations while, at the same time, strengthening democratic institutions that would be guided by civilians and responsive to the people as a whole (not merely to established elites). In writing about this development in the year 2000, I maintained that "in Argentina, these processes ultimately mattered because it brought officials to power whose identity and ideology allowed them to frame nuclear development and bilateral relations in a new way. In short, the redefinition of the nuclear confidence-building regime was placed in the context of building democratic security" (Paupp 2000, 63–64).

Because of this paradigm shift in governance at both the national and regional levels, it is clear that the Alfonsin government of Argentina was able to assert effective civilian control over Argentine-Brazilian relations, thereby ensuring that the Argentine military was marginalized in foreign and military matters throughout the entire Alfonsin government. The central lesson to be learned from this case study is that the Argentine-Brazilian experience fits well with the observation that expectations about other states, while not empirically grounded, if shared, can become self-confirming (Paupp 2000, 64). Robert Kennedy understood this point very well. That emerging reality in political affairs helps to explain, at least in part, why RFK often spoke about the need for a new approach to global relations, wherein:

> The Latin American nations should increasingly share in the councils of the West—not after a decision has been made, but in a sincere and determined effort to draw upon their wisdom in advance of crisis and action. This effort is the mutual responsibility of Latin America, the nations of Europe, and the United States. Regular channels of communication and consultation should be established for continuing discussion of the great challenges to peace—from Southeast Asia to Berlin. This should not be an effort to bind any country to the policies of any other country; rather it should be to draw upon Latin American ideas and imagination, and to insure this continent that place of partnership which its history and the limitless prospects of its future demand. (Ross 1968, 435)

This was Robert Kennedy's hope for Latin America: a partnership with the rest of the world, and continuing dialogue with it as an equal partner. This would not be the view or policy of either Nixon or Kissinger. Those who came to power in the White House of 1969 immediately sought to dismantle the Alliance for Progress and to ignore its lessons. The Nixon-Kissinger team embraced the old and broken policies of linking US foreign policy with dictators and suppressing social movements and democratic elections that called for changes to the status quo, and sought instead to revive the practices associated with the "behemoth of the North." They completely lacked Kennedy's sensitivity to the relevance of social-justice concerns and the need to extend human rights, and utterly failed to comprehend the dangers of alliances with dictators and military juntas (Schmitz 1999, 293–309; Schmitz 2006, 72–111; Saull 2007, 126–142; Afkhami 2009, 448;

Zepezauer 2003, 8, 13–14, 25–26, 54, 63, 103, 123–125; Barry, Wood, Preusch 1983,6; Gerassi 1965, 242; Lawrence 2008, 269–288). Guided by the neoliberal economic model of Milton Friedman and the Chicago boys, the Nixon-Kissinger team rejected the Kennedy legacy embodied in the Alliance for Progress and instead embraced the neoliberal cause against the socialist agenda of the Allende government.

According to Juan Gabriel Valdes, an advisor to Chile's Minister of Finances, it was evident that "from 1974 to 1978, the military regime of General Pinochet developed a radical economic liberalization program based on the indiscriminate use of market mechanisms, the dismantling and reduction of the state, deregulation of the financial sector, and a discourse that ascribed to market forces the ability to solve practically any problem in society" (Valdes 1995, 7). In this struggle, the neoliberals focused strictly on the battle against inflation, while the goals of the socialist and left-progressive forces dedicated to redistribution and economic reactivation were entirely abandoned. The only thing that remained true for both sides in this struggle was that "in the language of the Allende period, both wished to bring about 'irreversible reform'" (Valdes 1995, 7). Within the right-wing conservative perspective of Nixon-Kissinger team and their allies, the historical record reveals that "the Nixon-Kissinger approach also reflected deep pessimism about underlying social and political trends in the region and the ability of the United States to alter the situation" (Lawrence 2008, 272). As RFK had predicted, there was a restless and revolutionary yearning for a better way of life across all of Latin America, yet a range of interlocking problems—poverty and population growth, urbanization and unemployment, illiteracy and corruption—was blocking progress. In response to these problems—and from the reflexive ideological matrix of Cold War concerns—the Nixon-Kissinger team, along with Nelson Rockefeller, came together in their shared conviction that radical upheavals "threatened to tarnish US credibility and, in the worse case, to create new opportunities for Soviet or Cuban meddling" (Lawrence 2008, 272).

In a letter to Nixon that served as a preface to his report on Latin America, Nelson Rockefeller attempted to explain the negative response that his mission to the continent had evoked. Rockefeller wrote: "There is a general frustration over the failure to achieve a more rapid improvement in standards of living. The United States, because of its identification with the failure of the Alliance for Progress to live up to expectations, is blamed. People in the countries concerned also used our visit as an opportunity to demonstrate their frustrations with the failure of the own governments to meet their needs. [In fact] . . .demonstrations that began over grievances were taken over and exacerbated by anti-US and subversive elements which sought to weaken the United States, and their own governments in the process" (Taffet 2007, 187). What Nelson Rockefeller's view seemed to embody was nothing less than a 1950s perspective on Latin America while, at the same time, setting forth a renunciation of the Alliance for Progress, arguing that any future solutions had to be different (Taffet 2007, 187).

Beyond advice from Rockefeller, Latin Americans were aggressive in suggesting other courses of action to Nixon. In mid-June 1969:

[Juan Gabriel Valdes, in his capacity as the Chilean foreign minister,] met with the president to deliver a statement crafted in Vina de Mar, Chile, by representatives of twenty-one Latin American nations. Valdes and the document he presented, which came to be known as 'The Consensus of Vina del Mar' argued that the United States should open its market to Latin American goods. Washington aggressively pushed Latin Americans to open their markets to US firms, but did not play fair by limiting the sale of Latin American goods in the United States. The United States, Valdes suggested, could become wealthy because of inter-American trade, but the same was not true of the Latin Americans (Taffet 2007, 188).

In short, the recalcitrance of the Nixon administration to Latin American calls for fairness in trade issues, along with the rejection of aid, constituted the kind of response that was conclusive evidence that the promise of the Alliance for Progress was officially dead.

In reflecting on these events in 1995, Valdes commented on the failure of the neoliberal economic model that had been imposed on Chile after the violent overthrow of the Allende government and the effects of the brutal dictatorship of the Pinochet regime upon the people of Chile. He wrote: "The recent history of Chile demonstrates . . . that only flexibility and a combination of political and economic measures, based on consensus through persuasion, can result in a viable development model" (Valdes 1995, 11). Valdes then concluded that the real costs of the neoliberal model had proven to be unsustainable and its promises illusory. As the Pinochet regime crumbled, in large measure due to its unwavering fidelity to the Nixon-Kissinger-Rockefeller-Friedman ideology of neoliberal thought, Valdes noted: "The massive, multi-class phenomenon of social disobedience known a the 'protests,' and the brutal repression employed by the regime to keep itself in power from 1983 to 1986, scared the dominant social sectors. It was forced to realize that social policies could not simply be discarded, and that *an ideology which reduced political decisions to a mere technical criteria was a dangerous illusion*" (Valdes 1995, 272, italics added). Robert Kennedy's sensitivity to Third World struggles, nationalism, and aspirations for human rights and dignity had been vindicated in the stream of history. His voice still echoes from a speech he made to the Canadian Press on April 14, 1964, when he cautioned that "*we . . . are a part of their revolution. At least we should be, and I believe that we must encourage them in their efforts to bring about improvements . . . Someone will share their aspirations and their leadership. If not the West, then some other system will make common cause with them to achieve their immediate goals*" (Ross 1968, 425, italics added).

With regard to Chile, after the coup of General Pinochet's military junta, it was clear that "Kissinger had gone out of his way to flatter and protect one of the most brutal regimes in the world" (Schmitz 2006, 110). After Nixon resigned the presidency and Ford replaced him, US policy with respect to Chile did not change. In fact, a review of the historical record indicates that, on the issue of human rights, "Kissinger left no doubt that the Ford Administration, despite sniping in the US Congress about human rights abuses, embraced the new strongman, Augusto Pinochet, and had little desire to see the restoration of democracy. During his trip to Santiago for an OAS meeting in June 1976, Kissinger said as much directly to Pinochet. The administration, he told the Chilean leader, had to respect concern in Congress about human rights abuses but did not share it. 'We are sympathetic with what you are trying to do here,' Kissinger affirmed. 'We wish your government well'" (Lawrence 2008, 283). When Jimmy Carter was inaugurated as the thirty-ninth president of the United States, his energy secretary, James Schlesinger, observed the differences between Carter and his predecessors, Nixon and Ford. In a biography on the Shah of Iran, the author relates Schlesinger's views on the three presidents' differing responses to human rights concerns, noting that "Carter was deeply concerned about human rights, which made him quite different from Nixon, who scoffed at the idea, or Ford, who paid little attention to it and was easily deflected from it by Kissinger, who, as Schlesinger also tells us, 'was not known to be a crusader on human rights'" (Afkhami 2009, 448).

In short, the Nixon-Kissinger team completely rejected President Kennedy's admonition in his inaugural address that *"if a free society cannot help the many who are poor, it cannot save the few who are rich*." Similarly, they adamantly rejected this admonition from Robert Kennedy: "*A better life for the people of Latin America can only come out of the progress toward a better, more democratic political and social structure*" (Ross 1968, 433). In so doing, those who came to power after Robert Kennedy betrayed his legacy of hope, human rights, and real social progress for millions of excluded and marginalized groups—especially the poor and the dispossessed. By the decade of the 1980s, President Ronald Reagan would do no better.

In the tradition of the Nixon-Kissinger team, Reagan embarked upon a "rollback" of socioeconomic gains across the Global South in an effort to buttress the profit-seeking priorities of multinational corporations, bankers, and business interests (Bello 2005, 7–11). For Reagan, as was the case with the Nixon-Kissinger team, all that mattered was the magic of the market. Reagan found himself building on the logic that authoritarian regimes were part of the free world. Therefore, he actively and illegally provided support for friendly right-wing governments that were under attack—such as El Salvador. The Iran-Contra affair emerged out of this very policy. Critics of the Vietnam War had been working along the lines suggested by Robert Kennedy in articulating a no-more-Vietnams approach to US foreign policy, emphasizing the principle of nonintervention and human rights. At the same time, some neoconservative thinkers from the Committee on the Present Danger (CPD) were actively developing an ideological defense of traditional Cold War policy. These neoconservatives rejected both détente and human rights as the basis for US foreign policy and sought a revival of the old containment theory.

It was in this distorted atmosphere of doublespeak that Reagan's eventual UN Ambassador, Jeanne Kirkpatrick, came up with an alleged distinction between two kinds of regimes, "authoritarian versus totalitarian." She blamed President Jimmy Carter for having emphasized human rights in US foreign policy because, in her view, it led to the ouster of the Shah of Iran and the collapse of the Somoza regime in Nicaragua. She argued that these traditional autocrats and right-wing dictators should be left in place because they could allegedly develop into democracies. On the other hand, the totalitarian communist states, she believed, could not evolve in the same way. Hence, right-wing dictators were a supposedly necessary stage of government for Third World nations (Schmitz 2006, 194–240). Following her logic would also lend credence to Reagan's support for the apartheid government of South

Africa. Therefore, the contrived distinction between authoritarian and totalitarian was an ideological rationale that was eventually employed by the Reagan administration to avoid seriously questioning human-rights abuses at any time, anywhere in the world. Hence, in the end, following this counterfactual logic would become the basis for providing Reagan with a stated rationale for supporting the apartheid government of South Africa. Completely oblivious to the moral, human rights, and global calls for social justice regarding the South African regime, Reagan blithely mused: "if we're going to sit down at a table and negotiate with the Russians, surely we can keep the door open and continue to negotiate with a friendly nation like South Africa" (Schmitz 2006, 220). Calls for social justice, economic justice, and political independence from US dictates would be met with violence, illegal military and CIA interventions, and efforts to economically strangle any socialist experiment that would dare to exclude US multinational corporations' business interests and/or banking and financial penetration into the marketplace. From the Middle East to Latin America, no region of the world was beyond the reach of this ideology or the threat that it embodied (Zepezauer 2003, ix).

With the brief interlude of the Kennedy years (1961–1963) as an exceptional departure from the US foreign policy norm, it is indisputable that from the end of World War II to the early decades of the twenty-first century, "American officials consciously and purposefully supported non-democratic rulers and forces in the pursuit of expanded trade and investments, anticommunism, and stability" (Schmitz 1999, 308). Between 1964 and 1968, Robert Kennedy attempted to restore his martyred brother's foreign policy of withdrawing aid from dictators who installed themselves by military coup. Robert also articulated his strong support for social movements that would advance the human rights of their people, strengthen national development over and above profit-seeking and exploitative multinational corporations, and assist with the installation of genuinely democratic regimes that would reflect the aspirations of the majority of the people. All of this ended on June 5, 1968. In the aftermath of Robert Kennedy's assassination, it also is indisputable that "the Nixon administration's commitment to containment and stability mandated support for right-wing dictators and enforced order, leading to an even greater reliance upon authoritarian regimes to maintain regional stability in various parts of the world. Thus, with a series of selected nations, such as Indonesia, Greece, Iran, and the Congo, the United States increased its arms sales and overall support despite domestic criticism of these regimes" (Schmitz 2006, 73). Human rights and the principle of nonintervention were effectively jettisoned by the US foreign policy establishment. The legacy of Robert Kennedy was to become memory, not a guide for future action among the elite power-brokers of Washington and Wall Street. Yet this would not be the last word. As Richard Barnet opined, it was becoming clear that *"the evidence is mounting that the costs of empire, not only financial but political and psychological, have weakened the United States. Indeed, the loss of American hegemony appears to be directly related to the strategies adopted to maintain it"* (Barnett 1972, 67, italics added).

15

Robert Kennedy's Enduring Legacy

Obviously, the reverberations of these aforementioned national and international struggles have continued to be felt throughout the period of the ensuing decades since the assassination of RFK in 1968. Without exception, an historical review of the stream of history during the decades of the 1970s, 1980s, 1990s, and on into the first decades of the twenty-first century reveals the relevance of the legacy, message, and mission of Robert Kennedy. The racial system of apartheid was finally buried in the 1990s and Nelson Mandela was elected South Africa's first black president. Also, Kennedy had predicted in 1968 that a black American would probably become president of the United States within 40 years—and his prediction was realized with the 2008 election of Barack Obama. These are just two examples of an updating of the RFK legacy that is not counterfactual at all, but rather a stunning testimony to Kennedy's visionary idealism in the face of great historical obstacles.

So, the salience and historical relevance of these struggles for human rights, for peace, for human development have not diminished—they have, in fact, intensified. To realize this reality of global relations is to be consciously positioned to appreciate and learn from the lessons that JFK and RFK taught by example and have left as their legacy. To appreciate the full spectrum of that legacy and its meaning is the central purpose of this book. Therefore, it is time to revisit, remember, and even perhaps appreciate for the first time the true dimensions, meaning, and message of the Kennedy legacy.

In particular, this book is primarily dedicated to an examination of Robert Kennedy's message—especially the last four years of his life as a senator and as a 1968 presidential candidate. That is largely because, in the aftermath of President Kennedy's assassination, it fell to Robert to take up the fallen standard of a political mission that he and his brother had carefully crafted over almost two decades. Between 1964 and 1968, we find that Robert Kennedy produced a more mature, radical, and revolutionary legacy that had only begun to be formulated and implemented during President Kennedy's legendary thousand days. Because they literally shared the presidency, Robert saw his work and message between 1964 and 1968 as seeking to carry out a restoration of the unfulfilled promise of the JFK legacy. To do this, however, RFK had to articulate his brother's vision within the context of a different time and through the lens of his own perceptions in a new and changed global environment. RFK embarked upon a journey that resulted in a rebirth of his political imagination in conjunction with the emerging needs and aspirations of a new era. Hence, it can be said that he engaged the US and the world at large with his own unique creativity.

Robert Kennedy's tenure in the JFK administration as Attorney General, head of the United States Department of Justice, had placed him in the role of chief law enforcement of the United States. His primary responsibilities involved following the dictates of the courts in the enforcement of civil and political rights. In association with his brother and in fidelity to recent Supreme Court decisions on the issue of civil rights—from desegregation of schools and other public facilities, subject to the Commerce Clause of the US Constitution and the doctrine of federalism—the use of power by the executive branch took on a very activist role in the task of enforcing a host of new legal decisions as authorized by the courts.

By early 1963, the effect of the Kennedy endorsement of these laws and their vigorous enforcement throughout all regions of the country would effectively diminish President Kennedy's support throughout many sections of the nation—especially in the bastions of the old Confederacy in the American South. During the course of the presidential campaign of 1968, Richard Nixon would seek to reclaim this region for the Republican Party by invoking the anger of a "silent majority," according to Nixon, who had unfavorably witnessed and resisted the efforts of the Kennedy brothers to peacefully bring about a Second Reconstruction. Nixon's infamous "Southern strategy" would play on the historic racism of the region and deprive the Democratic Party of its electoral votes in the decades to come (Kotlowski 2001, 259–271).

Yet, for both John and Robert Kennedy, it was morally necessary to commit both themselves and the nation to fulfilling the unfinished task of the first Reconstruction. For the Kennedy brothers, it was vital for the nation to recognize and act upon the promise of the Fourteenth

Amendment and its guarantee of equal protection under the law. In this task, both JFK and RFK committed themselves and the Kennedy administration to a legislative program that was faithful to the constitutionally mandated pursuit of the long political task of constructing a new cultural, social, and political consensus in which race would no longer be a limiting criteria for the enjoyment of housing rights, employment rights, or educational rights in America. In short, their commitment was to a shared social-justice vision that would forever change the face and character of America's civil society. The domestic social revolution that the Kennedys came to lead was largely inspired by civil society itself, especially the Southern Leadership Conference under the direction of Dr. Martin Luther King, Jr. (Garrow 1986; Branch 1988; Oates 1982).

Historians would later ascribe even greater importance to the social movements for change that emanated from the African American community itself. Yet, in the totality of events, the Kennedy commitment to the demands from these movements was still essential for American society to begin the process of coming full circle. Dr. King's role was central in helping to define the direction that change would take insofar as the "Negro revolution" of the 1960s. The Kennedy brothers, in turn, gave governmental legitimacy to a social revolution that was viewed with hostility by elements of the government's own institutional bureaucracy. This was especially true with respect to the FBI and the CIA (Melanson 1991).

Only in 1979 did a more complete history of the FBI's war on Dr. King and the rest of the civil rights movement come to light. Lingering questions about the possibility of conspiracies in the assassinations of both President Kennedy and Dr. King had forced the US House of Representatives to set up a three-year investigation into the murders. With the release of the *Report of the Select Committee on Assassinations—US House of Representatives*, it was revealed that the FBI had set up a "counterintelligence program" (COINTELPRO) to not only monitor Dr. King and his movements, but also to intimidate and threaten Dr. King. The authors of the report disclosed that the FBI had launched a campaign against Dr. King. Under Hoover's direction, COINTELPRO was used to get certain newspapers, such as the *Globe-Democrat*, to print editorials hostile to Dr. King. These editorials, it was found, had many similarities to disparaging remarks that were also present in FBI memorandum. In reaction to these discoveries, the authors of the House report asserted: "*Not only did this conduct contribute to the hostile climate that surrounded Dr. King, it was morally reprehensible, illegal, felonious, and unconstitutional. There is no place in a free society for such governmental conduct. It deserves the strongest condemnation"* (US House of Representatives 1979, 580, italics added).

The recalcitrance of J. Edgar Hoover and his FBI to constitutionally legitimate calls for social justice were a hallmark of the 1960s. These calls for social justice from black America found a receptive audience with the political commitment and moral idealism of the Kennedy brothers. However, regardless of the political demands for social justice from a broad coalition of groups within America's civil society, the FBI chose to simply ignore the demands of democratic governance and acted as a law unto itself under the directorship of J. Edgar Hoover (Summers 1993). Within the Kennedy administration—with Robert Kennedy in place as attorney general of the United States—the clashes with Hoover became more intense and more ominous for both the Kennedy brothers and Dr. King. In this critical struggle, the historical record makes it clear that both the Kennedy brothers and Dr. King were operating in a dangerous and hostile environment. Yet, a receptive and compassionate presidential leadership in the Kennedy White House would eventually converge with social movements for racial justice. In this convergence there would come, in the words of Robert Kennedy, a political force that would "sweep down the mightiest walls of oppression and resistance." It was a theme to which RFK would return again and again with respect to the revolutionary tides for the recognition of civil and human rights in South Africa, Latin America, and Southeast Asia. In the America of the 1960s, the force of these social movements would find their convergence in a dramatic and searing combination of racial riots and nonviolent protests. It was a dynamic that was fueled by the crisis of minority unemployment, job discrimination, and obstacles to voting rights. The resolution of these injustices would come about through a radical reexamination and remaking of the entire structure of American society itself (Nelson 2001; Borstelmann 201; Gerstle 2001).

The demands for the full recognition of civil and political rights invariably led to claims beginning to be made for the wider fulfillment of these rights in substantive ways within the socioeconomic order. By 1967, RFK would note: "Of all our failures in dealing with the problems of the poor, the greatest is the failure to provide jobs. Here is an aspect of our cities' problems almost untouched by Federal action. No government program now operating gives any substantial promise of meeting the problem of unemployment in the inner city, and thus of any way to avoid the inefficient, wastefully expensive, degrading and self-defeating system of welfare" (Kennedy 1967, 33). What RFK detested most about the welfare system was that, in his words, it denied the person on welfare to "stand as a man among other men," that it destroyed families just as it destroyed the possibility of a genuine community. The welfare system, as Kennedy perceived it, was a political mechanism that reinforced socioeconomic and sociopolitical exclusion. Further, this was a problem that could not be divorced from the larger problem of poverty. In an address before the Day Care Council of New York, on May 8, 1967, Kennedy asked:

> Can we not respond to the aspirations of our fellow citizens?
>
> Do we not have the ingenuity to involve private enterprise in the process of providing adequate housing for the 43 percent of Negroes who now live in substandard dwellings?
>
> Do we not have the wherewithal to bring health services to the poor on a neighborhood scale, with family physicians, and aides who bring preventive care to the ghetto for the first time?
>
> Do we not have the ability to devise manpower programs which create not just jobs, but jobs with possibilities for further education and advancement over time?
>
> Do we not have the capacity to reorganize our welfare system so the ghetto resident is not confronted with a bewildering fragmented array of agencies, but rather is served by a rational system he can understand, with expediters or workers from his own community to help him obtain aid?
>
> Do we not have all the skill to bring government back to the community, back to Lewis Mumford's "face-to-face" scale, before it is too late?
>
> We have begun to some of these things, here in New York and across the country. But having begun, we must do more. And in all of this there must be an overriding theme and goal—the involvement of the community, of those who have the greatest stake in the quality of the services they receive. (Ross 1968, 155)

Kennedy sought to enact policies that were inclusive, that strengthened both the individual and the community—that gave real opportunities to the poor, the excluded, and those victimized by persistent racism. Hence RFK became an advocate and an architect of social change by taking on a trinity of problems simultaneously: poverty, the welfare system, and jobs. He was intelligent enough and empathetic enough to see that the dignity and worth of the person could only be preserved by uniting the efforts and the investments of the public sector with the private sector. But this insight amounted to more than just a material calculation undertaken in reference to a narrowly defined concept of markets and capitalist profit margins. Rather, Kennedy placed these various considerations within the framework of a wider context—the context of what constitutes a vibrant and sustainable community.

At both the local and the national level, RFK was concerned with the kind of human community being constructed—and whether it met the needs of the individual so that the fulfillment of the individual and group needs could be met together in harmony and not fragmented by either an insensitive bureaucracy or the forces of greed, waste, and private gain at the expense of public good. Kennedy had studied these problems for years —first as attorney general, and then as a senator from New York. By the time he declared for the presidency in 1968, he had also read the *Report of the National Advisory Commission on Civil Disorders* (the Kerner Report), which clearly stated:

> The disorders are not simply a problem of the racial ghetto or the city. As we have seen, they are symptoms of social ills that have become endemic in our society and now affect every American—black or white, businessman or factory worker, suburban commuter or slum dweller. None of us can escape the consequences of the continuing economic and social decay of the central city and the closely related problem of rural poverty. The convergence of these conditions in the racial ghetto and the resulting discontent and disruption threaten democratic values fundamental to our progress as a free society. The essential fact is that neither existing conditions nor the garrison state offer acceptable alternatives for the future of this country. Only a greatly enlarged commitment to national action—compassionate, massive and sustained, backed by the will and resources of the most powerful and the richest nation on this earth—can shape a future that is compatible with the historic ideals of American society. (*Report of the National Advisory Commission on Civil Disorders* 1968, 410)

16

Robert Kennedy's Agenda to Empower American Democracy

As a senator representing the state of New York, he made the city of Bedford-Stuyvesant his personal experiment in "slum self-regeneration." He sought to embark on a new path to socioeconomic reform by enlisting three different constituencies to work in conjunction with one another as never before: government, private enterprise, and the residents of Bedford-Stuyvesant themselves. Kennedy believed that if Jeffersonian democratic ideals were to be realized in practice, then the previously excluded residents of the slum must be given a seat at the table of decision-making over matters that affected their own lives. Therefore, RFK began his programmatic agenda by acknowledging that "government at all levels—Federal, state and local—will have to play key roles in any such program. But total reliance on government would be a mistake" (Kennedy 1967, 41). Therefore, he argued, "that is why it is imperative that we enlist the energies, resources and talents of private enterprise in this most urgent national level" (Kennedy 1967, 41). Government and business interests from the private enterprise sector would combine with the third and most critically vital organizational component: the Community Development Corporation (CDC).

According to Kennedy, "the heart not only of the private enterprise program, but of nearly all programs aimed at alleviating slum conditions should be the creation of Community Development Corporations. Such corporations might be financed by an initial contribution of capital from the Federal government; but for their ongoing activities, they would need and receive no significantly greater subsidy than is ordinarily available to non-profit corporations under present law" (Kennedy 1967, 45). At the core of the CDC, Kennedy asserted, "the critical element in the structure, financial and otherwise, of these community corporations should be the full and dominant participation by the residents of the community concerned" (Kennedy 1967, 46). By making sure that this Jeffersonian principle of self-determination was built into the structure of the governing structure of CDCs in poverty areas, it was Kennedy's belief that "they would have the opportunity to make every government program, and many private efforts, more effective than ever before. . . . Such corporations, each devoted to improving the conditions of a single community, could go far to changing our techniques for meeting urban needs" (Kennedy 1967, 46).

Kennedy's approach to slum regeneration and urban renewal had effectively made possible a policy revolution. Not only was he moving in the stream of history by giving a practical voice to the ideals embodied in FDR's Second Bill of Rights, but he was also acting as an advocate for excluded and marginalized members of American society who wanted nothing more than an opportunity to claim their rights as citizens of the nation. In order to fully realize his vision, he also proposed a logical and effective mechanism for limiting an overly intrusive governmental role by curtailing its proclivity to dominant democratic affairs. His plan offered a special role to business and private enterprise in combination with a mandate for democratic accountability to the residents of the affected neighborhoods by delegating final decision-making power to the members of the community elected to sit on local CDC boards. These representatives would guide the Community Development Corporation in the task of determining which businesses were actually needed in their community to meet the unique needs of that community. Hence accountability, authority, and decision-making responsibilities would be shared by all under the umbrella of the CDC structure. RFK hoped that his vision to make civil and human rights real and effective in New York would become a blueprint for the entire United States. Beyond that, he also hoped that it would offer insights for development and modernization throughout the Third World.

In this critical regard, he was seeking to launch a national and international human rights revolution that would finally unite the pursuit of civil and political rights with the not-yet-fully-articulated human rights to peace and development. By so doing, he sought to make a linkage in policy and practice that was prefigured in FDR's Second Bill of Rights, had matured under the guidance of JFK's New Frontier, and then was interrupted by the policy departures undertaken by Lyndon Johnson. Despite these obstacles, Robert sought to elaborate and implement the idea of a human right to development that went beyond the all-encompassing nature of a right or even the language in which it is embodied. He did so by seeking to merge theory with practice—to move beyond mere legal pronouncements and convert the promise of civil and human rights law into the practice of politics and the realities of social life. The "human right to development," which RFK defined as the basis of human dignity and freedom, was as much a call to action as it was an ideal to be articulated in laws, policies, and programs. As a statesman, Robert sought to bring US foreign policy into more direct correspondence with the ideals of America. At the same time, he was also actively seeking to resolve the domestic contradictions between American ideals and practices within the nation itself. In short, he was involved in a struggle on two fronts, but with a complementary purpose: to advance the human right to development in such a way that the dignity of the individual person would be guaranteed by a moral, legal, and ethical consensus.

In retrospect, it would seem that Kennedy's greatest challenge in his efforts to advance the human right to development is perhaps best summed up by professor Bonny Ibhawoh's observation about the difference between the critics and the proponents of the human right to development. Ibhawoh astutely describes these opposing worldviews by noting: "Critics contend that the right to development is devoid of meaning and unenforceable because of its scope and the inability of states to ever realize all of its components.... Such conclusions are often based on the assumption that the value of the discourse on the right to development can only truly be measured by its 'tangible' outcomes such as the creation of binding international legal instruments and the emergence of effective enforcement mechanisms. Often overlooked are the intangible outcomes of the discourse in terms of clarifying concepts, mobilizing opinions, challenging orthodoxies, and building consensus on key issues" (Ibhawoh 2011, 77–78).

Robert Kennedy's approach was to engage in a political discourse that was dedicated to clarifying concepts about human dignity, freedom, and rights. As such, he was seeking to build a groundswell of support for social movements that were dedicated to the improvement of conditions that would allow for the flourishing of human rights, instead of their denial and/or subordination to other values and priorities. Kennedy found himself constantly giving speeches throughout Latin America, South Africa, and within the United States that stressed his belief about the need to mobilize public opinion on behalf of the poor, the marginalized, and dispossessed, while also actively seeking to challenge those status-quo barriers to the realization of human rights and human development. In this fundamental respect, Robert Kennedy's legacy is ultimately one of challenging and confronting orthodoxies that reinforce practices of oppression and subordination while, at the same time, working to build a consensus on key issues that would, in his words, "sweep down the mightiest walls of oppression and resistance" (Guthman and Allen 1993, 244). RFK's promise of revolutionary change is contained within a graduation speech that he delivered on June 6, 1966, to the graduating class at the University of Cape Town, South Africa. In what is perhaps one of his most remembered and often quoted statements, the larger context in which it is found reads as follows: "Each time a man stands up for an ideal, or acts to improve the lot of others, or strikes out against injustice, he sends forth a tiny ripple of hope, and crossing each other from a million different centers of energy and daring, those ripples build a current which can sweep down the mightiest walls of oppression and resistance. . . . Few men are willing to brave the disapproval of their fellows, the censure of their colleagues, the wrath of their society. Moral courage is a rarer commodity than bravery in battle or great intelligence. Yet, it is the one essential, vital quality of those who seek to change a world which yields most painfully to change" (Guthman and Allen 1993, 243–245).

In the decades following RFK's assassination, there has been a perceptible shift away from the idealism, policies, and goals that Kennedy had hoped to set for the Untied States. Gar Alperovitz, professor of political economy at the University of Maryland, noted that: "In the 1960s roughly two out of three regularly told pollsters that they believed government was run 'for the benefit of all.' Asked in 1999, 'Would you say government is pretty much run by a few big interests looking out for themselves, or that it is run for the benefit of all the people,' a mere 19 percent said that it is run for all. Fully 75 percent now felt that government was run for the benefit of special interests" (Alperovitz 2005, 10). Another political scientist, Carl Boggs, is even less restrained: "[T]he largest corporations are able to dominate virtually every phase of economic, political, and cultural life; they set the agenda for nearly every dimension of public policy" (Boggs 2000, 70–71). Democracy's steady decline, theorist Michael Sandel laments, is ultimately evidenced in "a widespread sense that we are caught in the grip of impersonal structures of power that defy our understanding and control" (Sandel 1996, 201–202). Kennedy foresaw this trend as early as 1966. In reaction to it,

Kennedy's call for reflection and readjustment stood in stark contrast to prevailing ideologies of both the political right, who saw no useful role for government outside of guaranteeing public safety, and the left, who had come to regard large-scale federal spending as the preferred remedy for any domestic ill.

Kennedy placed himself outside the mainstream of his own time when he warned about the dangers associated with the mainstream's affection for modernity, the fascination with the new, and the constant celebration of the big. On September 17, 1966, he spoke at a community college dedication in Worthington, Minnesota, where he prophetically noted:

> Even as the drive toward bigness [and] concentration . . . has reached heights never dreamt of in the past, we have come suddenly to realize how heavy a price we have paid: in overcrowding and pollution of the atmosphere, and impersonality; in growth of organizations, particularly government, so large and powerful that individual effort and importance seem lost; and in loss of the values of nature and community and local diversity that found their nurture in the smaller towns and rural areas of America. And we can see—as we enter the last third of the twentieth century—that the price has been too high. Bigness, loss of community, organizations and society grown far past the human scale—these are the besetting sins of the twentieth century, which threaten to paralyze our very capacity to act, or our ability to preserve the traditions and values of our past in a time of swirling, constant change. To these central dangers . . . we can trace a hundred others [in] the signs around us that all is not well with the republic: spreading violence, unconcern for others, too many seeking to escape in noninvolvement or in drugs, debate becoming acerbic and bad-tempered, and overall a sense that no one is listening. Therefore, the time has come . . . when we must actively fight bigness and over-concentration, and seek instead to bring the engines of governments, of technology, of the economy, fully under the control of our citizens, to recapture and reinforce the values of a more human time and place. (Guthman and Allen 1993, 211–212)

Kennedy's speech concluded with his version of a communitarian vision for the United States as a restored republic. He saw the centrality of democratic citizenship in action as the antidote to bigness, to corporate-creep, and to the associated problems of national decline. In outlining the dimensions, characteristics, and meaning of his communitarian vision, Kennedy unequivocally stated:

> It is not more bigness that should be our goal. We must attempt, rather, to being people back to . . . the warmth of community, to the

> worth of individual effort and responsibility . . . and of individuals working together as a community, to better their lives and their children's future . . . And it is the lesson that if this country is to move ahead in the last third of this critical century, it will not be by making everything bigger, not by piling all our people further on top of one another in huge cities, not be reducing the citizen to the role of passive consumer and recipient of the official vision, the official product. (Guthman and Allen 1993, 212)

In the leadership vacuum left in the wake of RFK's death, we discover that by the time of the early 1980s, there were already numerous signs that his warnings had been essentially ignored by the American power-structure. In place of the march of Kennedy's agenda for social change, we find that the continued centralization of vast and essentially unaccountable private power had manifested itself. Corporate ascendancy could be seen both from the victory of large corporations in the political struggles over restructuring the US economy to successful efforts to consolidate their strength against potential challengers to the corporate regime (Gordon 1996). By the early 1980s, prevailing pro-business strategies shared three basic principles, according to three progressive economists, Samuel Bowles, David Gordon, and Thomas Weisskopf: "profit-led growth, market-based allocation, and arms for economic power" (Bowles, Gordon, Weisskopf 1983, 256). In assessing the situation, we discover that "the first of these principles involves a transfer of resources to the wealthiest and largest corporations. The second extends the dominion and reduces the accountability of corporate decisions—by insisting on the primacy of profitability in economic life. The third strengthens the hand of corporate interests against those abroad while sacrificing the needs of the poor in the United States for the sake of military spending" (Bowles, Gordon, Weisskopf 1983, 256). The implications of their findings offer support to what Kennedy had predicted as early as 1966. They unanimously conclude:

> It is clear to us that democracy will suffer if any of the pro-business strategies is pursued. Either people will cower before the reassertion of corporate interests, paving the way for rapid centralization of private power and the erosion of popular rights, or popular forces will mobilize, insisting on the importance of their own needs and interests. If this latter tendency is strong, but does not succeed in displacing a pro-business strategy, then corporations will be likely to waste even more of our economic resources to curtail popular power—building up their bureaucratic empires and extending their influence over the

> government. And they may move directly to curb democratic rights and privileges. (Bowles, Gordon, Weisskopf 1983, 256)

Just twenty years later, in 2003, we find that their predictions about the victory of corporate power over popular civic forces for a change in the status quo had lamentably come true. The corporate constriction of popular movements and democratic demands was advancing with great rapidity. Under the administration of George W. Bush, the USA Patriot Act was passed by Congress and signed by the president, allowing for the formal suspension of many Constitutional rights, all in the name of fighting terrorism, in much the same way that the McCarthy-era of the 1950s had been a time when the fear of communism was used to silence dissenters and allow the military to continue its buildup throughout every corner of American society and culture (Raskin and Spero 2007, 93–106). At the dawn of the twenty-first century, the government and media of the United States itself was now increasingly referring to America as the "homeland," conjuring up unfavorable historical parallels to the Third Reich's depiction of its national self as the "Fatherland." In this new era, increasingly being described by government leaders and corporate-media masters as the "age of terrorism," the imagined gravity of the threat served to give new meaning to the task of defending the American homeland. This new role for the United States now provided the ideological justification for massive expenditures attendant to the building and maintenance of a massive multi-billion-dollar bureaucracy, which was dubbed the "Department of Homeland Security." America had not only become a corporate state, it was now being turned into a police state (Raskin and Spero 2007).

A neoliberal trend converged with a fascist/corporate drift that had overwhelmed the nation by 2003. Acting unilaterally, the Bush administration had invaded the sovereign nation of Iraq under a false pretext, alleging that it harbored weapons of mass destruction and also that it had been engaged in the September 11, 2001, attack on the World Trade Center in New York. The administration further alleged that Iraq was offering a safe harbor for Middle Eastern terrorists who were allegedly still conspiring against the United States. The domestic effects of this form and style of foreign policy proved to be equally damaging for the rule of law within the United States. Along with the USA Patriot Act, a host of other insidious bureaucratic measures were quickly put into place that tore the Constitutional rug out from under the average citizen while placing civil disobedience and basic human rights at risk. Racial profiling and spying on domestic communities allowed for blank-check violations of civil liberties by the FBI, while the CIA engaged in "renditions" of suspected enemies of the state, to be tortured at "undisclosed locations" in foreign nations.

When viewed in combination, all these trends represented an emerging and dangerous political, cultural, social, and economic phenomenon that Sheldon Wolin, professor emeritus of politics at Princeton University, had termed "managed democracy" and "inverted totalitarianism," under the auspices of a United States government acting in its capacity as a "Superpower." According to Wolin, the term "Superpower" stands for "the projection of power outwards," while "inverted totalitarianism" stands for the unlimited and virtually unconstrained projection of power "inwards" (Wolin 2008, xiii). In his book, *Democracy Incorporated: Managed Democracy and the Specter of Inverted Totalitarianism,* Wolin identifies and defines a new national and global political reality, wherein we discover a new world order: ***"'Superpower,' 'empire,' and 'globalization' all presuppose and depend upon inequalities of power while maintaining the illusion that somehow those inequalities are not retrojected into the homeland, that the refinement of methods of controlling 'crowds' or the denial of due process to American citizens is, at worst, an aberration rather than a prerequisite of Superpower and a contribution to inverted totalitarianism. In fact, empire and Superpower undermine and implicitly oppose two presumably fundamental principles of American political ideology: that the Constitution provides the standard for a government of limited powers—and that American governance and politics are democratic"*** (Wolin 2008, 237, italics and bold added).

While Robert Kennedy sought to change the course of America's foreign policy and take the nation and the world in a radically different direction aimed toward no more Vietnams, the post-Kennedy decades have borne witness to more Vietnams, more illegal interventions, and more violations of human rights and human dignity, all of which were taken in support of the US empire and the maintenance of US hegemony on a global scale. Hence professor Carl Boggs has observed that, in the aftermath of Robert Kennedy's assassination: "Leftist and progressive movements capable of posing effective alternatives to an increasingly bankrupt political order scarcely exist" (Boggs 2011, 251). To make matters even worse, it should be remembered that "Democrats are beholden to the same corporate and military interests—and subscribe to the same broad political outlook—as Republicans" (Boggs 2011, 251). So much for the value of the much-heralded virtue and ideal of "bipartisanship." In light of these trends, it can only be assumed that "these voracious interests exhibit no readiness to abandon their vast network of privilege and power, nor relinquish the 'grand illusions' vital to perpetuating their hegemony" (Boggs 2011, 251).

By 2011, the policies of both major political parties had come to reflect a total reversal of the priorities that defined Robert Kennedy's career, policies, and message for progressive change (Kuttner 2013; Stockman 2013; Chossudovsky and Marshall 2010). By late summer of that year, a debt deal forged by the Republicans with little real resistance from the Democrats reflected both parties' convergence on $1.5 trillion in budget cuts. On one side of the budgetary ledger, items placed on the chopping block and targeted for cuts included: $650 billion for special education, student aid, and assistance to poor schools; $310 billion from the National Institutes of Health; $100 billion from the Centers for Disease Control and the FDA; $98 billion from Head Start and child care programs; $47 billion from energy grants to help poor families afford heat; $20 billion from job training for the unemployed; and $11 billion from after-school tutoring programs (Dickinson 2011, 57). On the other side of the budgetary ledger, those items exempted from cuts—that resulted in tax breaks and subsidies for the rich—included: $690 billion remaining from the Bush tax cuts for the wealthiest 2 percent; $321 billion in itemized deductions for top-bracket taxpayers; $129 billion in subsidies for foreign profits; $97.5 billion in subsidies for business inventories; $44 billion in subsidies for oil and gas companies; $21.4 billion in a carried-interest loophole for hedge-fund managers; and $10 billion in tax breaks on loans for vacation homes and yachts (Dickinson 2011, 57).

17

Robert Kennedy's Approach to Modernization and Development

In setting the historical stage for explicating and understanding Robert Kennedy's more humanistic/humanitarian approach to the challenges of twentieth century modernization and development, and of US foreign policy in Asia, it is analytically necessary to identify his situation in the stream of history in juxtaposition with some of the most dominant intellectual elements of an earlier era: that of Europe's eighteenth-century Enlightenment. In the late eighteenth century, a number of prominent European political thinkers—such as Diderot, Kant, and Herder—attacked imperialism as it was practiced by various European nation-states. They undertook their critique of and their opposition to European imperialism by not only defending the human rights and dignity of non-European peoples against the injustices of European imperial rule, as some earlier modern thinkers had already done, but also by directly challenging the idea that Europeans had any right to subjugate, colonize, and "civilize" the rest of the world (Muthu 2003, 1). The arrogance of the European "civilizing mission" that had begun in earnest in the eighteenth century continued into the first half of the twentieth century. This mission was undertaken, according to Diderot, Kant, and Herder, with a disdain for the moral universalism that underscored the dissenters' version of cosmopolitan justice. We find that "Kant defends the lives, the freedom, and the independence of peoples remarkably different from his own both as incommensurably diverse and as similarly human . . . For Kant, to respect the incommensurable pluralism of both individual and collective lives, either at home or abroad, is to respect our shared humanity" (Muthu 2003, 209). The same could be said of Robert Kennedy's own view and perspective more than two hundred years after Kant.

Kennedy expressed his moral outrage about the human costs and horror of the Vietnam War in a moving speech on the floor of the US Senate on March 2, 1967:

> Few of us are directly involved while the rest of us continue our lives and pursue our ambitions undisturbed by the sounds and fears of battle. To the Vietnamese, however, it must seem the fulfillment of the prophesy of Saint John the Divine: "*And I looked, and beheld a pale horse: and his name that sat on him was Death, and hell followed with him. And power was given unto them over the fourth part of the earth, to kill with sword, and with hunger, and with death . . .*" Let us reflect for a moment not on the wisdom and necessity of our cause, nor on the valor of the South Vietnamese, but on the horror. For although the world's imperfections may call forth the acts of war, righteousness cannot obscure the agony and pain those acts bring to a single child. (Ross 1968, 535, italics added)

These words from Robert Kennedy reveal what separates him from the politicians of his time and those who have come after. Kennedy could feel the pain, identify with victims, articulate the moral concerns involved, and remind his audience about the oft-forgotten realities of human dignity and rights in a world victimized by war, imperialism, and greed. In this regard, Kennedy was unique, because he forced his audience to consider their personal responsibility for allowing the war to proceed in all of its horrific dimensions. In his own words, from the March 2, 1967 speech, we hear Kennedy's voice remind his listeners that: "***All we say and all we do must be informed by our awareness that this horror is partly our responsibility; not just a nation's responsibility, but yours and mine. It is we who live in abundance and send our young men to die. It is our chemicals that scorch the children and our bombs that level the villages. We are all participants***" (Ross 1968, 536, italics and bold added).

Like Kant more than two hundred years before, Kennedy felt obligated to remind his audience that we all share a common humanity—and it is this common humanity that demands and deserves respect. As Professor Sankar Muthu has observed: "For Kant, to respect the incommensurable pluralism of both individual and collective lives, either at home or abroad, is to respect our shared humanity" (Muthu 2003, 209). Robert Kennedy clearly understood this as well, which is why he undertook a moral and practical critique of the Vietnam War that implicated every one of his fellow citizens as participants who shared a moral responsibility for the horrors that were being inflicted on a foreign people in their name. It is this moral and philosophical perspective that so intimately serves to connect Robert Kennedy with Kant and the anti-imperialists of the eighteenth century Enlightenment era. In the stream of history, we discover that the themes of human rights, human dignity, anti-imperialism, and anti-colonialism all have their roots in a history that centralizes the importance of our interconnected moral universe beyond the artificial boundaries of culture, nation-states, and ephemeral "national interest." We discover that over the course of passing centuries, there remain certain constants or enduring themes that define what is most crucially human about us as human beings—thereby positing some lasting hints about our ultimate purpose and where the human future ought to be headed. Professor Muthu has observed: "A study of Enlightenment anti-imperialism offers a richer and more accurate portrait of eighteenth-century political thought and illuminates the under-appreciated philosophical interconnections between human unity and human diversity, and between moral universalism and moral incommensurability" (Muthu 2003, 3). As the twentieth century evolved and as the remnants of European colonialism and imperialism were invariably in a state of political and ideological collapse—caught up in a hopeless trajectory of decline—these last vestiges of imperial practices were being dismantled by a global consensus of emerging states throughout the Third World. These Third World nations, working in alliance with other progressive movements and anti-imperialists on every continent, asserted the principles of human freedom through the newly emerging international law concepts of self-determination, independence, human rights, and self-reliance.

By the 1960s, Robert Kennedy was engaged in the center of this struggle, both within the civil rights struggles of the United States, and also in the anti-apartheid movement in South Africa, the land-reform efforts of Latin American nations, and the growing global human-rights movement—all of which reinforced and refocused attention on the struggle to centralize the claims of human dignity over and above the hierarchies of power, profit, and privilege. The Vietnam War of Lyndon Johnson, in particular, became the focus of rage and opposition by global progressive forces that renounced imperial pretensions in whatever garb such pretensions were draped, and under whatever ideological mandates they sought refuge. For Robert Kennedy, like Kant in the eighteenth century, there could be no justification for the colonial subjugation of foreign peoples and cultures under the auspices of imperial state interventions that resulted in the denial of the cosmopolitan right of one's "innate right of humanity"—that is, the right to a distinctively human freedom, or cultural agency, that all human possess by virtue of their humanity (Muthu 2003, 173). For Robert Kennedy, from 1966 onward there could be no moral justification for the human agony that US imperialism had imposed on either the people of Vietnam or on the American people themselves. Abroad, the Vietnam War had created a crisis of conscience—as well as international law. Further, the Vietnam War created a crisis with respect to adherence to international law standards by virtue of the United States violating long-established norms such as the Nuremberg Principles. At home, the economic and social costs of the Vietnam War could be measured in the toll exacted by depriving and diverting needed economic resources from the tasks of eliminating hunger and poverty, educating the young, strengthening the bonds of community, and meeting the challenges connected with racial reconciliation, job creation, and the renewal and renovation of America's decaying cities.

America's domestic crisis was further complicated by long-standing practices of a paternalistic state that all too often reinforced bureaucratic policies and practices that were antithetical to the realization of human dignity. This was another arena in which the insights of Kant informed some of Robert Kennedy's perceptions of America's problems and their solutions. We find in the political writings of Kant a persistent proclivity to engage in a critique of modern society and politics that is reflective of a strong anti-paternalism toward the state because of the danger it posed to his understanding of human freedom. Ultimately, Kant was committed to individual and collective self-determination (Muthu 2003, 155). In the final analysis, an examination of Kantian precepts serves to demonstrate the strongly held view that "even if some of the most unequal and despotic state-sanctioned institutions were eliminated, Kant believed that the power of European sates would continue to be a problem to reckon with both domestically and internationally" (Muthu 2003, 156). Therefore, it followed that the "worst forms of brutality and the ominous sense of insecurity that our social tensions foster can be held in check, Kant asserts, by a non-despotic public power," but "not all of our rights are created externally through our actions and then secured by public power. There is, Kant argues, one innate right, ***'that which belongs to everyone by nature, independently of any act that would establish a right . . . Freedom (independence from being constrained by another's choice), insofar as it can coexist with the freedom of every other in accordance with***

a universal law, is the only original right belonging to every man by virtue of his humanity.' This is precisely the kind of freedom . . . that underlies Kant's understanding of humanity as cultural agency' (Muthu 2003, 156-157, italics and bold added).

Similarly, Robert Kennedy opposed the nature of the US welfare system for its proclivity to be paternalistic and destructive of self-worth by depriving welfare recipients of their own opportunity to be heard in the making of decisions that affected their very lives. The jobless, hopeless, and endemic dependency engendered by the US welfare state was an object of Kennedy's contempt because it deprived individuals of their dignity and communities of bonds of solidarity. The net result of these trends were disastrous effects on the ideals of democratic participation, public debate, and decision-making over investment and distributional issues. It was a global and a national challenge. As early as the eighteenth century, this was a problem insofar as human freedom itself was placed in jeopardy. Political freedom does not entail the total elimination of conflict. Our political goal, Kant argues, should be to construct "a society which has not only the greatest freedom, and therefore a continual antagonism among its members, but also the precise specification and preservation of the limits of this freedom in order that it can co-exist with the freedom of others" (Muthu 2003, 158).

Upon further reflection, twenty-first century scholars in the fields of economics and politics have come to conclude that Kantian socioeconomic theory serves to conceptualize human beings as moral agents who are engaged in balancing moral preferences with the practical challenges of evolving political, economic, and social norms. What ultimately matters is doing one's duty—no matter what the cost—because doing what is right is central in the Kantian moral equation. In short, unlike the nineteenth century utilitarians, such as Jeremy Bentham and John Stuart Mill—who embraced a system of ethics that judges the morality of actions by the goodness (or "utility") of their consequences—we discover that Kant rejects using a numerical index that measures doing right in terms of either money or time (White 2011, 2–3). Kant—like Amartya Sen in the late twentieth century and early twenty-first century—believed that one's commitment is of central importance in making the determination of goodness. That is because commitment cuts across and against preferences, severing the connection between preference and choice (White 2011, 3–4). In short, the pursuit of one's duties does not bend to opportunity costs, because duties are not traded off or compromised when circumstances change.

Both John and Robert Kennedy often used the word "commitment" in addressing their policy preferences and their decisions to pursue one course over another, and in making moral appeals in support of particular political goals.

In this respect, Robert Kennedy summed up the Kantian position in his own political formulation of moral choice when he noted in an address at Fordham University, New York, on June 10, 1967, that "if there was one thing that President Kennedy stood for that touched the most profound feelings of young people across the world, it was the belief that idealism, high aspirations and deep convictions are not incompatible with the most practical and efficient of programs—that there is no basic inconsistency between ideals and realistic possibilities—no separation between the deepest desires of heart and mind and the rational application of human effort to human problems"(Ross 1968, 14). Kennedy then proceeded to undermine the basis of utilitarian logic: "It is not realistic or hardheaded to solve problems and take action unguided by ultimate moral aims and values. It is thoughtless folly. For it ignores the realities of human faith and passion and belief; forces ultimately more powerful than all the calculations of economists or generals" (Ross 1968, 14). Kennedy concluded his remarks with a Kantian affirmation of duty that applies to a situation when it is the right thing to do, regardless of other factors or circumstances.

Kennedy concluded: "Of course to adhere to standards, to idealism, to vision, in the midst of immediate dangers takes courage and self-confidence. But we also know that only those who dare to fail greatly, can ever achieve greatly" (Ross 1968, 14). In making this point, Kennedy emphasized his commitment to a particular political path as a matter of moral obligation, civic obligation, and moral duty. Hence, we discover here that Kennedy rejects the consequentialist or teleological (goal-oriented) ethics of utilitarianism and embraces the deontological ethics of Kant as the basis for forms of action that serve to advance human dignity, rights, and the value of persons—irrespective of some illusion of a guarantee of success that is merely predicated upon a numerical calculation of risk or some form of cost-benefit analysis. For Kennedy, the bane of modernization in the twentieth century is that the ideology of modernization had been taken captive by a form of utilitarian calculation that severed moral concerns, idealism, and a more humane vision for the human future from human commitments in the political world. Such an approach, Kennedy believed, left the political, economic, and social realms of human life devoid of moral meaning and content, and left them hopelessly crippled by an ideology of convenience. In Kennedy's view, such a result inevitably left structures and situations of injustice safely in place. In turn, it was a path that left powerful forces and hierarchies of privilege unaccountable, while leaving demands for moral claims for greater human freedom in abeyance while structural violence and injustices continued to mount.

From the eighteenth century Enlightenment insights of Kant on into the twentieth-century struggles for national and personal liberation, there was an evolving theme in the stream of history in which Robert Kennedy found himself immersed: how best to assert human freedom such that the dignity of the person could find public expression in a public space that was advantageous to the realization of human rights. Hence, upon reflection, it can be argued that what Kant advocated about human freedom and dignity in the eighteenth century may also be said of the world order that emerged out of the post-World War II twentieth century—a trend that reached its moral, social, cultural, and ideological apex in the 1960s. The calls for greater human freedom and dignity reached a new crescendo in the US and around the world. The 1960s was the crucial decade in which Robert Kennedy emerged as not only a national figure within the context of United States leadership, but also as a global statesman who combined sensitivity toward the exercise of political power with a clear recognition of the moral, communal, and international connections attendant to the exercise of that power.

The nature of this battle has persisted well beyond Kennedy's time and has reemerged with stark intensity in the late twentieth and early twenty-first century. According to Naomi Klein:

> In *The Shock Doctrine*, I explore how the right-wing has systematically used crises—real and trumped up—to push through a brutal ideological agenda designed not to solve the problems that created the crises but rather to enrich elites. As the climate crisis begins to bite, it will be no exception. This is entirely predictable. Finding new ways to privatize the commons and to profit from disaster are what our current system is built to do. The process is already well under way. The only wild card is whether some countervailing popular movement will step up to provide a viable alternative to this grim future. That means not just an alternative set of policy proposals but an alternative worldview to rival the one at the heart of the ecological crisis—this time embedded in interdependence rather than hyper-individualism, reciprocity rather than dominance and cooperation rather than hierarchy. (Klein November 28, 2011, 19)

The kind of response that Klein has advocated is also rather Kantian, insofar as it points toward the need to embrace an economic model of decision-making that is based on non-consequentialist ethics—specifically the moral duty that Kant endorsed in which the nature of the actions themselves, rather than their moral consequences, determines their moral worth. For Robert Kennedy, the same was true. Speaking in 1967 at Fordham University in New York, Kennedy quoted the Chinese curse that says: "May you live in interesting times." He then told his audience: "Like it or not we live in interesting times. They are times of danger and uncertainty; but they are also more open to the creative energy of men than any other time in history. Everyone here will ultimately be judged—will ultimately judge himself—on the effort he has contributed to building a new world society and the extent to which his ideals and goals have shaped that effort" (Ross 1968, 14–15).

As both a national leader and as a global statesman, Robert Kennedy adopted a largely Kantian view of human dignity. He did so by giving high priority to the power of human agency—the universal and undifferentiated worth of the individual person. His political message was designed to inspire people to recognize that one person can make a difference to advance the collective good. Kennedy's vision had both national and international implications. On September 29, 1964, in a statement following a speech he delivered at the University of Rochester, he said:

> If President Kennedy's life stood for anything, it was for the fact that an individual can make a difference—that an individual has an obligation and a responsibility to try to make a difference. I think that whether in the field of civil rights or in the field of housing, the problems that are facing us in Latin America or Asia or Berlin or any of these places, all of us make some kind of sacrifice—make some kind of effort—on behalf of our country, and on behalf of our own fellow citizens, and on behalf of the citizens of the world—it is absolutely essential. (Ross 1968, 9)

This statement provides us with solid evidence that Robert Kennedy was a statesman, a national leader who also viewed himself as a citizen of the world, able to look beyond a narrowly tailored nationalistic message and embrace the larger demands of global citizenship and acknowledge the existence of global responsibilities. Not content with merely winning electoral contests as ends in themselves, Kennedy sought to use the platform of electoral office to empower himself and others to literally change the world. This is the central and most profound insight that unites Kennedy's vision with that of Kant. Professor Mark White has noted: "Kantian dignity is a relatively simple concept, and a very appealing one to the modern person (although shocking in his day). As Hill puts it, '*the root idea of dignity is simply that virtually everyone, regardless of social station, talents, accomplishments, or moral record, should be regarded with respect as a human being*.' Despite its simplicity, the Kantian conception of dignity has very strong implications for how persons may be treated, by other persons as well as by the state (and themselves)" (White 2011, 21–22, italics added). This is the central insight that connects Kant's philosophy and ethics with the politics, message, and policies of Robert Kennedy.

This Kantian perspective served to complement and to reflect Kennedy's own uniquely communitarian view of the importance of human community in advancing not only the collective well-being of one's fellows through a sense of shared solidarity, but also through offering a call to service that united the pursuit of one's individual interests and preferences with those of the community of which one was a part. Hence, Kennedy did not acknowledge some kind of artificial separation between the pursuit of what classical economists refer to as self-interest and one's personal preference—a rather stilted conceptualization of choice that assumes there is something that needs to be axiomatically divorced from a conception of the common good, or from the larger concerns of the national and/or global community. Rather, Kennedy's own incorporation of a Kantian view of human dignity supplied him with the rationale to argue, like Kant, that every citizen needed to recognize the moral and categorical imperative to feel a sense of obligation toward those in need and those who suffer. A good example of Kennedy's view on the matter: when he responded to critics of his visit to California with a form letter explaining, "I was in California because the problems which migrant farm workers face are not, as you suggest, a California problem, but a national concern. They are the lowest paid, least protected group of workers in our economy. In addition, I have specific legislative responsibilities in regard to farm problems. I am a member of the Senate Subcommittee on Migratory Labor, and pursuant to that responsibility, I have visited a number of migrant worker camps throughout the country in connection with specific legislative proposals now before our committee" (Bender 2008, 35). It was this sense of obligation that, in Kennedy's view, supplied not only a political rationale but a political and moral duty to contribute to improving and enhancing the lives of others—thereby enhancing one's own well-being as a member of a community, as a citizen of a national and world community. In other words, Kennedy took Kant's concept of the categorical imperative and turned it into a political duty, a moral call to action that would necessitate a confrontation with one's personal conscience as an individual and one's conscience as a citizen—a citizen who owed a duty to the larger community of which one was a part and a participant.

In explicating this view, Kennedy communicated a vision for both the national and global community that made human well-being, human rights, and human dignity the essential building blocks of a more humane future. Kennedy understood that the mere aggrandizement of wealth—of more *things*—and the mania of the consumer society could ultimately neither satisfy the demands of personal improvement or a definition of national growth and progress that was worthy of truly free individuals in a viable democracy. It was clear to Robert Kennedy that the essential and ongoing requirements of a democracy and democratic citizenship required a renewal of the Athenian notion of citizenship—as defined by participation in public affairs—combined with a Kantian notion of duty and obligation to a greater moral and ethical good, to be undertaken by citizens irrespective of some kind of utilitarian calculus. Nowhere was this commitment more evident in Kennedy's life than with respect to his concern for American Indians. Historian Edward Schmitt noted: "Whatever the political calculation that may have factored into Kennedy's decision to spend time on Indian affairs in the midst of the primary races, it was certainly unconventional. When aide Fred Dutton tried to convince him that the Native American vote was insubstantial, telling him *'he should knock off the Injuns,'* the candidate dashed off a note in response: *'Those of you who think you're running my campaign don't love Indians the way I do. You're a bunch of bastards'*" (Schmitt 2010, 204, italics added).

When Dutton admonished Kennedy to give up providing his time and attention to the plight and suffering of the American Indian community, he was violating the Kantian premise of the categorical imperative by treating people as mere means to an end—that is, as means to campaigning for a large electoral vote as the ultimate goal of Robert Kennedy's political efforts. It is clear that Robert Kennedy rejected Dutton's advice because "Kantian ethics are demanding only in what one must *not* do, not in what one must do instead; there is much room for judgment in what the agent actually chooses to do in fulfillment of [their] duties" (White 2011, 23, italics in original). As a free moral agent confronted with moral and political choices of great consequence, Kennedy—as the historical record reveals—rejected Dutton's advice because he did not accept the narrow confines of the electoral game of American politics. Rather, Kennedy was the embodiment of the new politics of 1968. Kennedy chose *not* to avoid committing to the cause of American Indians, deciding instead to take some of his time away from the traditional confines of electoral campaigning to be with the American Indian community—exposing the nature of their suffering, their needs, and their aspirations to the American people. In this situation, we discover that Kennedy made a very personal choice to embrace the cause of the neglected and oppressed American Indian community by fulfilling both his personal and political perception of what he owed them, and what he believed the nation as a whole owed to those who suffered under unjust conditions and circumstances that could be addressed once exposed. Kennedy viewed the plight, suffering, and struggles of the American Indian community as a community that was a part of the larger national and global community of persons who suffer—and who do not deserve to suffer the denial of their human rights and dignity as persons of infinite worth. Like Kant, Robert Kennedy believed that we share with one another a moral duty to act in such a way that we seek to advance what is right, regardless of whether a particular consequence is achieved. What matters is that we try, that we make an effort, that we seek the higher good and not the lowest common denominator.

This is the philosophical and moral bridge that best explains Robert Kennedy's enduring commitment to human rights and his enduring, consistent efforts to wipe out the ghettos that separated the poor from the rest of society. At the same time, he was painfully aware that there would be no quick or immediate resolution to the problem of the ghettos and, by extrapolation, what that meant to the lives of those still trapped within the confines of ghetto existence, with its attendant and endemic culture of poverty. Commenting on the quandary in which Kennedy found himself in 1966, historian Edward Schmitt writes:

> Wisconsin senator William Proxmire challenged Kennedy on the wisdom of building in the ghetto when economists were suggesting that jobs were moving out of the city, but Kennedy contended that despite the trend, ghettos would continue to exist. As he had proposed in the first of his three January 1966 speeches, he conceded that mobility for blacks was vital but asserted: "For a long time to come in the future

> there are just going to be very, very few Negroes who are going to be in a class where they are able to move out of the ghettos . . . It will be hard for them to know how to find jobs [in the suburbs] and for their children to keep up in these schools." (Schmitt 2010, 203)

RFK's commitment to eliminating poverty as a barrier to human dignity and human community provides us with the moral and philosophical touchstone of his unique brand of politics. Kennedy's view ultimately reflects a path and program that provide a common denominator for action and judgment in dealing with the problems of social injustice and social exclusion—a view that explains his policies from the slums of Bedford-Stuyvesant in New York to the slums of Latin America and South Africa. Now the question becomes: *What is the philosophical, political, economic, and human rights connection between the social experiment of Bedford Stuyvesant with the Alliance for Progress and Robert Kennedy's advocacy for ending racial apartheid in South Africa as well as the American south?* Kennedy's own answer is best summed up in his famous 1966 graduation speech to the young people of South Africa, which also served as the *Postscript* to his book, *To Seek a Newer World*:

> Each nation has different obstacles and different goals, shaped by the vagaries of history and experience. Yet, as I talk to young people around the world I am impressed not by the diversity but by the closeness of their goals, their desires and concerns and hope for the future. There is discrimination in New York, apartheid in South Africa, and serfdom in the mountains of Peru. People starve to death in the streets of India; intellectuals go to jail in Russia; thousands are slaughtered in Indonesia; wealth is lavished on armaments everywhere. These are differing evils, but they are the common works of man. They reflect the imperfections of human justice, the inadequacy of human compassion, the defectiveness of our sensibility toward the suffering of our fellow; they mark the limit of our ability to use knowledge for the well-being of others. And therefore, they call upon common qualities of conscience and of indignation, a shared determination to wipe away the unnecessary sufferings of our fellow human beings at home and around the world. (Kennedy 1967, 229–230)

Forty four years later, writing in her book entitled *Creating Capabilities: The Human Development Approach*, professor Martha C. Nussbaum noted: "All over the world people are struggling for lives that are worthy of their human dignity. Leaders of countries often focus on national economic growth alone, but their people, meanwhile, are striving for something different: meaningful lives for themselves" (Nussbaum 2011, 1). She continues: *All nations . . . contain struggles for lives worthy of human dignity, and all contain struggles for equality and justice . . . All nations, then, are developing nations, in that they contain problems of human development and struggles for a fully adequate quality of life and for minimal justice. All are currently failing at the aim of ensuring dignity and opportunity for each person*" (Nussbaum 2011, 16, italics added). Nussbaum reminds us of what Robert Kennedy sought to teach both the national and the global community throughout his career: that for the people of the United States, South Africa, Latin America, and elsewhere, the challenges posed by the pursuit of human development are basically—at the most fundamental level—a set of challenges that center on the question of how to respect and honor the core human dignity of every person. The central message of the lesson, which began in earnest with Kant, is that this challenge is a truly universal one.

Whatever historical distinctions or commonalities may be cited, the reality is that all human beings over the last decades are confronting the global realities of how we must transcend our past history if we are to truly claim the present time in which we live. Robert Kennedy understood this insight better than anyone. He summed up the daunting nature of these new global realities with profound insight on June 10, 1967, at Fordham University:

> Everywhere, new technologies and communications bring men and nations closer together, the concerns of one inevitably becoming the concerns of all. But our new closeness has not yet stripped away the false masks, the illusions of difference which are the root of injustice and hate and war. Earthbound man still clings to the dark and poisoning superstition that his world is bounded by the nearest hill, his universe ended at river shore, his common humanity enclosed in the tight circle of those who share his views and his town and the color of his skin. And therefore the survival of the human species itself depends on our ability to strip the last remnants of that ancient, cruel belief from the civilization of man. (Ross 1968, 11–12)

More than four decades later, Naomi Klein echoed Kennedy's sentiments on the subject with her own observation: "In the rocky future that we have already made inevitable, an unshakable belief in the rights of all people, and a capacity for deep compassion, will be the only things standing between humanity and barbarism" (Klein 2011, 21).

On June 6, 1966, at the University of Cape Town, Robert Kennedy began his remarks to the graduating South African students with this observation:

> I came here because of my deep interest and affection for a land settled by the Dutch in the mid-seventeenth century, then taken over by the British, and at last independent; a land in which the native inhabitants were at first subdued, but relations with whom remain a problem to this day; a land which defined itself on a hostile frontier; a land which has tamed natural resources through the energetic application of modern technology; a land which once imported slaves, and now must struggle to wipe out the last traces of that former bondage. I refer, of course, to the United States of America. (Kennedy 1966, 237)

With a wry sense of humor, Kennedy came full circle in helping his audience to see that all nations share common problems and are in the process of slowly emerging from a similar place in the stream of history. Robert Kennedy understood that the success of social movements for change would be critically determined by the wider social and political context in which struggles for social justice were undertaken. The outcome of these struggles is never certain. What was certain from Kennedy's perspective is that persons should be seen as ends in themselves and not as means to some other end.

Like Kant, Kennedy was committed to the principle that every person is endowed with dignity, possessing an incalculable and incomparable worth. Holding true to this view provided Kennedy with a substantive basis for his political positions and for his moral view of where the world should be changed and transformed. As with Kant, Kennedy was not content to allow the oligarchs of corporate capitalism to use, exploit, and oppress people in such a way that they would become little more than the means to an end—such as the narrow pursuit of profit for the sake of profit. Just as centuries before, when the doctrine of the eighteenth century monarchs as expressed in the notion of the "Divine Right of Kings" was rejected by the Enlightenment's leading philosophers and thousands of patriots in the American and French Revolutions, so, too, countless others in the twentieth century decided that the "Divine Right of Capital" had to be rejected as well—and for starkly similar reasons. By the twentieth century, the intellectual terrain had expanded beyond merely civil and political rights, and economic rights, social rights, and cultural rights now come under the rubric of human rights, itself, in turn, under the ambit of governmental action and state responsibility.

In Kennedy's view, fidelity to human rights should take precedence over capitalism's insatiable drive for profit (so often undertaken irrespective of the human cost in attaining those profits). Whether the group in question was migrant laborers, American Indians, or black citizens trapped in poverty or the grip of apartheid, Kennedy naturally associated himself with a tradition of humanistic and socially oriented moral philosophers whose moral arguments allowed him to become a practical political advocate for change on behalf of the powerless, the excluded, the marginalized, and the dispossessed (Fletcher and Gapasin 2008; Shaw 2008; Somers 2008; Crepaz 2008; Hing 2010; Vargas 2005; Bosniak 2006; Barkan 2007; Ngai 2004; Echo-Hawk 2010; Pommersheim 2009; Blackburn 2011; Klein 2003; Marable, Ness, and Wilson 2006). In this crucial respect, it is manifestly clear from the historical record that Kennedy believed in the principle that one person could make a difference. Therefore, he committed himself and the policies that he pursued to making a difference that would reroute the stream of history in his own time. Kennedy's commitment to opposing the human-rights violations of the American empire, the abuses of an international structure of white supremacy, and the demonization of the other has been a continuing struggle since his 1968 assassination (Kelley 2006, 57–69). Inspired by RFK's legacy, many other people around the globe have engaged in the struggle to advance human rights and oppose the continuing violations of those rights. Further, there have been significant efforts to expand and redefine human rights—as exemplified in the proliferation of National Human Rights Institutions (NHRIs), newly passed UN protections for indigenous peoples, and a greater attention to the actions of multinational corporations that have stolen the natural resources of peoples and exploited their environments and their livelihoods (Paupp 2014).

Part of Kennedy's strategy was to participate in a national and global sea change of sensibility in the 1960s. Decolonization had been the first step, in the aftermath of World War II. The civil rights movement in the United States was in harmony with national liberation struggles taking place throughout the Third World (Fredrickson 1995; Winant 2001). What was happening within the context of South Africa's liberation struggles, driven by the African National Congress (ANC), would resonate within the civil- and human-rights struggles taking place in the United States and elsewhere. History was changing course in the 1960s, and Kennedy sensed it, spoke about its demands, and added his principled voice to articulating its challenge to the status quo.

On October 28, 1967, Kennedy outlined his position in no uncertain terms in a speech on the fate of underdeveloped nations, declaring:

> Reform and progress, the economy of the twentieth century, cannot and will not be planned and managed by leaders and social structures that were outmoded in the eighteenth. Men will not strive to learn, to improve lands they do not own, in whose proceeds they do not share. They will not save and sacrifice to develop a nation and an economy in which the fruits of their labor are reserved for the privileged few. If our assistance finds its way only to those who would perpetuate privilege, it will buy for us only contempt and hate which will plague our children for generations to come. Justice cannot be a luxury for the rich—it must be the sustenance and hope of the many; it is the only real way to progress. (Ross 1968, 444)

Similarly, what is required of us in our own day and generation is that we must—as people of conscience with a recognizable common bond to others in a condition of shared human solidarity—come to recognize this emerging twenty-first century global reality: a higher degree of respect, commitment, and universal understanding must be given to the realization of human dignity, human rights, and human capabilities, if we are to effectively and collectively traverse a more humane path that honors each and every person. This commitment is reflective not only of the legacy of Kant and Kennedy, it is also an essential part of the moral argument against global poverty and social injustices that has been offered by philosopher Thomas W. Pogge. Following in the tradition of Kant and Kennedy, as well as John Rawls, Martha Nussbaum and Amaryta Sen, Pogge offers his own moral assessment of our national and global orders. In so doing, he argues that both the political and economic orders of national communities, as well as the global community itself, remain too undemocratic to allow for the necessary participation and access for all persons who are negatively affected by these structures—with the exception of a tiny oligarchical minority who unjustly benefit from a global order of exploitation. It is for this reason that Pogge condemns the global economic order, because it fails to meet two minimal requirements that would make the world more just and allow the majority of people access to avenues for peaceful change. Pogge states: "The first minimal requirement is that, at least within the limits of what justice allows, social rules should be liable to peaceful change by any large majority of those on whom they are imposed" (Pogge 2002, 96). This was precisely one of the claims that Robert Kennedy was making when he criticized South Africa's apartheid regime—as well as the Jim Crow laws of his own country. Pogge also states: "The second minimal requirement is that avoidable life-threatening poverty must be avoided" (Pogge 2002, 96). This insight returns us to Nussbaum's twenty-first century rendition of Kennedy's ideal with respect to honoring and empowering the capabilities and human rights of the person at the dawn of the twenty-first century.

Nussbaum makes a strong case for the fundamental proposition that "for all, then, the *Capabilities Approach* supplies insight" (Nussbaum 2011, 16, italics added). Nussbaum defines the Capabilities Approach thusly: "the approach takes each person as end, asking not just about the total or average well-being but about the opportunities available to each person. It is focused on choice or freedom, holding that the crucial good societies should be promoting for their people is a set of opportunities, or substantial freedoms, which people then may or may not exercise in action: the choice is theirs. It thus commits itself to respect for people's power of self-definition" (Nussbaum 2011, 18). What Kant, Kennedy, Pogge, and Nussbaum—as well as Rawls and Sen—all share is a commitment to making sure that national and global structures of power, both economic and political, respect and protect the ability of persons to define themselves—as autonomous moral agents, to be sure, but also as active citizens who are members of local, national, and global communities who have sought to achieve and to maintain the capacity and power of the popular masses of people to participate in decision-making, dialogue, and democratic discourses on matters of shared concern.

Unfortunately, this is not the case within most countries, including the United States. This is largely because far too many of the aforementioned minimal conditions associated with inclusion, access, and participation have not been met. In fact, they have been effectively blocked by the dominant forces of the status quo. Professor Carl Boggs has examined American institutions and discovered that "to be a functioning system, democracy requires certain minimum conditions: universal and open suffrage, constitutional rights and freedoms, popular access to economic and political institutions, free party competition offering genuine alternatives, local governance, and developed norms of citizen participation. It cannot survive, moreover, in the absence of popular involvement based on readily accessible and diverse sources of information. Any ideal of democracy confined to formal procedures or governmental processes alone is ultimately flawed since economic and social life, integral to the commons, must be subject to roughly the same criteria of access and participation" (Boggs 2011, 5). By this criteria, the United States of the early twenty-first century is critically flawed and dysfunctional. In large measure this has been the result of the intrusion of corporate power into every arena of the public and governmental spheres.

Both civil society and government of the people, by the people, and for the people has been taken hostage by virtue of a hostile take-over of corporate media, corporate oligarchs, and a corporate war machine that runs a permanent war economy (Boggs 2011, 145–196). The situation is so critical that the question has been raised as to whether the United States has lapsed into a kind of "American Fascism" (Boggs 2011, 227–251). Whether it has already become essentially fascist, or is about to, there is one essential fact that is no longer in dispute. Since the death of Robert Kennedy, the United States has been increasingly transformed into a "phantom democracy"—a species of political governance where public access, institutional accountability, and free communications scarcely define the political system or shape arenas of daily life such as the workplace, media, education, and local communities (Boggs 2011).

One rather prominent arena of discourse where this phenomenon is prevalent is discernible in the US debate over climate change. Not only have corporatist interests and right-wing corporatist power come to dominate the right-wing side of the debate, but these same interests have seriously compromised the left and progressive wings as well. The result is that there is no Robert Kennedy to stand as a statesman-like voice to offer a competing paradigm or to offer an alternative that could prove to be a viable antidote to the power of corporate and right-wing ideology. According to Naomi Klein, we find at the dawn of the early twenty-first century that:

Half of the problem is that progressives—their hands full with soaring unemployment and multiple wars—tend to assume that the big green groups have the climate issue covered. The other half is that many of those big green groups have avoided, with phobic precision, any serious debate on the blindly obvious roots of the climate crisis: globalization, deregulation, and contemporary capitalism's quest for perpetual growth (the same forces that are responsible for the destruction of the rest of the economy)... The right-wing, meanwhile, has a free hand to exploit the global economic crisis to cast climate action as a recipe for economic Armageddon, a surefire way to spike household costs and to block much-needed jobs drilling for oil and laying new pipelines. With virtually no loud voices offering a competing vision of how a new economic paradigm could provide a way out of both the economic and ecological crises, this fear mongering has had ready audience (Klein 2011, 20).

This early twenty-first century has some parallels to the Cold War paradigm wars of the 1960s—with the exception that John and Robert Kennedy, as well as Martin Luther King, offered their voices to articulate an alternative and transformative paradigm for social justice and for human dignity—thereby providing for a new way to re-conceptualize and remake the social, economic, and political order. It was only with their deaths by assassination that the entrenched oligarchy of the status quo was ultimately able to survive the popular democratic assault on its privileges, domination, and hierarchy. In the 1960s, the decade of people power was on a collision course with the forces of corporate rule, oligarchy, and plutocracy. It was a decade that was characterized by the desire of a new people's power for self-definition, not only within the United States, but in Asia, Africa, and Latin America.

With regard to respecting people's power for self-definition, it would be helpful to return once more to the history of the Alliance for Progress as a model for what Robert Kennedy had in mind for a program dedicated to advancing human rights, development, and the capabilities of people. Under the leadership of JFK, the Alliance was intended to pursue a social-reform program. The Alliance was to be dedicated to not only to the pursuit of economic growth, but to the actual restructuring of the political and social institutions of Latin American societies that had remained trapped by feudal land arrangements, in which dictators and large landowners exploited the vast majority of their people to serve a small, elite oligarchy. In this environment, the dictators and oligarchy of Latin America had created a dangerous situation, and the Alliance for Progress—as envisioned by John and Robert Kennedy—sought to create the political space for the people to become engaged in democratic social movements designed to bring about the eventual overthrow of these outdated and unjust arrangements. In this critical respect, the Kennedy brothers sought genuine reform in accordance with the demands of realizing human rights, rather than mechanically following old economic formulas about growth.

Guided by current theories about modernization and development, however, the Alliance ran into unexpected problems between 1962 and 1963 when the forces of oligarchic control within Latin America aligned themselves with the counter-reform offensive that had been launched by US business interests, bankers, and US financiers who had come to dominate both Wall Street and the corporate boardrooms of the business community. As a result, one historian commented that "the US commitment to 'peaceful revolution' and democracy soon evaporated. When liberal reforms created political conflict, the United States abandoned them in favor of immediate security goals. Where the Alliance had promised progressive structural change in opposition to oligarchic control, US policymakers came to embrace visions of 'military modernization' and threw their support behind a brutal counterinsurgency war. The idea that post-colonial militaries could play pivotal roles in accelerating modernization provided an easy way to reconcile support for development with the empowerment of security forces" (Latham 2011, 131).

This broad historical assessment omits the fact that Robert Kennedy himself never endorsed these shifts by the US government or the theoretical assumptions that legitimated them. Rather, RFK rejected these changes to the Alliance when he argued:

> We spend nearly twice as much to train foreign military personnel here as we do for all the operations of the Voice of America; yet we do not, apparently, pay enough attention to whether they leave these shores with a proper respect for the constitutional processes which it is our stated purpose to defend. All too many of the young officers who have intervened in politics, in Latin America and elsewhere in the world, have been trained in the United States. *We would do better to try to help them move toward a role in the work of economic and social development.* (Kennedy, 1967, 123, italics added)

Various other historical accounts of these years have done a better job in shedding light on the most critical distinctions between the Kennedy leadership of the Alliance versus the policies that were pursued under Lyndon Johnson from 1964 to 1968. Professor Brian Loveman has astutely noted:

> Ultimately, the Alliance for Progress had many unintended consequences. The counterinsurgency operations and the expanded political and economic roles of the armed forces further militarized politics, eroded civil liberties and rights, and weakened civilian institutions. Even where civilian governments finally survived, military officials, garrisons, patrols, and courts became de facto governments in rural hinterlands and in regional towns and cities . . . While the United States had employed contradictory rhetoric and policies in responding to Latin American coups from 1961 to 1964, President

> Johnson and his principal advisors on the region decided that military governments were preferable to either "more Cubas" or to nationalist, populist disorder. (Loveman 1999, 177–178)

That perspective was not shared by Robert Kennedy. Rather, RFK sided with the interests of the poor, the nationalist aspirations of people emerging from colonialism, and the need he perceived to embrace the revolutionary tide of the 1960s or to be swept away with the debris of history (Brands 2010, 44–48; Cullather 2010, 253).

To the chagrin of RFK, in the aftermath of his brother's assassination, President Lyndon Johnson had effectively sought to eliminate the social-reform elements of the Alliance and turn it into little more than a conduit for weapons and arms sales to Latin America's dictators (Brands 2010). Robert Kennedy was appalled. He remained actively dedicated to trying to maintain the original purpose of the Alliance and to explain to all of America's citizens—and, in particular the citizens of Latin America—what the real intent of the Alliance had been when JFK launched it in 1961 (Brands 2010, 44–49). Further, in both the US context and in the context of Latin America, the associated problems of poverty, crime, unemployment, the alienation of the young, and the emerging needs of the cities had all combined to present policy makers and citizens with nothing less than a social crisis that needed to be addressed. In fact, it needs to be addressed with even more urgency at the dawn of the twenty-first century because of the forces of globalization, an unregulated free market ideology that has dwarfed and diminished the sphere of democratic and civic life, and the nearly unmitigated culture of greed that has eroded past gains in the areas of civil and human rights.

In the context of the early twenty-first century, as expressed in the words of Margaret Somers, we find that:

> Today, global society is drastically out of balance. With the United States in the vanguard, we are in an era in which market fundamentalism—the drive to subject all social life and the public sphere to market mechanisms—has become the prevailing ideational regime... Through the alarm of "citizenship imperiled," I caution that the rise of market fundamentalism to the position of dominant ideational regime has created a radically unbalanced power dynamic between the market and the state on the one side, and civil society on the other. Inequality in America has reached a level not seen since the Gilded Age, as a once thriving middle class feels itself on the brink of collapse into the ranks of the invisible working poor. Indeed, three decades of

> what has become market-driven governance are transforming growing numbers of once rights-bearing citizens into socially excluded internally right-less and stateless persons. A political culture that tolerates, even legitimates, these brute disparities in life chances has a corrosive effect not only on citizenship and human rights, but equally on perceptions of what we owe each other as fellow human beings. (Somers 2008, 2)

This view has been expanded upon by other scholars who, having observed these trends, have noted that:

> The accumulation of forces within neoliberal globalization presents, in Bennett Harrison's terms, a "credible threat" to workers in the Global North. In other words, workers and their communities believe that regardless of whether a particular corporation will relocate, it *can* relocate. Neoliberal globalization has come to mean that companies have the ability to move (and certain trade agreements impede efforts to stop them) or the ability to threaten or imply that they will move. Thus, at a moment when the material basis for international working-class solidarity is greater than it has ever been, workers are being forced into a race to the bottom. (Fletcher and Gapasoin 2008, 93)

In this new twenty-first century Gilded Age of growing inequality, greed, and economic brutality, the legacy of Robert Kennedy retains a vital and vibrant capacity to teach forgotten lessons and to provide a path out of our current darkness. As Joseph Stiglitz has recognized, "Markets, by themselves, even when they are stable, often lead to high levels of inequality, outcomes that are widely viewed as unfair" (2012, xiii). In his assessment of the true price of inequality, Stiglitz concludes: "We can reshape these market forces in ways that promote *more* equality. We can make markets work, or at least work better. Similarly, we will never create a system with full equality of opportunity, but we can at least create *more* equality of opportunity. The Great Recession did not create the country's inequality, but it made it much worse, so much so that it made it hard to ignore, and it further limited a large segment of the population's access to opportunity" (2012, 287).

From the slums of Bedford-Stuyvesant, New York, to the ghettos of Oakland, Watts, Detroit, and Newark, RFK embarked upon a campaign of change for national renewal (Clarke 2008). His vision involved not only a material investment in physical structures, but the renewal of hope and purpose within the hearts of the nation's citizenry. From the disaffected to the most privileged, Kennedy sought to bring about a new conception of justice that was inclusive enough so as to realize Lincoln's promise at Gettysburg, just one hundred years earlier, that "this nation should have a new birth of freedom" and that this "government of the people, by the people, and for the people should not perish from the earth." This was Kennedy's vision as well. It was not only his vision for America as a nation, but was also instructive for his global vision of what a "newer world" would actually look like.

As an advocate for what has been termed "the open society," we find in Robert Kennedy's legacy a well-worked-out philosophy of life, of how to make more human choices, and of how to construct human-rights-oriented \structures of governance that augment, protect, and respect the ideals of rationality, meaning, democracy, and equal justice for all. As expressed by Karl Popper in the conclusion to his classic two-volume work, *The Open Society and Its Enemies*, the actual human choices and possibilities that we have are not automatically given to us because "neither nature nor history can tell us what we ought to do. Facts, whether those of nature or history, cannot make the decision for us, they cannot determine the ends we are going to choose. It is we who introduce purpose and meaning into nature and into history. Men are not equal; but we can decide to fight for equal rights. Human institutions such as the state are not rational, but we can decide to fight to make them more rational . . . We can make it our fight for the open society against its enemies . . . and we can interpret it accordingly" (Popper 1971, 278). In large measure, RFK's commitment to this vision goes a long way in explaining why he detested the Vietnam War policies of Lyndon Johnson. It was this shared vision that helps to account for the reason that he had become, along with Martin Luther King, the leading political figure of his time in opposition to both the Vietnam War and the military-industrial complex.

The inclusive nature of Kennedy's vision for the world connected his commitments across a broad range of issues and involvements. It would be seen in not only his personal commitment to the purposes of the 1963 Nuclear Test Ban Treaty, but his desire to move toward nuclear abolition and an end to the Cold War. It explains why he sought a negotiated end to the Vietnam War, even at a time when such a position was politically unpopular in many quarters. The inclusive and humane policies that RFK came to endorse and propose for the people of not only the Third World, but of every continent and in every region of the world, also serves to explain the nature of his deep commitment to social justice, human dignity, and human rights, as well as his empathy for those who suffered from exploitation, imperial domination, and racist policies from South Africa to Latin America, from Southeast Asia to the Middle East.

On the night of Martin Luther King's assassination, RFK quoted from the wisdom of the ancient Greeks and said that, like them, it should be our purpose "to tame the savageness of man and make gentle the life of the world." This was the essential vision and purpose that informed and shaped Robert Kennedy's own unique conception of what constituted community—community at the local, state, federal, and international levels (Thomas 2000, 389–390). It was the expression of this vision that made him more than an ordinary politician. It was a vision that transformed him into a statesman of his own time and for all time. It is for this reason that the RFK legacy endures into the twenty-first century as a transformative call, reminding us that "we can do better." In all of the various arenas and issue-areas of human endeavor that he touched and addressed, this commitment to taming the savagery of humankind was Robert Kennedy's most basic and guiding principle. As such, this guiding principle serves as a challenge for others to make their own enduring commitment—at the dawn of the twenty-first century—to creating the "newer world" to which Kennedy committed his career and for which he sacrificed his life. In fact, his commitment to this principle endures as a beacon of light in dark times, and still points the way to meeting our greatest collective need on this planet.

Bibliography

Abramovitz, Mimi. 2011. "The US Welfare State: A Battleground for Human Rights." In *Human Rights in the United States: Beyond Exceptionalism*, edited by Shareen Hertel and Kathryn Libal. New York: Cambridge University Press.

Afkhami, Gholam Reza. 2009. *The Life and Times of the Shah*. Berkeley: University of California Press.

Albert, Michael. 2010. "Why Participatory Economics?" *Z-Magazine* 23, no. 7, July.

Alexander, Michelle. 2010. *The New Jim Crow: Mass Incarceration in the Age of Colorblindness*. New York: The New Press.

Ali, Tariq. 2006. *Pirates of the Caribbean: Axis of Hope*. New York: Verso.

Alperovitz, Gar. 2005. *America Beyond Capitalism: Reclaiming Our Wealth, Our Liberty, and Our Democracy*. New Jersey: John Wiley & Sons, Inc.

Amenta, Edwin. 1998. *Bold Relief: Institutional Politics and the Origins of Modern American Social Policy*. New Jersey: Princeton University Press.

Bacon, David. 2010. "Down Prison Road." *Z- Magazine*, October.

Baker, Dean. 2011. "Why We Aren't Like Greece." *The Nation*. August 29–September 5: 8–9.

Balkin, Jack M. 2011. *Constitutional Redemption: Political Faith in an Unjust World*. Cambridge, MA: Harvard University Press.

Barber, Benjamin R. 1984. *Strong Democracy: Participatory Politics for a New Age*. Berkeley: University of California Press.

Barkan, Elliott Robert. 2007. *From All Points: America's Immigrant West, 1870s–1952*. Bloomington: Indiana University Press.

Barnet, Richard J. 1972. *Roots of War: The Men and Institutions behind U.S. Foreign Policy*. Baltimore: Penguin Books, Inc.

Barry, Tom. 1995. *Zapata's Revenge: Free Trade and the Farm Crisis in Mexico*. Boston: South End Press.

Barry, Tom, Beth Wood, and Deb Preusch. 1983. *Dollars & Dictators: A Guide to Central America*. New York: Grove Press, Inc.

Bello, Walden. 2005. *Dilemmas of Domination: The Unmaking of the American Empire*. New York: Metropolitan Books.

Bender, Steven W. 2008. *One Night in America: Robert Kennedy, Cesar Chavez, and the Dream of Dignity*. Boulder, CO: Paradigm Publishers.

Bernstein, Irving. 1991. *Promises Kept: John F. Kennedy's New Frontier*. New York: Oxford University Press.
———. 1996. *Guns or Butter: The Presidency of Lyndon Johnson*. New York: Oxford University Press.
Bernstein, Michael A. 2001. *A Perilous Progress: Economists and Public Purpose in Twentieth-Century America*. New Jersey: Princeton University Press.
Berry, Mary Frances. 1994. *Black Resistance—White Law: A History of Constitutional Racism in America*. New York: Allen Lane/The Penguin Press.
Bertram, Eva, and Morris Blachman, Kenneth Sharpe, and Peter Andreas. 1996. *Drug War Politics: The Price of Denial*. Berkeley: University of California Press.
Bird, Kai. 1998. *The Color of Truth: McGeorge Bundy and William Bundy—Brothers in Arms*. New York: Simon & Schuster.
Black, Earle, and Merle Black. 2002. *The Rise of the Southern Republicans*. Cambridge, Massachusetts: The Belknap Press of Harvard University.
Blackburn, Robin. 2011. *The American Crucible: Slavery, Emancipation and Human Rights*. New York: Verso.
Blackmon, Douglas A. 2008. *Slavery by Another Name: The Re-Enslavement of Black People in America from the Civil War to World War II*. New York: Doubleday.
Block, Fred, Richard A. Cloward, Barbara Ehrenreich, and Frances Fox Piven. 1987. *The Mean Season: The Attack on the Welfare State*. New York: Pantheon Books.
Boggs, Carl. 2000. *The End of Politics: Corporate Power and the Decline of the Public Sphere*. New York: Guilford Press.
———. 2011. *Phantom Democracy: Corporate Interests and Political Power in America*. New York: Palgrave-Macmillan.
Borgwardt, Elizabeth. 2008. "FDR's Four Freedoms and Wartime Transformations in America's Discourse of Rights." In *Bringing Human Rights Home: A History of Human Rights in the United States, Volume I*, edited by Cynthia Soohoo, Catherine Albisa, and Martha F. Davis. Westport, CT: Praeger.
Borstelmann, Thomas. 2001. *The Cold War and the Color Line: American Race Relations in the Global Arena*. Cambridge, Massachusetts: Harvard University Press.
Bosniak, Linda. 2006. *The Citizen and the Alien: Dilemmas of Contemporary Membership*. New Jersey: Princeton University Press.
Bowles, Samuel, David M. Gordon, and Thomas E. Weisskopf. 1983. *Beyond the Waste Land: A Democratic Alternative to Economic Decline*. New York: Anchor Press/Doubleday.
Bowles, Samuel, and Herbert Gintis. 1986. *Democracy and Capitalism: Property, Community, and the Contradictions of Modern Social Thought*. New York: Basic Books, Inc.
Branch, Taylor. 1988. *Parting the Waters: America in the King Years, 1954–63*. New York: Simon & Schuster.
———. 1998. *Pillar of Fire: America in the King Years, 1963–65*. New York: Simon & Schuster.

———. 2006. *At Canaan's Edge: America in the King Years (1965–68).* New York: Simon & Schuster.

Brands, Hal. 2010. *Latin America's Cold War*. Cambridge, MA: Harvard University Press.

Brauer, Carl M. 1977. *John F. Kennedy and the Second Reconstruction.* New York: Columbia University Press.

Braun, Denny. 1998. *The Rich Get Richer: The Rise of Income Inequality in the United States and the World.* Chicago: Nelson-Hall Publishers.

Bremmer, Ian. 2010. *The End of the Free Market: Who Wins the War Between States and Corporations?* New York: Portfolio.

Brinkley, Alan. 1995. *The End of Reform: New Deal Liberalism in Recession and War.* New York: Alfred A. Knopf.

———. 1998. "1968 and the Unraveling of Liberal America." In *1968: The World Transformed,* edited by Carole Fink, Philip Gassert, and Detlef Junker. New York: Cambridge University Press.

Brown, Michael K. 1999. *Race, Money, and American Welfare State.* Ithaca: Cornell University Press.

Bunch, Will. 2009. *Tear Down This Myth: How the Reagan Legacy Has Distorted Our Politics and Haunts Our Future.* New York: Free Press.

Carnoy, Martin. 1994. *Faded Dreams: The Politics and Economics of Race in America.* New York: Cambridge University Press.

Carson, Clayborne. 1991. *Malcolm X: The FBI Files.* Edited by David Gallen. New York: Carroll & Graf Publishers, Inc.

Carter, Dan T. 1995. *The Politics of Rage: George Wallace, the Origins of the New Conservatism, and the Transformation of American Politics.* New York: Simon & Schuster.

Carter, David C. 2009. *The Music Has Gone Out of the Movement: Civil Rights and the Johnson Administration, 1965–1968.* Chapel Hill, NC: University of North Carolina Press.

Chambliss, William J. 1999. *Power, Politics, and Crime.* Boulder, CO: Westview Press.

Chemerinsky, Erwin. 2010. *The Conservative Assault on the Constitution.* New York: Simon & Schuster.

Chomsky, Noam. 1991. *Deterring Democracy.* New York: Verso.

Chossudovsky, Michel, and Andrew Gavin Marshall, eds. 2010. *The Global Economic Crisis: The Great Depression of the XXI Century.* Quebec, Canada: Global Research.

Clarke, Thurston. 2008. *The Last Campaign: Robert F. Kennedy and 82 Days That Inspired America.* New York: Henry Holt and Company.

Cockcroft, James D. 2006. "Imperialism, State and Social Movements in Latin America." In *Imperialism, Neoliberalism, and Social Struggles in Latin America,* edited by Richard A. Dello Buono and Jose Bell Lara. Chicago: Haymarket Books.

Cohen, Joshua. 2003. "For a Democratic Society." In *The Cambridge Companion to Rawls,* edited by Samuel Freeman. New York: Cambridge University Press.

Cohen, Joshua, and Joel Rogers. 1983. *On Democracy*. New York: Penguin Books.

Colby, Gerald, and Charlotte Dennett. 1995. *Thy Will Be Done: The Conquest of the Amazon: Nelson Rockefeller and Evangelism in the Age of Oil*. New York: Harper-Collins Publishers.

Cole, David. 1999. *No Equal Justice: Race and Class in the American Criminal Justice System*. New York: The New Press.

Crepaz, Markus M. L. 2008. *Trust Beyond Borders: Immigration, the Welfare State, and Identity in Modern Societies*. Ann Arbor: The University of Michigan Press.

Cullather, Nick. 2010. *The Hungry World: America's Cold War Battle Against Poverty in Asia*. Cambridge, MA: Harvard University Press.

Dallek, Robert. 2003. *An Unfinished Life: John F. Kennedy (1917–1963)*. New York: Little, Brown and Company.

———. 2007. *Nixon and Kissinger: Partners in Power*. New York: Harper-Collins Publishers.

Dallek, Robert, and Terry Golway. 2006. *Let Every Nation Know: John F. Kennedy in His Own Words*. Naperville, IL: Sourcebooks Media Fusion.

De Sousa Santos, Boaventura. 2005. "General Introduction: Reinventing Social Emancipation Toward New Manifestos." In *Democratizing Democracy: Beyond the Liberal Democratic Canon*, edited by Boaventura De Sousa Santos. New York: Verso.

Dickinson, Tim. 2011. "The Party of the Rich: How the Republicans abandoned the poor and the middle class to pursue their relentless agenda of tax cuts for the wealthiest one percent." *Rolling Stone Magazine*, November 24, 46–57.

Diggins, John Patrick. 1996. *Max Weber: Politics and Spirit of Tragedy*. New York: Basic Books.

Dobos, Ned. 2011. "Introduction." In *Global Financial Crisis: The Ethical Issues*, edited by Ned Dobos, Christian Barry, and Thomas Pogge. New York: Palgrave-Macmillan.

Donovan, John C. 1967. *The Politics of Poverty*. New York: Western Publishing Company.

Donziger, Steven R., ed. 1996. *The Real War on Crime: The Report of the National Criminal Justice Commission*. New York: Harper-Perennial.

Doran, Charles F. 2009. "Statecraft Today: Regional Predicaments, Global Conundrums." In *Imbalance of Power: US Hegemony and International Order*, edited by I. William Zartman. Boulder, CO: Lynne Rienner Publishers.

Douglass, James W. 2008. *JFK and the Unspeakable: Why He Died and Why It Matters*. New York: Orbis Books.

Dudziak, Mary L. 2000. *Cold War Civil Rights: Race and the Image of American Democracy*. New Jersey: Princeton University Press.

Dworkin, Ronald. 2000. *Sovereign Virtue: The Theory and Practice of Equality*. Cambridge, MA: Harvard University Press.

Dworkin, Ronald. 2008. *The Supreme Court Phalanx: The Court's New Right-Wing Bloc*. New York: New York Review of Books.

Dyer, Joel. 2000. *The Perpetual Prisoner Machine: How America Profits from Crime*. Boulder: Westview Press.

Dyson, Michael Eric. 2000. *I May Not Get There With You: The True Martin Luther King, Jr.* New York: The Free Press.

Echo-Hawk, Walter R. 2010. *The Courts of the Conqueror: The 10 Worst Indian Law Cases Ever Decided.* Golden, CO: Fulcrum.

Edelman, Peter. 1997. "The Worst Thing Bill Clinton Has Done." *The Atlantic Monthly* 279 (3), March.

———. 2001. *Searching for America's Heart: RFK and the Renewal of Hope.* Boston: Houghton Mifflin Company.

Edsall, Thomas Byrne. 1984. *The New Politics of Inequality.* New York: W.W. Norton & Company.

Ensalaco, Mark. 2000. *Chile Under Pinochet: Recovering the Truth.* Philadelphia: University of Pennsylvania Press.

Fairclough. Adam. 2001. *Better Day Coming: Blacks and Equality, 1890–2000.* New York: Viking.

Fanon, Frantz. 1968. *The Wretched of the Earth,* translated by Constance Farrington. New York: Grove Press, Inc.

Farnsworth, Kevin. 2004. *Corporate Power and Social Policy in a Global Economy: British Welfare under the Influence.* Great Britain: The Policy Press.

Feder, Ernest. 1970. "Counter-Reform." In *Agrarian Problems and Peasant Movements in Latin America,* edited by Rodolfo Stavenhagen. New York: Anchor Books/Doubleday & Company, Inc.

Fitzgerald, Frances. 2008. "Ideas Floating Free: War as Demonstration Model." In *Lessons from Iraq: Avoiding the Next War,* edited by Miriam Pemberton and William D. Hartung. Boulder, CO: Paradigm Publishers.

Flamm, Michael W. 2005. *Law and Order: Street Crime, Civil Unrest, and the Crisis of Liberalism in the 1960s.* New York: Columbia University Press.

Fletcher, Bill, and Fernando Gapasin. *Solidarity Divided: The Crisis in Organized Labor and a New Path Toward Social Justice.* Berkeley: University of California Press.

Fredrickson, George M. 1981. *White Supremacy: A Comparative Study in American and South African History.* New York: Oxford University Press.

———. 1995. *Black Liberation: A Comparative History of Black Ideologies in the United States and South Africa.* New York: Oxford University Press.

———. 1997. *The Comparative Imagination: On the History of Racism, Nationalism, and Social Movements.* Berkeley, CA: University of California Press.

Friedly, Michael, and David Gallen. 1993. *Martin Luther King, Jr.: The FBI File.* New York: Carroll & Graf Publishers, Inc.

Fuchs, Doris. 2007. *Business Power in Global Governance.* Boulder, CO: Lynne Rienner Publishers.

Galbraith, James K. 1998. *Created Unequal: The Crisis in American Pay.* New York: The Free Press.

———. 2008. *The Predator State: How Conservatives Abandoned the Free Market and Why Liberals Should Too.* New York: The Free Press.

Garrow, David J. 1983. *The FBI and Martin Luther King, Jr.* New York: Penguin Books.

———. 1986. *Bearing the Cross: Martin Luther King, Jr. and the Southern Leadership Conference.* New York: William Morrow and Company.

Gartner, Alan, Colin Greer, and Frank Riessman, editors. 1982. *What Reagan Is Doing to Us*. New York: Perennial Library.

Gerassi, John. 1973. *The Great Fear in Latin America*. New York: Collier Books.

Gerstle, Gary. 2001. *American Crucible: Race and Nation in the Twentieth Century*. New Jersey: Princeton University Press.

Gest, Ted. 2001. *Crime and Politics: Big Government's Erratic Campaign for Law and Order*. New York: Oxford University Press.

Gibson, Donald. 1994. *Battling Wall Street: The Kennedy Presidency*. New York: Sheridan Square Press.

Gill, Stephen R. 1993. "Neo-Liberalism and the Shift Towards a US-Centered Transnational Hegemony." In *Restructuring Hegemony in the Global Political Economy: The Rise of Transnational Neo-Liberalism in the 1980s*, edited by Henk Overbeek. New York: Routledge.

Gilmore, Glenda E. 2008. *Defying Dixie: The Radical Roots of Civil Rights, 1919–1950*. New York: W. W. Norton & Company.

Gilmore, Ruth W. 2007. *Golden Gulag: Prisons, Surplus, Crisis, and Opposition in Globalizing California*. Berkeley: University of California Press.

Goldstein, Gordon M. 2008. *Lessons in Disaster: McGeorge Bundy and the Path to War in Vietnam*. New York: Times Books.

Goldstone, Lawrence. 2005. *Dark Bargain: Slavery, Profits, and the Struggle for the Constitution*. New York: Walker & Company.

———. 2011. *Inherently Unequal: The Betrayal of Equal Rights by the Supreme Court, 1865–1903*. New York: Walker & Company.

Gordon, David M. 1996. *Fat and Mean: The Corporate Squeeze of Working Americans and the Myth of Managerial "Downsizing."* New York: The Free Press.

Greenberg, Jack. 1994. *Crusaders in the Courts: How a Dedicated Band of Lawyers Fought for the Civil Rights Revolution*. New York: Basic Books.

Greenfield, Kent. 2006. *The Failure of Corporate Law: Fundamental Flaws and Progressive Possibilities*. Chicago: The University of Chicago Press.

Gross, Bertram. 1980. *Friendly Fascism: The New Face of Power in America*. New York: M. Evans and Company, Inc.

Guthman, Edwin, and C. Richard Allen. 1993. *RFK: Collected Speeches—Edited and Introduced by Edwin O. Guthman and C. Richard Allen*. New York: Viking.

Habermas, Juergen. 1975. *Legitimation Crisis*. Boston: Beacon Press.

Harcourt, Bernard E. 2011. *The Illusion of Free Markets: Punishment and the Myth of Natural Order*. Cambridge, Massachusetts: Harvard University Press.

Hardin, Russell. 2000. "The Public Trust." In *Disaffected Democracies: What's Troubling the Trilateral Countries?*, edited by Susan J. Pharr and Robert D. Putnam. New Jersey: Princeton University Press.

Harrington, Michael. 1962. *The Other America: Poverty in the United States*. New York: The Macmillan Company.

Hedges, Christopher. 2011. "Occupy Wall Street is a Movement Too Big to Fail." AlterNet, October 17. http://www.alternet.org/story/152761/occupy_wall_street_is_a_movement_too_big_to_fail

Heymann, Jody, and Alison Earle. 2010. *Raising the Global Floor: Dismantling the Myth That We Can't Afford Good Working Conditions for Everyone.* Stanford: Stanford University Press.

Hill, Herbert. 1977. *Black Labor and the American Legal System: Race, Work, and the Law.* Washington, DC: The Bureau of National Affairs, Inc.

Hilty, James W. 1997. *Robert Kennedy: Brother Protector.* Philadelphia, PA: Temple University Press.

Hing, Bill Ong. 2010. *Ethical Borders: NAFTA, Globalization, and Mexican Migration.* Philadelphia: Temple University Press.

Hoffmann, Stanley. 2011. "A Cure for a Sick Country?" *The New York Review of Books,* October 27.

Hogue, Ilyse. 2011. "Downgrading Democracy." *The Nation,* August 29–September 5, 6–8.

Holland, Robert, ed. 1994. *Emergencies and Disorder in the European Empires after 1945.* London: Frank Cass.

Honey, Michael K. 2007. *Going Down Jericho Road: The Memphis Strike, Martin Luther Kings's Last Campaign.* New York: W. W. Norton & Company.

Hopkins, Thomas A., ed. 1964. *Rights for Americans: The Speeches of Robert F. Kennedy.* New York: The Bobbs-Merrill Company, Inc.

Howell, David R. 2005. "Unemployment and Labor Market Institutions: An Assessment." In *Fighting Unemployment: The Limits of Free Market Orthodoxy.* New York: Oxford University Press.

Hudson, Michael. 2005. *Global Fracture: The New International Economic Order—New Edition.* London: Pluto Press.

Huneeus, Carlos. 2007. *The Pinochet Regime,* translated by Lake Sagaris. Boulder, CO: Lynne Reinner Publishers.

Ibhawoh, Bonny. 2011. "The Right to Development: The Politics and Polemics of Power and Resistance." *Human Rights Quarterly,* 33 (1), February.

Jackson, Thomas F. 2007. *From Civil Rights to Human Rights: Martin Luther King, Jr., and the Struggle for Economic Justice.* Philadelphia: University of Pennsylvania Press.

Jones, Howard. 2003. *Death Of A Generation: How the Assassinations of Diem and JFK Prolonged the Vietnam War.* New York: Oxford University Press.

Jones, Jacqueline. 1992. *The Dispossessed: America's Underclasses from the Civil War to the Present.* New York: Basic Books.

———. 1998. *American Work: Four Centuries of Black and White Labor.* New York: W. W. Norton & Company.

Josephson, Matthew. 1962. *The Robber Barons: The Great American Capitalists, 1861–1901.* New York: Harcourt Brace Jovanovich.

Kahlenberg, Richard D. 1996. *The Remedy: Class, Race, and Affirmative Action.* New York: A New Republic Book/Basic Books.

Kaiser, David. 2000. *American Tragedy: Kennedy, Johnson, and the Origins of the Vietnam War.* Cambridge, MA: The Belknap Press of Harvard University Press.

Kaldor, Mary, Helmut Anheier, and Marlies Glasius. 2003. "Global Civil Society in an Era of Regressive Globalization." In *Global Civil Society 2003,* edited by Helmut Anheier, Marlies Glasius, and Mary Kaldor. Oxford: Oxford University Press

Kang, Susan L. 2009. "The Unsettled Relationship of Economic and Social Rights and the West: A Response to Whelan and Donnelly." *Human Rights Quarterly*, 31 (4), November.

Katz, Michael B., ed. 1993. *The "Underclass" Debate: Views from History.* Princeton, NJ: Princeton University Press.

Katz, Michael B. 2008. *The Price of Citizenship: Redefining the American Welfare State—Updated Edition.* Philadelphia: University of Pennsylvania Press.

Katznelson, Ira. 2013. *Fear Itself: The New Deal and the Origins of Our Time.* New York: Liveright Publishing Corporation.

Keck, Thomas M. 2004. *The Most Activist Supreme Court in History: The Road to Modern Judicial Conservatism.* Chicago: The University of Chicago Press.

Kelley, Robin D. G. 2006. "Labor Against Empire: At Home and Abroad." In *Race and Labor Matters in the New US Economy,* edited by Manning Marable, Immanuel Ness, and Joseph Wilson. Lanham, MD: Rowman & Littlefield Publishers, Inc.

Kennedy, John F. 1964. *Public Papers of the Presidents of the United States—John F. Kennedy—Containing the Public Message, Speeches, and Statements of the President, January 1 to November 22, 1963.* Washington, DC: United States Government Printing Office.

Kennedy, Paul. 1987. *The Rise and Fall of the Great Powers: Economic Challenge and Military Conflict from 1500 to 2000.* New York: Random House.

Kennedy, Robert F. 1967. *To Seek A Newer World.* New York: Doubleday & Company, Inc.

———. 1968a. Quoted in John Herbert, "Kennedy Calling U.S. Power-Obsessed, Appeals for a New Policy," *NYT,* April 18, 1968, 34. Cited in Rakove, Robert B. 2013. *Kennedy, Johnson, and the Nonaligned World.* New York: Cambridge University Press, 254.

———. 1968b. "Address by Robert F. Kennedy at the University of Indiana on '*No More Vietnams,*'" Robert F. Kennedy Senate Papers, Speeches, April 24, 1968.

Kern, William S. 1998. "Current Welfare Reform: A Return to the Principles of 1834." *Journal of Economic Issues,* 32 (2), 427.

King, Martin Luther. 1967. *Where Do We Go From Here: Chaos or Community?* Boston: Beacon Press.

———. 2011. *"All Labor Has Dignity,"* edited by Michael K. Honey. Boston: Beacon Press.

Klarman, Michael J. 2004. *From Jim Crow to Civil Rights: The Supreme Court and the Struggle for Racial Equality.* New York: Oxford University Press.

Klein, Jennifer. 2003. *For All These Rights: Business, Labor, and the Shaping of America's Public-Private Welfare State.* New Jersey: Princeton University Press.

Klein, Naomi. 2011. "Capitalism vs. The Climate: What the right gets—and the left doesn't—about the revolutionary power of climate change." In *The Nation,* November 28.

Klinkner, Philip A. 1999. "Bill Clinton and the Politics of the New Liberalism." In *Without Justice for All: The New Liberalism and Our Retreat from Racial Equality*, edited by Adolph Reed Jr. Boulder, CO: Westview Press.

Klinkner and Smith. 1999. *The Unsteady March: The Rise and Decline of Racial Equality in America*. Chicago: University of Chicago Press.

Koetting, Mark G., and Vincent Schiraldi. 1997. "Singapore West: The Incarceration of 200,000 Californians." *Social Justice: A Journal of Crime, Conflict & World Order*, 24 (1), 1997.

Kornbluh, Peter. 2003. *The Pinochet File: A Declassified Dossier on Atrocity and Accountability*. New York: The New Press.

Kotolowski, Dean J. 2001. *Nixon's Civil Rights: Politics, Principle, and Policy*. Cambridge, MA: Harvard University Press.

Kozul-Wright, Richard, and Paul Rayment. 2007. *The Resistible Rise of Market Fundamentalism: Rethinking Development Policy in an Unbalanced World*. London: Zed Books.

Krippner, Greta R. 2011. *Capitalizing On Crisis: The Political Origins of the Rise of Finance*. Cambridge, MA: Harvard University Press.

Kulish, Nicholas. 2011. "Protests Rise Around Globe as Faith in the Vote Wanes: Many Are Driven by Contempt of Political Class." *The New York Times*, September 28, A-1 and A-8.

Kuttner, Robert. 1984. *The Economic Illusion: False Choices Between Prosperity and Social Justice*. Boston: Houghton Mifflin Company.

Kuttner, Robert. 2013. *Debtors' Prison: The Politics of Austerity Versus Possibility*. New York: Alfred A. Knopf.

Lane, Mark. 1991. *Plausible Denial: Was the CIA Involved in the Assassination of JFK?* New York: Thunders' Mouth Press.

Latham, Michael E. 2011. *The Right Kind of Revolution: Modernization, Development, and US Foreign Policy from the Cold War to the Present*. Ithaca: Cornell University Press.

Lawrence, Mark Atwood. 2008. "History from Below: The United States and Latin America in the Nixon Years." In *Nixon in the World: American Foreign Relations, 1969–1977*, edited by Fredrik Logevall and Andrew Preston. New York: Oxford University Press.

Lee, Steven Hugh. 1995. *Outposts of Empire: Korea, Vietnam, and the Origins of the Cold War in Asia, 1949–1954*. Montreal: McGill-Queens University Press.

Leffler, Melvyn. 1992. *A Preponderance of Power: National Security, the Truman Administration, and the Cold War*. Stanford, CA: Stanford University Press.

Lemann, Nicholas. 1988. "The Unfinished War: The Inside Story of the Wars Behind the War on Poverty—Part I." *The Atlantic Monthly*, 262 (6), December 1988.

———. 1989. "The Unfinished War: The Inside Story of the Wars Behind the Wars on Poverty—Part II." *The Atlantic Monthly*, 263 (1), January 1989.

———. 1991. *The Promised Land: The Great Black Migration and How It Changed America*. New York: Alfred A. Knopf.

Lesher, Stephan. 1994. *George Wallace: American Populist*. Reading, MA: Addison-Wesley Publishing Company.

Leuchtenburg, William E. 1995. *The FDR Years: On Roosevelt and His Legacy*. New York: Columbia University Press.
Levinson, Jerome, and de Onis, Juan. 1970. *The Alliance That Lost Its Way: A Critical Report on the Alliance for Progress—A Twentieth Century Fund Study*. Chicago: Quadrangle Books.
Lieberman, Robert C. 1998. *Shifting the Color Line: Race and the American Welfare State*. Cambridge, MA: Harvard University Press.
Lindblom, Charles E. 1977. *Politics and Markets: The World's Political-Economic Systems*. New York: Basic Books, Inc., Publishers.
———. 1984. "The Market as Prison." In *The Political Economy: Readings in the Politics and Economics of American Public Policy*, edited by Thomas Ferguson and Joel Rogers. New York: M. E. Sharpe, Inc.
———. 2001. *The Market System: What It Is, How It Works, and What To Make of It*. New Haven: Yale University Press.
Logevall, Fredrik. 1999. *Choosing War: The Lost Chance for Peace and the Escalation of the Vietnam War*. Berkeley, CA: University of California Press.
Logevall, Fredrick. 2012. *Embers of War: The Fall of an Empire and the Making of America's Vietnam*. New York: Random House.
Lopez, Ian F. Haney. 1996. *White by Law: The Legal Construction of Race*. New York: New York University Press.
Loveman, Brian. 1999. *For la Patria: Politics and the Armed Forces in Latin America*. Wilmington, Delaware: Scholarly Resources, Inc.
Luttwak, Edward. 1999. *Turbo-Capitalism: Winners and Losers in the Global Economy*. New York: HarperCollins-Publishers.
Lynn, Barry C. 2010. *Cornered: The New Monopoly Capitalism and the Economics of Destruction*. New Jersey: John Wiley & Sons, Inc.
Mahoney, Richard D. 1983. *JFK: Ordeal in Africa*. New York: Oxford University Press.
Manela, Erez. 2007. *The Wilsonian Moment: Self-Determination and the International Origins of Anticolonial Nationalism*. New York: Oxford University Press.
Marable, Manning. 2011. *Malcolm X: A Life of Reinvention*. New York: Viking.
Marable, Manning, Immanuel Ness, and Joseph Wilson, eds. 2006. *Race and Labor Matters in the New US Economy*. Lanham, MD: Rowman & Littlefield Publishers, Inc.
Martinez, Mark A. 2009. *The Myth of the Free Market: The Role of the State in a Capitalist Economy*. Sterling: Kumarian Press.
Marx, Anthony W. 1998. *Making Race and Nation: A Comparison of South Africa, the United States, and Brazil*. New York: Cambridge University Press.
Massey, Douglas S., and Nancy A. Denton. 1993. *American Apartheid: Segregation and the Making of the Underclass*. Cambridge, MA: Harvard University Press.
Massie, Robert K. 1997. *Loosing the Bonds: The United States and South Africa in the Apartheid Years*. New York: Doubleday.
Mauer, Marc. 1994. "The Fragility of Criminal Justice Reform." *Social Justice: A Journal of Crime, Conflict & World Order*. 23 (3), issue 57, Fall.

——. 1999. *Race to Incarcerate—The Sentencing Project*. New York: The New Press.

McNamara, Robert S. 1995. *In Retrospect: The Tragedy and Lessons of Vietnam*. New York: Times Books.

McNamara, Robert S., Thomas Biersteker, and Herbert Schandler. 1999. *Argument Without End: In Search of Answers to the Vietnam Tragedy*. New York: Public Affairs.

Melanson, Philip H. 1991. *The Martin Luther King Assassination: New Revelations on the Conspiracy and Cover-Up, 1968–1991*. New York: Shapolsky Publishers, Inc.

Melman, Seymour. 2001. *After Capitalism: From Managerialism to Workplace Democracy*. New York: Alfred A. Knopf.

Miller, Jerome G. 1996. *Search and Destroy: African-American Males in the Criminal Justice System*. New York: Cambridge University Press.

Miller, Richard L. 1996. *Drug Warriors and Their Prey: From Police Power to Police State*. Westport, CT: Praeger.

Mills, C. Wright. 1956. *The Power Elite*. New York: Oxford University Press.

Milne, David. 2008. *America's Rasputin: Walt Rostow and the Vietnam War*. New York: Hill and Wang.

Muehlenbeck, Philip E. 2012. *Betting on the Africans: John F. Kennedy's Courting of African Nationalist Leaders*. New York: Oxford University Press.

Muhammad, Khalil Gibran. 2010. *The Condemnation of Blackness: Race, Crime, and the Making of Modern Urban America*. Cambridge, MA: Harvard University Press.

Munck, Ronaldo. 2005. *Globalization and Social Exclusion: A Transformationalist Perspective*. CT: Kumarian Press, Inc.

Murphy, Paul L. 1972. *The Constitution in Crisis Times, 1918–1969*. New York: Harper & Row, Publishers.

Muthu, Sankar. 2003. *Enlightenment Against Empire*. New Jersey: Princeton University Press.

Nelson, Bruce. 2001. *Divided We Stand: American Workers and the Struggle for Black Equality*. New Jersey: Princeton University Press.

Newfield, Jack. 1969. *Robert Kennedy: A Memoir*. New York: Bantam Books.

Newman, John M. 1992. *JFK and Vietnam: Deception, Intrigue, and the Struggle for Power*. New York: Warner Books.

Ngai, Mae M. 2004. *Impossible Subjects: Illegal Aliens and the Making of Modern America*. New Jersey: Princeton University Press.

Nussbaum, Martha C. 2011. *Creating Capabilities: The Human Development Approach*. Cambridge, MA: Harvard University Press.

Oates, Stephen B. 1982. *Let the Trumpet Sound: The Life of Martin Luther King, Jr.* New York: Harper & Row, Publishers.

O'Connor, James. 1984. *Accumulation Crisis*. New York: Basil Blackwell.

O'Reilly, Kenneth. 1989. *"Racial Matters": The FBI's Secret File on Black America, 1960–1972*. New York: The Free Press.

Palermo, Joseph A. 2001. *In His Own Right: The Political Odyssey of Senator Robert F. Kennedy*. New York: Columbia University Press.

Parker, Jason C. 2006. "Small Victory, Missed Chance: The Eisenhower Administration, the Bandung Conference, and the Turning of the Cold War." In *The Eisenhower Administration, the Third World, and the Globalization of the Cold War*, edited by Kathryn C. Statler and Andrew L. Johns. Lanham, MD: Rowman & Littlefield Publishers, Inc.

Parker, Richard. *John Kenneth Galbraith: His Life, His Politics, His Economics*. New York: Farrar, Straus and Giroux.

Parmet, Herbert S. 1980. *Jack: The Struggles of John F. Kennedy*. New York: The Dial Press.

Paupp, Terrence E. 2000. *Achieving Inclusionary Governance: Advancing Peace and Development in First and Third World Nations*. New York: Transnational Publishers, Inc.

———. 2007. *Exodus from Empire: The Fall of America's Empire and the Rise of the Global Community*. London: Pluto Press.

———. 2009. *The Future of Global Relations: Crumbling Walls, Rising Regions*. New York: Palgrave-Macmillan.

———. 2012. *Beyond Global Crisis: Remedies and Road Maps by Daisaku Ikeda and His Contemporaries*. New Jersey: Transaction Publishers.

———. 2014. *Redefining Human Rights in the Struggle for Peace and Development*. New York: Cambridge University Press.

Penn, Michael L., and Aditi Malik. 2010. "The Protection and Development of the Human Spirit: An Expanded Focus for Human Rights Discourse." *Human Rights Quarterly*, 32 (3).

Pepper, William F. 2003. *An Act of State: The Execution of Martin Luther King*. New York: Verso.

Perelman, Michael. 2007. *The Confiscation of American Prosperity: From Right-Wing Extremism and Economic Ideology to the Next Great Depression*. New York: Palgrave-Macmillan.

Perry, Michael J. 1999. *We the People: The Fourteenth Amendment and the Supreme Court*. New York: Oxford University Press.

Petras, James. 2003. *The New Development Politics: The Age of Empire Building and New Social Movements*. Hants, England: Ashgate.

Petras, James, and Henry Veltmeyer. 2003. *System In Crisis: The Dynamics of Free Market Capitalism*. New York: Zed Books.

———. 2005. *Empire With Imperialism: The Globalizing Dynamics of Neo-Liberal Capitalism*. New York: Zed Books.

———. 2007. *Multinationals on Trial: Foreign Investment Matters*. Hampshire, England: Ashgate.

———. 2009. *What's Left in Latin America?—Regime Change in New Times*. Surrey, England: Ashgate.

Phillips, Kevin. 2008. *Bad Money: Reckless Finance, Failed Politics, and the Global Crisis of American Capitalism*. New York: Viking.

Phillips, Peter. 2010. "Poverty and Social Inequality." In *The Global Economic Crisis: The Great Depression of the XXI Century*, edited by Michel Chossudovsky and Andrew Gavin Marshall. Canada: Global Research Publishers.

Piven, Frances Fox, and Richard A. Cloward. 1987. "The Contemporary Relief Debate." In *The Mean Season: The Attack on the Welfare State*, edited by

Fred Block, Richard A. Cloward, Barbara Ehrenreich, and Frances Fox Piven. New York: Pantheon Books.

———. 1993. *Regulating the Poor: The Functions of Public Welfare—Updated Edition*. New York: Vintage Books.

———. 1997. *The Breaking of the American Social Compact*. New York: The New Press.

Plotke, David. 1996. *Building a Democratic Political Order: Reshaping American Liberalism in the 1930s and 1940s*. New York: Cambridge University Press.

Pogge, Thomas W. 2002. *World Poverty and Human Rights: Cosmopolitan Responsibilities and Reforms*. Malden, MA: Polity.

———. 2011. "The Achilles' Heel of Competitive/Adversarial Systems." In *Global Financial Crisis: The Ethical Issues*, edited by Ned Dobos, Christian Barry, and Thomas Pogge. New York: Palgrave-Macmillan.

Pollin, Robert. 2003. *Contours of Descent: US Economic Fractures and the Landscape of Global Austerity*. New York: Verso.

Pomfret, Richard. 2011. *The Age of Equality: The Twentieth Century in Economic Perspective*. Cambridge, MA: The Belknap Press of Harvard University Press.

Pommersheim, Frank. 2009. *Broken Landscape: Indians, Indian Tribes, and the Constitution*. New York: Oxford University Press.

Popper, Karl R. 1971. *The Open Society and Its Enemies, Vol. 2: The High Tide of Prophesy: Hegel, Marx, and the Aftermath*. New Jersey: Princeton University Press.

Porter, Gareth. 2005. *Perils of Dominance: Imbalance of Power and the Road to War in Vietnam*. Berkeley: University of California Press.

Posner, Richard A. 2010. *The Crisis of Capitalist Democracy*. Cambridge, MA: Harvard University Press.

Poveda, Tony G. 1994. "Clinton, Crime, and the Justice Department." *Social Justice: A Journal of Crime, Conflict & World Order*, 21 (3), issue 57, Fall.

Prashad, Vijay. 2007. *The Darker Nations: A People's History of the Third World*. New York: The New Press.

———. 2012. *The Poorer Nations: A Possible History of the Global South*. London: Verso.

Prouty, L. Fletcher. 1973. *The Secret Team: The CIA and Its Allies in Control of the United States and the World*. New Jersey: Prentice-Hall, Inc.

———. 1992. *JFK: The CIA, Vietnam and the Plot to Assassinate John F. Kennedy*. New York: Birch Lane Press.

Quadagno, Jill. 1994. *The Color of Welfare: How Racism Undermined the War on Poverty*. New York: Oxford University Press.

———. 2004. "Promoting Civil Rights through the Welfare State: How Medicare Integrated Southern Hospitals." In *Social Problems, Law, and Society*, edited by A. Kathryn Strout, Richard A. Dello Buono, and William J. Chambliss. Lanham, MD: Rowman & Littlefield Publishers, Inc.

Rabe, Stephen G. 1999. *The Most Dangerous Place in the World: John F. Kennedy Confronts Communist Revolution in Latin America*. Chapel Hill: The University of North Carolina Press.

Rakove, Robert B. 2013. *Kennedy, Johnson, and the Nonaligned World.* New York: Cambridge University Press.
Rana, Aziz. 2010. *The Two Faces of American Freedom.* Cambridge, MA: Harvard University Press.
Raskin, Marcus, and Robert Spero. 2007. *The Four Freedoms under Siege: The Clear and Present Danger from Our National Security State.* Westport, CT: Praeger.
Rasmus, Jack. 2010. *Epic Recession: Prelude to Global Depression.* London: Pluto Press.
———. 2012. *Obama's Economy: Recovery for the Few.* London: Pluto Press.
Reinarman, Craig, and Harry G. Levine, editors. 1997. *Crack in America: Demon Drugs and Social Justice.* Berkeley: University of California Press.
Rich, Michael J. 1993. *Federal Policymaking and the Poor: National Goals, Local Choices, and Distributional Outcomes.* Princeton, NJ: Princeton University Press.
Rieder, Jonathan. 1989. "The Rise of the 'Silent Majority.'" In *The Rise and Fall of the New Deal Order, 1930–1980.* New Jersey: Princeton.
Rodgers, Daniel T. 2011. *Age of Fracture.* Cambridge, MA: The Belknap Press of Harvard University Press.
Roht-Arriaza, Naomi. 2005. *The Pinochet Effect: Transnational Justice in the Age of Human Rights.* Philadelphia: University of Pennsylvania Press.
Roosevelt, Franklin D. 1972. *Complete Presidential Press Conferences of Franklin D. Roosevelt.* New York: DaCapo.
Rose, Stephen M. 1970. *Community Action Programs: The Relationship Between Initial Conception of the Poverty Problem, Derived Intervention Strategy, and Program Implementation*—A Dissertation Presented to the Faculty of the Florence Heller Graduate School for Advanced Studies in Social Welfare, Brandeis University. May 1970. Ann Arbor, Michigan: University Microfilms, Inc.
Rosenblatt, Elihu, ed. 1996. *Criminal Injustice: Confronting the Prison Crisis.* Boston: South End Press.
Ross, Douglas. 1968. *Robert F. Kennedy: Apostle of Change.* New York: Pocket Books.
Rude, Christopher. 2009. "The Role of Financial Discipline in Imperial Strategy." In *American Empire and the Political Economy of Global Finance,* edited by Leo Panitch and Martijn Konings. New York: Palgrave-Macmillan.
Russell, Judith. 2004. *Economics, Bureaucracy, and Race: How Keynesians Misguided the War on Poverty.* New York: Columbia University Press.
Sachs, Jeffrey D. 2013. *To Move the World: JFK's Quest for Peace.* New York: Random House.
Sandel, Michael J. 1996. *Democracy's Discontent: America in Search of a Public Philosophy.* Cambridge: The Belknap Press of Harvard University Press.
Sanders, Jerry W. 1983. *Peddlers of Crisis: The Committee on the Present Danger and the Politics of Containment.* Boston: South End Press.
Satter, Beryl. 2009. *Family Properties: Race, Real Estate, and the Exploitation of Black Urban America.* New York: Metropolitan Books.

Saull, Richard. 2007. *The Cold War and After: Capitalism, Revolution and Superpower Politics*. London: Pluto Press.

Schlesinger, Arthur M. 1978. *Robert Kennedy and His Times*. Boston: Houghton Mifflin Company.

———. 1986. *The Cycles of American History*. Boston: Houghton Mifflin Company.

Schmitt, Edward R. 2010. *President of the Other America: Robert Kennedy and the Politics of Poverty*. Amherst and Boston: University of Massachusetts Press.

Schmitz, David F. 1999. *Thank God They're On Our Side: The United States and Right-Wing Dictatorships, 1921–1965*. Chapel Hill: The University of North Carolina Press.

———. 2006. *The United States and Right-Wing Dictatorships, 1965–1989*. New York: Cambridge University Press.

Schwartz, Herman, ed. 2002. *The Rehnquist Court: Judicial Activism on the Right*. New York: Hill and Wang.

Schwartz, Herman. 2004. *Right Wing Justice: The Conservative Campaign to Take Over the Courts*. New York: Nation Books.

Scott, Peter Dale. 1993. *Deep Politics and the Death of JFK*. Berkeley: University of California Press.

Selznick, Philip. 1992. *The Moral Commonwealth: Social Theory and the Promise of Community*. Berkeley: University of California Press.

Shaw, Randy. 2008. *Beyond the Fields: Cesar Chavez, The UFW, and the Struggle for Justice in the 21s Century*. Berkeley: University of California Press.

Siff, Ezra Y. 1999. *Why The Senate Slept: The Gulf of Tonkin Resolution and the Beginning of America's Vietnam War*. Westport, CT: Praeger.

Simon, Jonathan. 2007. *Governing Through Crime: How the War on Crime Transformed American Democracy and Created a Culture of Fear*. New York: Oxford University Press.

Simpson, A. W. Brian. 2001. *Human Rights and the End of Empire: Britain and the Genesis of the European Convention*. New York: Oxford University Press.

Sklar, Holly. 1980. "Trilateralism: Managing Dependence and Democracy—An Overview." In *Trilateralism: The Trilateral Commission and Elite Planning for World Management*. Boston: South End Press.

Smiley, Tavis, and Cornel West. 2012. *The Rich and the Rest of Us: A Poverty Manifesto*. New York: Smiley Books.

Smith, Michael Peter. 1988. *City, State, and Market: The Political Economy of Urban Society*. Cambridge: Basil Blackwell.

Smith, Rogers M. 1997. *Civic Ideals: Conflicting Visions of Citizenship in US History*. New Haven: Yale University Press.

Somers, Margaret R. *Genealogies of Citizenship: Markets, Statelessness, and the Right to Have Rights*. New York: Cambridge University Press.

Starr, Amory. 2005. *Global Revolt: A Guide to the Movements Against Globalization*. New York: Zed Books.

Statler, Kathryn C., and Andrew L. Johns, eds. 2006. *The Eisenhower Administration, the Third World, and the Globalization of the Cold War*. Lanham, MD: Rowman & Littlefield Publishers, Inc.

Stiglitz, Joseph. 2003. *The Roaring Nineties: A New History of the World's Most Prosperous Decade*. New York: W. W. Norton & Company.

———. 2012. *The Price of Inequality: How Today's Divided Society Endangers Our Future*. New York: W. W. Norton & Company.

Stiglitz, Joseph E., and Linda J. Bilmes. 2008. *The Three Trillion Dollar War: The True Cost of the Iraq Conflict*. New York: W. W. Norton & Company.

Stiglitz, Joseph, Amartya Sen, and Jean-Paul Fitoussi. 2010. *Mis-Measuring Our Lives: Why GDP Doesn't Add Up—The Report by the Commission on the Measurement of Economic Performance and Social Progress*. New York: The New Press.

Stockman, David A. 2013. *The Great Deformation: The Corruption of Capitalism in America*. New York: Public Affairs.

Stricker, Frank. 2007. *Why America Lost the War on Poverty—And How to Win It*. Chapel Hill: The University of North Carolina Press.

Sugrue, Thomas J. 2008. *Sweet Land of Liberty: The Forgotten Struggle for Civil Rights in the North*. New York: Random House.

Summers, Anthony. 1993. *Official and Confidential: The Secret Life of J. Edgar Hoover*. New York: G. P. Putnam's Sons.

Sunstein, Cass R. 2004. *The Second Bill of Rights: FDR's Unfinished Revolution and Why We Need It More Than Ever*. New York: Basic Books.

Taffet, Jeffrey F. 2007. *Foreign Aid as Foreign Policy: The Alliance for Progress in Latin America*. New York: Routledge.

Talbot, David. 2007. *Brothers: The Hidden History of the Kennedy Years*. New York: Free Press.

Tan, See Seng, and Amitav Acharya, eds. 2008. *Bandung Revisited: The Legacy of the 1955 Asian-African Conference for International Order*. Singapore: National University of Singapore.

Taylor, Lance. 2010. *Maynard's Revenge: The Collapse of Free Market Macroeconomics*. Cambridge, MA: Harvard University Press.

Thomas, Evan. 2000. *Robert Kennedy: His Life*. New York: Simon & Schuster.

Tonry, Michael. 1995. *Malign Neglect: Race, Crime, and Punishment in America*. New York: Oxford University Press.

———. 1996. *Sentencing Matters*. New York: Oxford University Press.

———. 2004. *Thinking about Crime: Sense and Sensibility in American Penal Culture*. New York: Oxford University Press.

Valdes, Juan Gabriel. 1995. *Pinochet's Economists: The Chicago School in Chile*. New York: Cambridge University Press.

Vanden Heuvel, William J., and Milton Gwirtzman. 1970. *On His Own: Robert F. Kennedy, 1964–1968*. New York: Doubleday & Company, Inc.

Vargas, Zaragosa. 2005. *Labor Rights Are Civil Rights: Mexican American Workers in Twentieth-Century America*. New Jersey: Princeton University Press.

Wacquant, Loic. 2009. *Punishing The Poor: The Neo-Liberal Government of Social Insecurity*. Durham: Duke University Press.

White, Mark D. 2011. *Kantian Ethics and Economics: Autonomy, Dignity, and Character*. Stanford: Stanford University Press.

Williams, Walter. 2003. *Reaganism and the Death of Representative Democracy.* Washington, DC: Georgetown University Press.

Wilson, William Julius. 1996. *When Work Disappears: The World of the New Urban Poor.* New York: Alfred A. Knopf.

Winant, Howard. 2001. *The World Is A Ghetto: Race and Democracy Since World War II.* New York: Basic Books.

Winn, Peter. 2004. "The Pinochet Era." In *Victims of the Chilean Miracles: Workers and Neo-Liberalism in the Pinochet Era, 1973–2002,* edited by Peter Winn. Durham: Duke University Press.

Wolfe, Alan. 1981. *America's Impasse: The Rise and Fall of the Politics of Growth.* New York: Pantheon.

Wolff, Edward N. 2002. *Top Heavy: The Increasing Inequality of Wealth in America and What Can Be Done About It.* New York: The New Press.

Wolin, Sheldon S. *Democracy Incorporated: Managed Democracy and the Specter of Inverted Totalitarianism.* New Jersey: Princeton University Press.

Wood, Mark David. 2000. *Cornel West and the Politics of Prophetic Pragmatism.* Chicago: University of Illinois Press.

Yergin, Daniel, and Joseph Stanislaw. 1998. *The Commanding Heights: The Battle Between Government and the Marketplace That Is Remaking the Modern World.* New York: Simon & Schuster.

Zarefsky, David. 1986. *President Johnson's War on Poverty: Rhetoric and History.* Alabama: The University of Alabama Press.

Zepezauer, Mark. 2003. *Boomerang! How Our Covert Wars Have Created Enemies Across the Middle East and Brought Terror to America.* Monroe, Maine: Common Courage Press.

Zimring, Franklin E., Gordon Hawkins, and Sam Kamin. 2001. *Punishment and Democracy: Three Strikes and You're Out in California.* New York: Oxford University Press.

Index

For Product Safety Concerns and Information please contact our EU representative GPSR@taylorandfrancis.com Taylor & Francis Verlag GmbH, Kaufingerstraße 24, 80331 München, Germany

Batch number: 08151583

Printed by Printforce, the Netherlands